NO

MORE

SCHOOL

NO MORE SCHOOL

Howard S. Rowland

WITHDRAWN

A Sunrise Book

E. P. DUTTON & CO., INC. | NEW YORK | 1975

DUTTON-SUNRISE, INC., A SUBSIDIARY OF E. P. DUTTON & CO., INC.

Library of Congress Cataloging in Publication Data

Rowland, Howard S
No more school.

"A Sunrise book."
1. Education—Experimental methods. 2. Free schools. 3. Domestic education. I. Title.
LB1027.R69   370.11   74-19068

Published simultaneously in Canada by Clarke, Irwin & Company Limited,
Toronto and Vancouver
ISBN: 0-87690-147-X
Designed by The Etheredges

To Beebee

—my joy, my love.

CONTENTS

PREFACE: LEARNING

WITHOUT CLASSROOMS,

TEACHERS, OR

CURRICULUM

No More School is an account of how my wife and I attempted to give our children a fresh start, to remove them from contemporary middle-class, TV-oriented, peer-group dominated, suburban American life—particularly from that unnatural children's society called school—and allow each of them to discover whatever it was he wanted and could get out of being alive.

The book covers a ten-month period from November 1969 to September 1970. The place, for the most part, is La Herradura, a remote fishing village in Spain, where we settled down with one thing in mind—a determination to free our children of teachers, textbooks, classrooms, and routine.

The idea was not only to cut them off from all of suburban America's cultural, social, and educational influences, but to create some new kind of society, family centered, in which the immediate concerns of education would be values and attitudes, the ability to associate ideas and draw conclusions, the experience of creation and discovery. Arithmetic, spelling, and vocabulary would be relegated to mechanical, supporting roles.

In La Herradura there were no prescribed subjects, only those that cropped up during a day of play and work and teased the children to pursue them further. Interests ranged from burial customs and bread baking to photography, city planning, and comparative education. The children followed their own needs and inclinations wherever they led—but never far away was Bea or me with books and suggestions, shouting or laughing encouragment, impatient, self-involved, sloppy, ill informed—nakedly ourselves.

We made almost no effort to keep our children up to grade level with the kids back home, yet we found that each of our children moved forward academically—that is, in the recognized formal disciplines—by leaps and bounds. It was as if the basic skills, so torturously categorized, lesson planned, and spaced out in school over a twelve-year period, were readily discovered and mastered in a fraction of the usual time when a child needed them, when he started doing things he wanted to do and that required these skills.

For example, Seth, a seven-year-old freckled Huck Finn, discovered an interest in arithmetic, in part because he wanted to pay for purchases in the local marketplace. In three months he went through four years of math and had to be stopped because of the problems he would face when he returned to his old school and third-grade arithmetic.

Adam's curiosity about science—he's a black-haired, black-eyed, wiry eleven-year-old—was whetted by family explorations along the rugged coast or by long solitary hours observing ants, rats, and people on the barren mountainside, watching the tides and the teeming sea life. On his own, in a period of intense study, he swept through a host of sciences: comparative anatomy, wind and sea currents, astronomy, principles of light, gravity, and even relativity.

Ariel, a warm and lovely nine-year-old, moderately retarded, painfully began the process of putting her thoughts on paper, of writing, because she knew that if she wanted to receive letters—like the rest of the family—she would have to write them too. Until then she had haltingly tooled out the full alphabet and "sentences" like *cat sees rat*, and that was all. When she had to say something in her letters, her writing lurched forward with astonishing speed from clumsy and inarticulate fragments of ideas to close approximations of how she normally spoke, increasingly coherent and purposeful.

And so for ten months we lived together as few families in suburban America can—not just sleeping and eating, but conversing, working, playing, and learning together. And without classes, schoolrooms, teachers, or specific things to learn, it was hard to tell what was work, what was play, and what was education.

When it was time to return to the States, to Westchester County and the Lakeland schools, the Rowland family was a tight and stable little society. Each child was secure in his interests, jealously independent and resourceful, and voraciously curious about the people about him and the world.

More than ever our children were rough and tumble, high spirited, and mischievous. But they had also achieved hard educational gains.

Adam had discovered city planning and photography (most of the photos in this book are his) and had produced two hundred pages of an adventure novel.

Seth, besides his three-month march through grade school mathematics, had become an avid reader and writer, maintaining a detailed and thoughtful diary of the family's experiences.

And Ariel—perhaps our chief concern—had been able to find a sense of personal identity and accomplishment through her dancing, her housekeeping, and her demonstrated ability to do conventional schoolwork. For by the time she left La Herradura, Ariel was not only writing, she was reading with understanding, adding three-column figures, doing subtraction, and even beginning to grasp division.

So when we returned, we had a sense of success. And though the children fell back into the routines of school, Bea returned to her free-lance writing and housewifery, and I resumed my job as a high school teacher, each of our lives had been separately and profoundly affected by the ten months at La Herradura. The rich fabric of family life remained, the vibrant tones and spirit of those careless days still animated the thoughts and actions of the children's lives.

Most important, Adam, Seth, and, to an extent, Ariel had the motivation and discipline to continue educating themselves and therefore were a little better prepared for the nonsense, the drudgery, the opportunities they would meet in contemporary America.

I.

A SCENE AND

ITS BACKGROUND

I did no work at all today. The waves were big and the wind strong. So we decided to go to our other beach where it looked like there aren't any waves and no strong wind. We got ready and left. We took a short cut but in a few places it was very slippery and right on a cliff. We were soon at the beach. It was warm outside. But realy freesing in the water. I could hardly get in. I stayed in all most as long as Daddy or as long as Daddy who stayed in longest. Inclueding all the times everybody went in put together and made into seconds, I and Daddy would of stayed in the longest. Adam got a fire started and we cooked steak on it and ate. Then I took another little swim. I got ajusted to the freesing . . . cold water very soon. When I was finnished I went to the rocks to play with the periwinkles. They were beaty . . . veld. I put them back on a rock and slowly they disapeared in to the water. While I was doing, I noticed some like the Iandian [?] chiton. It looked just like in the book. I thought for a while then ran for daddy saying I found the iandian chiton. Daddy came running and sure enough I was right. We found plenty others but we only took the one I had found to mommy. I had found the best one there. After I showed Mommy the chiton I went and put him back. I told Adam that I had found some muscles and cooked them over the fire. The muscles were good. We soon left. When we got home we went to the village. We brought Cosshess [a stray cat]. On the way back we saw many baby goats. We saw baby goats trieing to get nursed by other Mothers. We got some warm milk straight from the goat. It tasted just like it did in Hiedi. Then we left.

SETH'S DIARY,
SUNDAY JUNE 14

1. LA HERRADURA—

SUNRISE TO

BEDTIME EDUCATION

It was 6:00 A.M. and not yet hot. At that hour in the United States, the schools were dark and locked up tight, teachers were still in bed, and textbooks and visual aids were stored in cabinets. Yet in this little Spanish fishing village, three American children were already busily at work educating themselves.

Seth, a red-headed seven-year-old, was hunched up in his bed, diary in hand, totally absorbed in the business of ordering and recording the tastes, thoughts, and events of yesterday. Outside on the lawn, Ariel, a nine-year-old retarded child, was gracefully going through her intricate dance exercises while glancing out now and then to watch the fishing boats laying their nets. And a mile down the beach in the village an eleven-year-old, Adam, barefoot and with camera slung over shoulder, was patiently searching out scenes and faces to photograph in the awakening marketplace.

Bea and I, the parents of the three children, were asleep.

By eight or nine or ten, the family would casually regroup for breakfast. Ariel would set the table. Adam, returned with stories from town, would take orders for eggs (everything from *huevos flamencos* to mushroom omelettes) and prepare them himself. Seth, seated at the dining room table, would be earnestly drawing up a list of multiplication and addition problems for Ariel, whom he had decided to tutor.

Breakfast was long. We would sit around for an hour or more, each of us telling what he planned to do that day, the rest offering suggestions or advice, arranging for materials. Then we slowly dispersed. Each day was different, and even what was planned occupied only a small portion of it. The children followed the sun and their own inclinations. Activities ranged over wide areas of interest, only occasionally related to school or classes back home. Adam could turn to designing another elaborate plan (economic, social, architectural) for a radically new urban development, writing a new chapter for his original adventure novel, playing soccer on the beach with some Spanish friends, fishing, or helping Ariel with her spelling. Seth might hole up silently in his room, racing word by word through one of the few books remaining unread in his private library, or climb along the rocky shore with Ariel picking up periwinkles, chitons, and gooseneck barnacles, or quietly set up a science experiment on refraction using mirrors and a glass of water. Ariel might help mommy clean up, write a painfully long letter to grandma, play store with Seth to practice her arithmetic, or read a story aloud with daddy to help her catch the rhythm and meaning.

Often we skipped lunch, preferring to drift into the kitchen to pick up a tangerine, a tomato, or a lush Valencia orange; to tear off a hunk of fresh crusty bread; or to take some cheese with goat's milk or the ten-cents-a-quart local wine. And in this way we got through till dinnertime. Sometimes we took a big bag of fruit or packed sandwiches and climbed down the steep coast to one of the small, barely accessible beaches and picnicked around a driftwood fire.

For the children the afternoons were full of horseplay and adventuring; of family mountain climbs and long delicious swims; of trips to town; of talks and visits with shepherds and farmers; of strolls through old cemeteries, ancient Moorish fortifications, clean austere village churches; of running, playing, sunbathing, dreaming, and musing.

And then the long evenings—of Bible reading, ghost stories,

and fairy tales; of star gazing, astronomy book in hand, long after normal bedtime; of Adam reading aloud to an attentive audience the latest chapter of his own, handwritten novel; of long family discussions on lovemaking and churchgoing, on values and life styles, on economics and politics, on ideas for the next day or week or the limitless future.

They were days rich with learning—not school days. The children were educating themselves, and they were going about it quickly and enthusiastically and with awesome independence and purposefulness. No schoolrooms, no peer grouping, no curricula, no teachers, no textbooks. It was exactly the sort of education we had wanted for our children.

2.

A CONCERNED FATHER

LOOKS AT THE SCHOOLS

I wanted my children to explore fully things that puzzled or intrigued them. I wanted them to see, to make, to do what they wanted with their time. I wanted them to discover and experience at their own speed without teacher, peer group, textbook, or system to get in their way, to hold them up or push them on. I wanted them to savor the sense of choice about what they wanted to know and what they decided not to know. I wanted them to resent fetters and routine. I wanted them to realize the pleasures of being alone, of musing and idling, of accepting oneself. I wanted them to respect the need for privacy. I wanted them to question the absolutes, to see life, not in terms of good and bad or right and wrong, but as fascinatingly intertwined, complex and human, subject to interpretation, prejudice, change. I wanted them to be disciplined so that they could decide to climb a mountain, dig out a cave, or study the stars; then plan well for the project and have the will and strength to complete the task. I wanted them to be always observant, open to new influences, enthusiastic, curious. I wanted them to be at ease and familiar with people of all ages, adults and children. I wanted them to have deeply and permanently embedded a sense of family; of loyalty, pride, shared responsibility; and most important, of total acceptance of each other without judgment. I wanted my children to see their parents not just as dinnertime presences but as whole people, concerned, intelligent, flawed, and fallible. I wanted them to be free of TV's acquisitive urgings; of the aimless, style-driven peer group, of the deluge of entertainments, diversions, momentary fads, and interests; of the glut of sight, sound, and taste treats that leave children at ten years of age jaded and cynical; of the gadgets, cars, games; of Little League; of after-school clubs; of an infinitely fragmented, meandering, soured middle-class society.

As a teacher I had come to realize that formal education as practiced in the United States is unable to do its assigned job. But it wasn't until my own children started attending our local schools that I fully comprehended the extent of damage taking place within the classroom.

For ten years I had taught high school English classes in Briarcliff Manor, an elite public school system in Westchester County, New York, which fluctuated between dull traditional and dull progressive in an effort to keep pace with the latest fashions in education. Before that I had been a vice-president of a major New York advertising agency, but had quit at the age of thirty and taken a two-thirds cut in salary because I wanted to teach.

The problem in advertising was that I felt I had pretty much exhausted the field. There seemed little new to be learned, and the prospect of churning out new campaign ideas for toilet paper or frozen vegetables for thirty more years was not a happy one —no matter the prestige and money involved.

The dramatic changes this financial plunge would entail in our standard of living would, of course, be felt most by Bea. But fortunately her values were not tied up with fancy restaurants, trips to Bermuda, prestigious communities, or fashionable clothes. So with her encouragement I sent a few letters to sub-urban school systems in the New York area. I had a B.A. from N.Y.U. and an M.A. in literature from Columbia, but not a single course in education.

Nevertheless, one school system, Briarcliff, found me enough of an oddity to offer me a job on the spot, and I accepted.

My colleagues and clients were split on the decision—remember it was made many years ago when the desirability of money and position was unquestioned. Some regarded it as a quixotic gesture; the rest—and there were more of them—as a mental and social aberration. Fortunately, Briarcliff, an upper-middle-class community of executives and professionals, bought the romance.

So within two months I had packed in my career and packed up our luxurious garden apartment, bought a four-acre chunk of forest fifty miles from New York City with a pond and a barn and a ramshackle bungalow—$5,000 down and $11,500 in mortgage—and become pretty much what I still am—a teacher.

Like many parents, I still remembered my own grim experiences in school, but I had assumed things had changed somehow with newer buildings, more visual aids, and better paid teachers. They hadn't. Underneath all the new trappings I found the same dead curriculum, the same set of values, the same timidity, rigidity, and ignorance. It was educacide, an institutionalized process whereby a child's curiosity, inventiveness, individuality, desire to learn were methodically destroyed. Any child who emerged from this system with any of these characteristics still intact was simply proof of the strong person's ability to withstand hostile forces.

Schoolroom education—as I had known it, as I saw it practiced by my colleagues, without malice but routinely and mechanically—was still unmistakably undermining all that was unique and vital about children. The very things that made them separate, unpredictable, happy youngsters were being tamed and broken. And what were being substituted in deadly daily rations of formal education were look-alike ideas; Tom, Jane, and Mary values; and an acceptance of the endless drudgery of pointless work.

If a child was tripping behind or shooting ahead, he was continuously lurched forward or back to keep pace with his class. If his interests or curiosity took him more deeply than required into a subject or led him into new areas, he was rudely reminded that he must keep up with his assigned work. If the work was insufferably repetitious or meaningless, he was compelled to remain attentive, to feign interest.

No wonder most children, eager to learn and finding their real needs veering off so often from the school's routine, abandoned each year a little more of their private direction and gradually accepted public tastes and goals as their own. Not surprisingly, many others coped with the system by what had become a contemporary phenomenon—youth cynicism: play the game and beat them. But my concern was no longer just professional. It had become personal. My own children were starting on their journeys through the school system. My writing for professional journals suggesting basic reforms in education and my work in my own classroom instituting these changes would do little to deflect the damage to my own children from the ongoing system.

By the time we removed them from their schools, I had already seen the eagerness with which each of them had first attended classes begin to fade. I knew it was only a matter of time before they too soured—or worse, acquired the herd behavior of their peer groups.

Adam, the fifth grader, bright and conscientious, had already adjusted to the routine and even the nonsense of school. Curious and respectful of learning, he was finding recognition and satisfaction in his academic success. As he became involved in the everyday business of school, many of his out-of-school activities were either accorded less emphasis or dropped entirely. There seemed no longer to be time for backyard football scrimmaging with neighborhood kids or for building tree houses, no longer any reason—with all the other demands on his time—to read unassigned books, no longer anything to be gained, for a conscientious student, from musing or idling. If he wanted to do well at school he had to bone up for tests, follow instructions, meet the teacher's standards, stay in line.

And so each day he returned from school still immersed in tests and exercise papers, with homework to be done and assigned chapters to be read, looking a little more sober and grown up. His openness to learning and delight in his own discoveries were being matter-of-factly displaced by the goals and standards the school prized. For Adam, learning had become a serious, frequently a grim, business.

Ariel was a slow learner, a brain-damaged child. To the world her most significant feature was, no doubt, her slowness. But to the boys, to Bea, and to me, she was a complete child: plump, soft, and awkward; amazingly persistent; warm, talkative, giggling and effervescent at times, then pouting and sullen; academically slow, but with a surprisingly sharp and accurate memory for social details. She lumbered when she walked, was swift and lithe when she ran, was graceful and poised in repose. Her dress and manners were impeccable, her love of company irre-pressible and sometimes embarrassing, her desire to please in-satiable. She was all this and much, much more.

We knew she would need special schooling. But our interest in Ariel's academic progress was negligible compared with our concern for her self-confidence and her feeling of acceptance, her ability to function outside of the classroom. And we soon learned that a formal school system was clearly unprepared to work toward a life for her beyond school walls.

After kindergarten, Ariel was quickly categorized, shunted off to a separate building, and forced each day to spend four hours at games, cut-outs, and other mark-time activities leavened with one hour of straight, hammer-it-home academic drill. We fretted and winced at the harm being done. For the first time, Ariel was seeing herself singled out as abnormal—not *different* as we believed and had made her understand at home. She was learning at school that most children were the same, except for a few strange ones like herself who had to be separated and given lots of busywork.

Seth, a boy with a swift and agile mind for numbers, a preco-cious taste in reading, and a flair for fabricating tall tales, was being systematically restrained or squelched by his school. When he was six Seth would figure out in his head in just a few seconds our change from a ten dollar bill before we paid a restaurant check. But it took the school only one year—by dint of countless assignments of simple addition, emphasis on neatness, torturous copying and repeating of the same figures in a never-ending stream of look-alike problems—to exhaust his natural reserve of wonder in numbers.

So too with reading. Seth had been picking out his own books in the neighborhood library, scanning the headlines of the local newspaper each evening, swiftly becoming a reader. But as the regularly paced, read-aloud school exercises each day brought him back to a slower, more elementary level of reading, his enthusiasm for reading ebbed and his speed actually re-gressed. He even returned to mouthing each word when he read to himself.

These were our three children before we called a halt to their formal education: a quick learner, a slow learner, and one whose potential could be brilliant. None was being adequately served by

the schools. In fact, we were convinced that the scho
doing them irreparable damage.

We weren't laying blame on a particular school or a
teachers. The indictment was general. Formal education was it
self the culprit. The goals, the methods, the people, the institution, the traditions were all flawed. They were also so complex
and interdependent as to be virtually incapable of radical change.
There were no malevolent forces at play, nothing manipulative
or sinister. It was simply a routine, everyday system that puzzled
even its practitioners as they observed their students slowly losing their enthusiasm and spirit and then yielding their values and
interests.

Something totally different had to be found. Such a system
could not be refashioned. With its massive framework of
schedules, course boundaries, groupings, and physical limitations, it would simply engulf and reduce to insignificance any
program of reforms. A completely fresh beginning was needed, a
reassessment of the most basic concepts: Why educate? For what?
By whom? Where and how?

Changing traditional grammar curricula to transformational
grammar; introducing "teacher accountability," programmed
learning, or modular scheduling; decreasing class sizes from
thirty to twenty-five pupils; lengthening the school year to forty-
eight weeks; teaching European rather than American history in
eighth grade—these alterations had nothing to do with what
children should learn, certainly not with what we wanted our
children to learn.

Even the hit-or-miss luck of getting a good teacher was, we
recognized, not the answer. In my own classes I prided myself on
a free-wheeling spirit, though I knew how slight an impact I was
making against a counterforce of forty other teachers and fourteen years of lockstep education. Historically, we may come to
see the good teacher working within the establishment as the
most inhibiting factor in effecting change in education because
he makes tolerable an otherwise pointless and destructive system.*

---

*We all remember particular teachers who enlivened a class, provided a sudden
insight into a field or activity, or made a personal remark that deeply affected us.
But we also carry with us memories of endless school hours spent dully with
disciplinarians, grammarians, term-paper addicts; with adults who were timid,
mechanical, repetitious, and rigid. We remember the forty-five-minute bells to

ıtter went beyond the classroom. The
d become alarmingly pervasive, spreading
ool buildings, beyond the nine-to-three
he five academic subjects. As a result our
ether Seth was learning to add two-digit
ıembering her alphabet. We worried about
operating so powerfully within the schools,
's tastes, values, individual perceptions. We
noted unhappily how the school increasingly assumed responsibility in nonacademic areas, how the range of these activities
grew steadily until it embraced almost all facets of a child's life:
sex education, driver education, and family relations; after-
school clubs to foster outside interests; entertainment, recreation, fund raising, and social activities for nights and weekends;
the services of psychologists and guidance counselors.*

We could see the school and its peer groups slowly taking
over the direction of our children. And as we watched in that
winter of 1969 we started questioning the whole educational
process:

- Are our family's values being subverted by unchallenged peer-
  group values operating within the schools?
- Are our children subordinating their sense of wonder and
  enthusiasm to the fuzzy goals and purposes of a fact-oriented
  educational system?
- Are our children being exposed to a world that exists or to a
  pedagogue's world, academically confined, anachronistic, isolated?
- When our children are grouped with other children, are the
  groupings inherently restrictive in limiting learning experiences?

---

turn on and turn off our interests, the novelty and then the resentment at being
assigned day after day to the same group, seat, room, teacher, and work; at having
to relinquish one's inclinations, tastes, needs, learning pace for the sake of the
group. These and many other features of the old days are still very much a part
of education today and make that innovative third-grade teacher or that inspiring
high school biology teacher stray sparks in an otherwise bleak and spirit-breaking
system.
*Many parents have come to believe that their major contribution to their child's
education is the annual payment of the school tax.

- Are our children's sense of privacy and individuality being violated?

- Are mathematics, English, science, languages, and history—no matter how stretched—the sole ingredients of all our children should learn until they are eighteen years of age?

But what alternative did we, did any parent, have? We had to send our children to school. There were state laws, there was the mother's expectation of free time—father, of course, went to work—and there was a general acceptance of the fact that a child at the age of five or six was shunted off to a schoolroom. There was no question of an alternative. Besides, what parents had the time, energy, skill, books, and materials—the presumption—to teach their children what had to be taught, when an entire system of specialists, facilities, and methods had been marshaled to do just that?

And so each day our three children returned from the system, and each day we saw some of the laughter and sudden insight, some of the enthusiasm waning. Bit by bit, our children were losing their confidence in their own judgments, their easy inclinations to be creative. School was not only filling their mornings and afternoons, but encroaching on their time at home, redirecting their interests, fusing their values with the school's values and with their peer groups' values. This was no arithmetic, spelling, and vocabulary curriculum. In those pleasant, well-lighted, brick buildings our children were being totally reworked.

Belaboring the school system clearly was not the answer. The problem was ours. Our children were rotting. They needed our attention, our time, our interest. After all, the school was going about its job as it saw fit. Its approach was general and statistical: Does your child's IQ fall below the median IQ? Has he completed all the required reading for the fifth grade? Has he been absent from school too often? The community would judge the school on these standards, the only standards it knew. As for Adam, Ariel, and Seth—the school enjoyed no blood relationship, had no personal stake in their futures. They might be delightful students, but they were part of a changing sea of faces, part of a flow of little people who had to be taught arithmetic, spelling, vocabulary; whose reading speed and comprehension had to be improved; who had to be tested, graded, and moved along. If more remained to be taught, if what was being taught was not important or might even be harmful, if peer groups operating unchallenged within the schools were imposing peer values, if the entire system was questionable, the problem was ours, the parents. We could submit, resign ourselves, bemoan the inadequacy of the schools. Or we could try ourselves to create an alternative.

3

THE ESCAPE

And thus it was that our misgivings about our children's education and our own inclinations to roam and make do led us to the novel idea of removing our children, all three of them, from school and whisking them off to a new, totally free environment where we could start fresh in establishing a new base for their education.

To do this, of course, money and time had to be provided. We were fortunate. I was eligible for a year's sabbatical leave from teaching, and my writing could provide an additional source of income. So it wasn't long before the idea was converted into a plan, and the plan into action.

Approval of the sabbatical was first obtained. Then the house was rented, arrangements made for picking up a car abroad, relatives and friends told of our intent, air transportation secured, and finally, finally, the children withdrawn from their schools. We were closely questioned by school authorities about how the children were to continue their education and how they would keep up with the required curricula. But by mumbling something about international schools abroad and accepting the solemnly proffered school textbooks, we were able to get off without further ado.

We flew from New York to Amsterdam, picked up our pre-purchased car, and set out on our adventure—without a schedule, a reservation, a single obligation. As our car careened along Leidschestraat, other drivers turned in surprise at the speeding vehicle and the five lusty voices singing, shouting in English, "No more schools, no more books, no more teachers' nasty looks." We had escaped.

II.

EIGHT WEEKS OF

COUNTEREDUCATION

4.

TRAVELING

RECAPTURING THE SENSES

When we informed the schools that we were withdrawing our children for a year, mumbling about plans for their education, we actually had few ideas about what we were going to do with them. Our generalities and vague principles would hardly have impressed a parent, much less an educator. Nevertheless, Bea and I—and gleefully, the children—were convinced that this was exactly the strength of the plan. We had not laid it out in advance. It would evolve and be created as it was needed.

And so in keeping with this loose structure, we set about rediscovering ourselves, starting at the most basic level. Each of the senses was separately coddled, teased, indulged. While traveling we rarely planned visits to places or museums and never made a reservation at a restaurant or hotel. Each hour, each day, each week was unassigned, unaccounted for. We were free to stop and explore an abandoned château that Ariel spotted high on a hill, and while wandering around the moat, crossing the drawbridge, and peeking into the courtyard ruins through the grillwork of the massive gates, we could wonder what it had been like to live in ancient times. We were free to eat in a provincial restaurant in champagne country and then wander through the vineyards feeling the rich soil, examining the dirt particles and the clay, and guessing why this produced better grapes or grapes at all.

It was like this day after day. If we heard of a local sight, felt hungry, saw a town in the distance, smelled the baking of fresh bread, felt thirsty, needed a bathroom, got tired of riding, felt like idling in our rooms, on a beach, in a café or museum or church, we did it. Bea and I were the eldest and therefore could claim more authority than the children, but since we had no adult plans or firm commitments and truly wanted them to discover their own tastes—without abandoning our own interests—the family ended up as a moderately democratic little society.

During these first weeks of unwinding from school learning, household chores, school teaching, and the special obligations we all had—to publishers, dance groups, Brownies, teachers, friends, relatives, and the neighborhood—we learned to feel no regret, no sense of lost time. We tasted, touched, saw, heard, and smelled again: the dank air in the bedchamber of the pope in Avignon and the decayed stone abutments of the crumbling castle wall; the little heaps of garbage left to fester at the side of some ancient chapel wall; the still-steaming dog turd on an elegant main street in Rotterdam; the fearsome voyage across Amsterdam streets in the face of a phalanx of moving bicycles; Ariel on skis, jealously competitive with the boys, doing so well in balancing herself as she slid down the hill, body slightly hunched over, waiting to fall; Seth warming his hands and backside at a workman's little outdoor fire in a flea market; Adam jumping and screaming happily at the top of his lungs as he took a cold shower; and after a visit to the Moët-Chandon cave and a company treat of a bottle of champagne, the three children red cheeked, singing, "Summertime and the living is easy . . ." even though it was the middle of winter and there was snow on the ground.

In all we spent about four weeks moseying south, including some time in Amsterdam, Belgium, and the wine country of France, and ten days in Switzerland at a little monastery-centered town called Einsiedeln where Seth was convinced Heidi still lived and where we would remain until the load of books we had shipped from the States arrived in Zurich. Ohh! The gleeful reception accorded those packages of books as they arrived on four separate days—an early indication of how important books would become in the children's lives while away from school. And then again south through Avignon and Nîmes, sleeping in converted windmills, eating in open-air marketplaces, wandering through unfamiliar streets.

This month of drifting was in fact a deep plunge into our sensory selves, a thorough displacement of the old classroom attitudes and responses and a discovery of an infinity of new possibilities, impressions, feelings—a world of sensation. Left far behind were the routine, the rigors of schooltime, the fixed surroundings, the known and knowing people, the expected sights, sounds, and planned events. Left behind was the carefully constructed and complex edifice of a working society. Left behind were the patterns, the standards, the hard facts to be accepted and learned on schedule. Left behind were method, fixed purpose, unalterable systems, institutions, authorities.

Yet strangely, the children did not change into little savages with insatiable demands and petulant responses. Their days were full and exhausting, and they seemed to look forward to the long nights without talk or movement, without television or friends, when they could quietly read or write letters or just lie in bed and stare at the ceiling, musing about the day or the morrow or simply nothing at all and feeling after a complete day's activity the physical sensations of well-being that come from muscles slowly untightening and senses idling and relaxed.

LEARNING FROM RANDOM EXPERIENCE

Although the children were enjoying a fresh awareness of their senses, those first few weeks never turned into an intellectual rout where they simply ate, romped, and slept. As a matter of fact, during this period we had any number of discussions on customs, history, sex, religion, government, freedom, love, security. We even made a few conventional cultural visits. The discussions were quite desultory and would take place while we were driving or eating, before bedtime, as we strolled down a village street, while we watched a soccer game, after we passed a schoolyard in which a class of well-disciplined students dressed in uniforms gazed at us quizzically, or when a toylike policeman, mechanical and correct in his street corner box, waved us on.

We didn't avoid the world of ideas, just as we didn't avoid museums and churches. But neither did we seek them out. If we saw a high steeple, passed a museum poster, or happened to remember, as at Rheims, that a famous site or building was there, we might consider a visit. More often we simply walked the streets of a village happily losing ourselves in a maze of alleys, finding a neighborhood café in which to warm up and look around while being looked at, or seeking out the schoolhouse where we peered into the darkened interior hoping to discover some feature to remark on.

The idea of visiting tourist sights—as the time many years ago when Bea and I had traveled all the way to Pisa to see the leaning tower and then later wondered, as we waited for the train back, why we had thought it so important to see—was anathema to us, and we saw no reason to force march our children through the "grand sights." If we did happen on an unusual scene or art gallery, it was always without design.

The one time we made specific plans to see a particular museum was in Belgium. I had long admired the bizarre paintings of Hieronymus Bosch, but had only seen printed reproductions of his large canvases, usually in black and white or in miniature in art books with coarse coloring. A guide in the Hague museum which we chanced on while visiting the bustling harbor in Rotterdam told us of a museum in Antwerp housing the best collection of Bosch's works, and we made plans to go.

The outcome of this little journey points up a moral that is highly appropriate for this family tale. We traveled a full four hours out of our way and spent the night on the outskirts of this drab industrial city, ate a cold and tasteless breakfast in a cafeteria in town, and after waiting in the damp for the tourist office to open, were finally able to inquire about the location of the museum. The agent laconically informed us that the museum was closed on Tuesdays. It was nine o'clock Tuesday morning. We had traveled many hours to get to this particular place, spent a night in accommodations we didn't enjoy, eaten a breakfast we wouldn't have ordered otherwise, and now heard that we would have to prolong this agony twenty-four more hours. We tramped back to the car, plopped in, and headed out—away from those

narrow grim streets, the damp dreary climate, the . . . *bang!* A
motorized scooter moving from a narrow, alleylike corridor into
our street had rammed the side of our car. Oh, Antwerp! Oh,
Bosch! Oh, planned sightseeing. We would never forget.

This fiasco helped reinforce our conviction that the unlooked-for experience is the only one worthwhile. Further reinforcement came later that very night. Hungry and cranky after
three hours of traveling, we entered an inn in southern Belgium
where a large family party was in progress. The host found a free
table for us and while we were waiting for the first course, our
children gaped at the loud and joyous conviviality. There were
singing, shouting, laughing . . . and before we knew what had
happened a stout, red-faced man had swept all three of our children into the circle of singers where, without a moment's pause,
arms were thrown around their shoulders and swaying back and
forth they were absorbed into the rhythm of the song. The children were bursting with embarrassment and delight, their faces
beet red, their smiles almost explosive. Before long they were
picking up phrases of the Flemish song and singing and rocking
along with the rest. When it was over, there was a loud cheer for
the three little Americans, and they ran back to us overwhelmed
with good-fellowship.

After the meal, we unobtrusively rose to leave, only to have
the whole party turn toward us and start singing auf wiedersehen.
We all wanted to sing back something American and homey, but
our minds went blank. All we could do was wave and smile and
with watery eyes slowly back out of the inn.

The incident gave rise to a family discussion that night and
in succeeding days. We talked much of the European extended
family of aunts and uncles and grandparents and cousins, of
gemütlichkeit and how little of this we enjoyed in the States. The
idea of family and belonging to something larger than oneself, we
pointed out to the children, had been scorned when we were
young; yet here we were overwhelmed and maudlin in its presence.

It was the sort of conversation not uncommon among articulate adults while traveling. What was uncommon was to have
three children exposed to a wide range of such discussions for
long hours each day weeks on end. In that first month Bea and
I often talked to one another about our impressions as we drove,
and frequently the conversations were animated. Adam, our eld-

est, listened occasionally. Traveling in a closed five- by eight-foot steel missile with few distractions, it was probably hard for him to block us out. It was just as hard for him to miss the distinction between his own perceptions and those of his parents. No doubt we seemed to be seeing a lot more than he and relating it to whole areas of life and experience totally foreign to him.

There was, of course, an easy way for Adam to handle such problems—the way most kids do at school when teachers talk at them. He could simply stop listening, and he often did. But we clearly were having good times and were not plotting to involve him in these talks. So either from envy or curiosity, it was not long before he was quietly trying to follow some of these parental conversations.

Passing through the narrow, high-walled streets of a French village, he might hear us remark at the sudden glimpse of a bright inner courtyard seen through an unshuttered window and its suggestion of a medieval legacy of well-guarded and private family living; at the seeming hundred-year lag between city and village life; at the new power lines, alien and incongruous, leaping across the countryside; at the differences between suburban and rural life.

He started betraying his interest occasionally by interrupting us to ask a related question or add an observation of his own. And because we too were a captive audience, with no nine-to-five job or household chores to distract us, he often received adult answers to his questions and adult responses to his observations— a heady experience for an American child.

Seth, emulating his brother, though proudly asserting an independent point of view, also began to enter the discussions. And then Ariel, not to be left out, did her best to participate too.

Long before we reached the Costa Brava, we could see that the children were demanding more and more from their daytime experiences. They were finding them dull or redundant unless something new was brought to them, an association, a sense of coherence. The raw, isolated incident or impression was losing its novelty and its appeal. And as it did the children became increasingly jealous and curious about our conversations and our allusions to other events or times. They began to pry, to learn more about what we knew and about our perspectives, not just as parents but as adults. Without any effort to force interest or supply specific packets of knowledge to the children, we found ourselves barraged with Why? and What? and How? Our conversations were interrupted, our attention insisted upon. Our children were again asking questions—as all children do until they are six, before they are slowly turned off by formal education—not an occasional question as back in the States on a Friday evening at home, or on an outing on Sunday, or when they were troubled with a problem in a school textbook. They were flooding us with questions. Clearly a lot was happening. Their parents were forever talking, obviously happy and enthusiastic—as most adults would doubtless be at the prospect of almost a year of long days and long nights, of eating and sleeping and doing what they wanted when and where they wanted—and the children wanted to share in it. They realized that the sights, sounds, and smells we were delighting in were not isolated happenings but parts of larger patterns that they were missing.

As a result we entered one of the most unanticipated periods in our ten-month sojourn. It was the time of "the discussion." Anything could trigger it—a face, an overheard comment, some men playing dominoes. But it always started with a child's question. Then before we knew it another discussion had opened and went catapulting through times and places randomly linking facts, ideas, events, ethics, insights. To an outsider, such discussions might look more like intellectual ramblings. But the elements were usually related to one another, and together they worked to present a somehow generous and more integrated view of a subject—not an isolated fragment of knowledge, sharp and clean in its separateness, but a spreading, unchanneled flow of adult thoughts and feelings. And as long as the discussions were initiated by the children, the children were predisposed to listen, comment, and question more. Their attention span proved considerable. However, if attention did lag, the discussions were cut off abruptly. We had no desire to force learning on them, and we wanted that to be clear. We could easily measure their interest by the number of interruptions and follow-up questions thrown at us. Curiously, the children often revealed a desire for continuity by asking us to return to a point veered off from as a result of one of their questions or our own tendency to ramble.

So without plan or subtle design, Bea and I found ourselves more and more engaged in explaining or relating happenings and sights to other happenings and sights. From the occasional conversation that stemmed from a critical remark on seeing another dingy French village and then broadened to a general discussion of the lagging French economy to the almost formal dinnertime lectures on subjects preselected by each child with jealous independence, we found "the discussion" assuming an unlooked-for importance. And the range of these discussions was astonishing. Each subject seemed to swell and spill over into neighboring areas until it inevitably reached beyond any neatly defined borders. The process of associating ideas freely became an exciting, if undisciplined, intellectual game for Bea and me, mixing knowledge, values, surmise, and insight. The children were fascinated by these new gymnastics and were soon participating eagerly in the fun.

Here are three examples of discussions that took place during our first two days in Spain.

COMPARISON SHOPPING. Shortly after crossing the border at Perpignan, we passed through a bustling marketplace. The abundance of fresh fruit and vegetables whetted our appetites, and we decided to picnic out. We bought oranges, tangerines, plums, a head of cauliflower (which the children enjoyed eating raw), some cheese, a round loaf of Spanish bread, a bottle of local wine, and out of curiosity, because the sizes of the cans and the net weights printed on each can were identical, four different brands of Spanish-packaged anchovies. Later, while picnicking, we opened each of the cans and inspected all of them together. We noted that the least expensive can costing nine and a half pesetas clearly contained many more anchovies than the others, which cost up to twenty-two pesetas. Adam, Seth, and Ariel were all gathered round, fascinated with the anchovy count, and we launched into a discussion of misleading packaging and labeling and the usefulness of a bureau of weights and measures. The conversation then moved out into current attempts to standardize packaging in the United States, and the new importance of consumer protection legislation in car manufacture, moneylending, meat and fish packaging; and from there into installment buying and funerals, the consumer as a victim of motivational research, the homogenization of tastes, the trend toward a homogenized world society, sound economics versus the quality of life.

THE LOCAL ECONOMY. As we headed south, we passed through new and luxurious Mediterranean resort centers, but occasionally detoured into the impoverished mountain villages. The children found the contrast of these separate societies, so close to one another, extraordinary. We talked about the foreigners who lived and played in the resorts and the unchanging lives of many Spaniards; of Franco's totalitarianism versus French democracy; of how industry and jobs affect life styles; of the tourist economy versus a self-sustaining economy and how each determines the pace of life, the type and quality of stores, and the physical amenities of a community; of the comparative value of services and foods in terms of costs in the United States; of exchange rates for U.S. dollars; of continuing American aid to Spain; of the old Marshall Plan; of the vagaries of war that had left our victorious allies with economic chaos and placed our enemies—Japan and Germany—on the road to prosperity.

LEONARDO DA VINCI AND DISSECTION. In an old Spanish cemetery Seth was surprised to see a burial wall made beehive style to receive caskets and each buried casket decorated on its exposed end with little mementos of the dead such as religious medals, silver candlesticks, tiny flags, miniature figures, pictures of the dead, and often beer and whiskey bottles. The discussion that followed covered burial customs including pyramids and cremation, the curious attempts of some to take possessions of this world with them, the burial of jewels and money—sometimes horses, servants, and wives; grave robbers and Leonardo da Vinci digging up corpses at night in order to dissect them and study human anatomy; Leonardo's paintings, inventions, endless curiosity; the Renaissance man; the difficulty of producing a Renaissance man today because of the knowledge explosion; the positive and negative features of specialization for the individual and also for society.

These were typical of our discussions, and for a period of about three weeks such rambling talks occurred two or three times each day. The point is not that Bea and I are unusually gifted people with encyclopedic minds—we are not!—but that we and millions of other college-educated parents have much to offer our children from our own backgrounds and that we can be immensely effective teachers because we offer a true one-to-one relationship, personal as opposed to professional interest, and a diversity of experience with the real nonschool world—all of which put the teacher's sphere of competence and concern to shame.

It is amazing how much residue has been quietly deposited in the literate adult mind. We were as surprised as the children at the information we were able to dredge up on a wide variety of subjects. The knowledge a teacher brings to the classroom is often closely bounded by the curriculum, his view of his job, his inhibitions, or his fears of disorder—and as a result his teaching becomes stale and repetitious. But in our novel situation, as parent-teachers, we found ourselves chided and challenged to discover information we had long since lost all trace of, to salvage and quickly reassimilate whatever was still there, and then to show how it was related to the immediate problems and events that generated the original questions as well as to an expansive network of broader concepts. As a result we were not only dredging up information, we ourselves were being forced to learn. It was clearly exciting to discover, then make use of, the accumulated detritus of more than thirty years. The spontaneity of our discoveries made the telling and handling of the information a fresh and creative experience for all of us—the tellers as well as the listeners. The children doubtless sensed this because on those occasions when Bea or I set about informing them on a subject of no particular interest to us their interest in turn waned as fast as if one of us had said, "Now children, let's open our grammar books."

Besides, when daddy or mommy was boring, the children could say so with an honesty most youngsters would not want to test out with the classroom teacher. Nor would they feel free to abruptly interrupt the teacher's clearly formulated lesson plans with shouted questions, challenges, and new thoughts. Perhaps that is why all three of our children caught on to the fun of an idea free-for-all and eagerly sought to play their full part. And it was not only in our discussions that they discovered the excitement of ideas, but in their exposure to random sights and happenings each day. Their impressions were no longer separate and fragmented. More and more we found them arranging and placing their observations. Our travels became a giant puzzle in which the children took visible pleasure in fitting separate experiences into larger patterns. Events and ideas that had been disconnected pieces during the first weeks started to have threads trailing from them which the children occasionally caught on to and tied together with other threads in little demonstrations of mental agility. Sometimes a network of threads would form around

a favorite subject—such as men at w
developed countries, underdeveloped pe
would seek out opportunities to return
themes kept developing, but old ones c
strength as more and more impressions fou
tions.

However, this random approach to learn
more threads and subjects were discovered—
itself too diffuse to satisfy the children. Nothing   ...u to
be completed or fully explored. And there were   ...ys the vast
dark caverns of information hinted at but inaccessible. Despite
their insatiable appetite for knowledge and new ideas, the children were often both tantalized and troubled at the end of one
of our discussions. The haphazard outpourings of information
seemed to have a cumulatively cloying effect on them.

I remember during a lengthy discussion of life on distant
stars noticing that the two boys, mouths open, were staring off
into space. I purposely paused midsentence to see if I had lost
them. Their expressions didn't change for two long seconds;
then Adam said, "Well, go on," and I nodded toward Seth, who
appeared to be in a stupor. After a full ten seconds, Seth turned
toward me and quietly asked a question relating to the very last
point I had made. When I answered his question, both boys sat
back exhausted, needing time to digest what they had been hearing, to relate it to other things they had heard or already knew,
to make it usable.

For the children were learning how to associate and connect
information on their own. They needed time for speculation, to
arrange their own thoughts. And as they began challenging us
with their own ideas, they started investigating new sources of
information and stimulation including other adults, books and
magazines, and their own and each other's observations. In time
the free-ranging parental discussions became less central to
them. (Though even today they will occasionally turn to us before
going to bed or at a quiet moment at dinner and say, "Let's have
a discussion.") The emphasis was shifting to activities wholly
initiated and carried out by the children themselves with little
supervision. And as our contributions became less and less dominant, their own horizons started to expand and their personal
channels of interest to deepen. We had puffed out their sails and
now they were running free.

IN LA HERRADURA

As we continued our journey south, hugging the Spanish coast, the views of the Mediterranean were spectacular, but somehow we felt separated from the Spain we had expected to see.

It was late December now and much of the rugged Costa Brava—encrusted with the handsome villas and bungalows of international vacation colonies—was silent and uninhabited. It was as if the narrow strip of coastline, cut off as it was from the interior of Spain by steep mountain ranges, was afflicted by a cancer of alien, lifeless habitations.

We began traveling more rapidly south through newly conceived and totally planned resort communities, silent and unpeopled, like unused movie sets; through the low and swampy shore land of the Gulf of Valencia; through isolated hamlets and cliff-hanging villages in the Sierra Nevada in settings of breathtaking natural splendor—bleak, desolate, rock-strewn terrain with gaping canyons and immense, ominous stone outcroppings rising everywhere, and then every once in a while, as the road pulled far enough away from the forbidding cliffs, a sudden, ghostlike view of the distant snow-covered peak, Cerro Mulhacén, one of the highest points in Europe, yet only a few miles from Africa. The convoluted mountain road finally wound its way back toward the coast and then down to the richly fertile, lush green delta of Almuñécar. There, for three weeks, we tried adjusting to a luxurious five-bedroom villa with a gardener and a full-time maid, a formal outdoor garden with fountains and archways, an interior garden and a circular free-standing living room fireplace—all for one hundred and fifty dollars a month.

It was far too elaborate for our tastes. During this period we took a few exploratory hikes, and once, after a particularly long trek along the coast further south, we discovered a little fishing village tucked into a hillside on a mile-long, seemingly deserted beach. From the road, the village couldn't be seen, and as a result it had been overlooked by tourists. But even so the land speculators had found it out and a small development of luxury villas (including the home of Andrés Segovia, we later discovered) had been built high up above the eastern end of the beach. Close to the development was the village itself, a line of stores (butcher shop, bakery, hardware store, café, grocery) fronting on the beach and then winding back to form a short main street where a row of open stalls was used mornings to market fruit, fish, meat, and vegetables. Rising up the hillside above the stalls were tiered levels of simple whitewashed homes fronted by narrow immaculately clean cobblestoned walkways that at the deepest recess in the hill joined a cart-sized cobblestoned path rising precipitously from the main street. In the one flat area on the hillside was the church square with a pert little church and an immense resounding bell. It was one of the two focal points of town life. The other was the café on the beach, where for much of the day groups of local men, including the mayor, would sit quietly sipping wine and playing dominoes.

Further along the beach the hills receded, leaving a large, flat, fertile area, richly cultivated, which bordered the shoreline. On the far side of the beach the hills closed in again and the shoreline turned rocky and rugged. It was here that we saw a lone white stucco house sitting placidly on a protected knoll. We cut across the beach and then climbed above it to gain a closer view. It was a large, modern, authentically Spanish villa affording a panoramic view of the bay of La Herradura on the left, a one-hundred-eighty-degree vista of the Mediterranean straight ahead, and on the right a landscape of open fields that dropped off into a gulley and then rose in stages to an immense stone-faced mountain. Some of the residents of La Herradura who had seen or been told of our walk across the beach (a family of strangers was an uncommon sight in La Herradura, particularly in January) were waiting for us on our return, and when we inquired, eagerly informed us that the house was untenanted, that Señor Rudi of Las Palmas (the name of the luxury development) was the man to see about rentals, that they hoped we would stay.

We climbed the steep hill to the development, sought out Rudi, a soft-spoken French expatriate and former World War II pilot, and inquired about the house across the bay. He immediately tried to dissuade us, offering instead a number of handsome villas in the development itself, where, he pointed out, we could enjoy not only his own and his wife's company but that of other cultured Europeans as well. Besides, we would have the services of maids, gardeners, and other amenities available in the development. We resisted, even when he insisted the house we had set our minds on would be unsuitable for our needs. Reluctantly he agreed to allow us to inspect it. We rode in his jeep down the hill to the shore (some townspeople waved familiarly as we passed), then across the long beach, fording a stream and avoiding numberless potholes, rocks, and boulders, and finally up the hill to the house itself. A small arched door led into a spacious, modern but sparsely furnished interior, and as the shutters of each room were opened we were treated to spectacular views on all sides. Most of the rooms opened on a huge stone-tiled deck that ran completely around the exterior of the house. There was no fancy furniture, but there were beds and built-in cabinets, a massive fieldstone living room fireplace, a modern refrigerator and stove (fed by bottled gas), and a large array of deck chairs. In addition there were no gardens to maintain (just a three-acre open field covered with wild flowers), no required maid (though we finally did have one come in mornings each day when we learned that the townspeople thought us unfair to run a house and not hire one of the local girls), no expatriate neighbors, no wind to buffet us, and a delightfully rugged shorefront with tidal pools, sea spray, and a sense of isolation. Rudi said the rental would be one hundred eighty dollars a month, a price he thought would discourage us, but without any haggling we took it, leaving him to mumble that we really didn't know how lonely it could be living in a place like this. He suggested that we try it for just a few weeks before settling in. But the children were already down by the shore, running across the field, exploring the gulley, discovering a stray cat, and we knew we had found a place to stay. In two days, after I learned how to navigate the beach in our Volvo, we were fully moved in. The townspeople had seen us crisscross a few times over the beach, and by the time we came into town to pick up our first supplies, we were familiar faces to the entire community—we were the 'Mericanos.

5.

COUNTERING

THE OLD VALUES

In this remote village, in which they and their values were alien, the children began finding some of their old ideas about what was right or wrong inappropriate, even ludicrous. Their peer groups, their schools, and the mass media could no longer provide convenient measuring sticks for much of what they were encountering. They had been exposed as travelers to a dizzying range of sights, customs, and ideas; and now as long-term residents in a strange setting they were being forced to reconcile many of their beliefs and habits with the mores and codes of this other specific society. The adjusting process seemed to provide them with fresh perspectives of what they had left behind in suburban America and insights into how defined and arbitrary their values had been.

Although a clean break with these old values had been our immediate purpose in going abroad, our eventual goal was to create a firm base of family and personal values that could stand up against the whims and changing fashions of McDonaldland. Because our children would be returning. But by then, hopefully, their value systems would be so intertwined with strong personal interests and privately arrived at attitudes that they could maintain a separate viewpoint on what was happening about them.

La Herradura was to provide a period of countereducation in which the influences of the peer group, the schools, and the mass media were to be effectively neutralized.

COUNTER PEER GROUP

I had long believed that the most insidious force working on the children was their own peer group, not because the group expressed a set of beliefs or a way of life that I quarreled with, but simply because the group believed in and adhered to nothing. This was not an embittered parent's or hard-line teacher's judgment. I was a "way out" teacher, a "cool" guy who "knew where it was at." The kids "leveled" with me, "Ya know, man. Ya know." The patched jeans and long hair, the random screwing in the woods behind the school, the shit, pills, horse, the "screw the flag, screw the church, screw the school, and the whole job-family-house kick, ya know, man, ya know." But I didn't know. And the more I listened and observed, the more I knew *they* didn't know.

Throughout history exceptional young people have questioned the moral and social orders of their times, but never before had a large percentage of the children of a nation rejected all order in society. We had all seen coming the loss of influence of the church but none had anticipated the rapidity with which religious codes of right and wrong would be neglected and then abandoned entirely by young people. Many of us had also carped at small-town loyalties, at regional pride, at national chauvinism, but again no one had anticipated that an entire generation of teenagers would jeer at its towns, decry regionalism, and openly scorn and mock its country. So, too, with the family. Until recently only playwrights and bachelors faulted the family, blaming it for warped lives, stifled talents, and enforced relationships. No one had thought that our children—armed with cars, money, and the knowledge that we, their parents, had shunted grandma off to a senior citizen's community—would regard with contempt our values, our way of life, our efforts to provide well for them. As for the law, we had all occasionally abused or used it for our own purposes, but again no one had expected a generation to move as quickly from high-minded social protest like the Birmingham sit-ins to outright ridicule of the police, the laws of the land, the very courts of justice. This was a generation turned off —turned off from patriotism, religion, community, law, family, turned off from all the traditional sources of values and moral order.

And what were they turned on to? A craze. A passing fad. The only serious agents at play in the game were the mass media and their commercial sponsors, who saw in these children a large malleable mass of consumers who could be easily excited and used for marketing products. Only they continued to exercise the last strings of control on these youngsters, who otherwise constituted a directionless herd unified only in feeling that each one's primary concern was to keep pace with the others, whether it was in music, dress, sex, protest, or acts of violence.

And that was exactly what I wanted to free my children from. I wanted them to know what they wanted to do with their time, their energies, and their lives; to know what their own tastes, their own interests, and their own values were. And if this awareness took them into protest, if it took them into communal life or suburban marriage, if it resulted in them spitting in the eyes of a policeman and calling him "Pig!" or in sober scholarship—so be it. I might have wished for something different or deeper or with more panache or humor, but I would not have felt the dread and helplessness of a parent seeing his child first sucked into a horde, then writhing and wriggling to the mad beat of the mob.

To counter the peer group, Bea and I proposed three forces: the family, the world of diversity, and the idea of self-determination. By family, of course, I mean primarily Bea and me and our values, hopefully worthwhile, free of commercialism or absolutism—and even if far short of ideal, at least offered with an acceptance of total responsibility. However, I also mean the children, who though stripped of their peer-group standards were nonetheless involved in effecting and changing our family values. Because during those first months abroad everything was tentative, even such mommy and daddy dicta as getting to bed on time, drinking lots of milk, and not talking to strangers. We, too, were affected by the unaccountability enjoyed by the traveler and the awareness that old patterns could no longer be followed.

What do you do when a country has no pasteurized milk?

The children drink goat's milk, exotic fruit juices, diluted wine. What do you do when a foreign setting offers evening sights and sounds and people? The children, goggle eyed and alert, adventure with you sometimes beyond midnight. What do you do when you're eager to know a people or sense a way of life? The children, like you, learn to abandon their reserve and become voluble and open with strangers.

As we moved from village to city, from one nation to another, new ideas, beliefs, and standards presented themselves one after another, adding new qualities and new relationships to a social awareness. The only values and standards that remained were those our family continued to carry with it from place to place, and these were constantly being challenged. The way things were done in New York City or America became simply other possibilities in this changing panorama. The only meaningful values were clearly seen as those each of us chose to adopt and, interestingly, those all of us in the family could mutually accept as we continued our journey.

In this way a fresh set of family values emerged, values such as a sense of family cohesion in which loyalty, pride, and shared responsibility played important roles; an acceptance of each other in the family without judgment, without comparison; a sense of belonging in a family that boasted a five-member identity and felt incomplete if any member was absent; a sense of personal identity as well, in a family that prized each individual's separate qualities as contributing to a family character; and an esprit de corps that sometimes expressed itself spontaneously— for example, after Bea prepared a flaming shish kebab dinner, she was greeted by the wild family cheer: "Kalamazoo, gazoo, gazam! Sonofabitch, god damn! Highty-tighty, Christamighty! Rah! Rah! Sheeeeeet!"—and sometimes more deliberately as when Bea and I were welcomed home from a couple of days away in Morocco with a children's show of Seth singing (original lyrics by his brother), Ariel dancing, and Adam playing his clarinet.

The children's involvement in creating our family life style while abroad gave them a sense of responsibility for family values. These were not group codes imposed from outside, but basic attitudes built up from each person's own judgments and adjustments in this miniature detached society. The emphasis on participation in forming values did more than strengthen family values; it enforced a continued recognition of the responsibility of each of us for his actions.

Once this feeling was established, the children were able to extend their sense of control into personal areas of interest—so that one child could study a chiton for a moment or a day and another could pursue a fascination with photography for an entire year—without any question about educational or social value. The occupations were what the children wanted to do, not authority-directed activities or peer-group fads. The children were intelligently and responsibly following their own interests. And they believed that to be good. It helped them to know that the other four members of the family also believed it to be good.

But opposing the peer group with what the family believed to be good or with a sudden emphasis on individual values would have had little effect had we not also moved the children out of familiar surroundings to strange environments. The sheer exposure to a multiplicity of life styles, dress, habits made them quickly realize not only that there exists incredible diversity in the world but that no one way is right or proper, that all of us have opportunities to pick and choose and perhaps even find a separate way.

Bea and I have always been curious about and open to other ways of living. And the children, observing us in these shifting environments, were quick to adopt, as children will, our attitude. They were soon regarding other cultures, not as zoolike exhibits to be goggled at, remarked upon, and left unrelated to what was thought true back home, but as alternatives. They were measuring and comparing all their old beliefs and the jargon, dress, and changing codes of their peers back home. They were also now able to see the peer group stripped of its importance and glamor, without support from those formidable allies, the schools and the mass media. These agencies not only reinforced the dominance of the peer group over each child but also wrought their own damage to each child as well.

COUNTERSCHOOL

Just as we wanted to end the uncontested authority of the peer group, so too did we want to stop the mechanical, morally empty education the children were receiving in their schools. It wasn't just a matter of countering what the schools were doing wrong—though that is the substance of much of the book—it was a conviction that too much of what needed doing in the schools wasn't being done at all.

NO CLASSROOMS. We felt that the physical structure of schools was itself a threat to meaningful education. To shut children into a room for six hours a day simply because it is economically more efficient and convenient to assemble them there, to store books, desks, and chairs, and to station teachers, shows a profound misunderstanding of the learning process. The device is not only painfully artificial but unquestionably ineffective educationally.

What is needed is not peer-group isolation in learning rooms but exposure to other parents and a wide range of adults; to older and younger children; to infants and young mothers and senior citizens; to the real world of industrial offices, construction projects, railroad yards, supermarkets, and department stores; to plumbers and lawyers and housewives and carpenters and draftsmen. The things to be learned are all around children and the books and visual aids and teachers can only help them to comprehend, cope with, and, hopefully, go beyond these things.

The most effective learning—for all but those who learn under any system—is not the result of abstract associations or simulation exercises in a room cut off from the community, but the outgrowth of real situations. And that is what we wanted to counter the schoolroom with—everything outside those four walls.

NO TEACHERS. We also wanted to do away with "the teacher" —that lonely adult, separated from the real world and locked in a room with thirty children for most of his working life. Who is to learn from whom—the children bringing with them thirty different sets of real experiences or the one adult with his schoolroom and unnatural child's world emphasis? Too often the teacher sees his job as no more than winning attention for his bag of school tricks and then selling a grade-level package of information and skills. For they are tricks, schoolroom games and exercises that at best can be shown to have some distant relevance to the children's lives. To make the children play his games in earnest, the teacher uses disciplinary rules and regulations, competitive marks, adult authority, and the threat of a lifetime of failure. The result is that most teachers become depersonalized agents of the establishment rather than adult persons worth listening to or modeling one's life after.

And that again, is what we wanted to counter. We wanted the whole community to be our children's teacher, not some bossy

Gulliver meddling in Lilliput. We didn't want learning to be thought of as prescribed packages purveyed at separate grade levels by grade-level educators. We wanted learning to be channeled and concentrated according to each child's inclinations and needs, with the teacher becoming simply one of many resources in and out of the school. We wanted knowledge and skills and values to be revealed as the concern of the entire community, not just of a single adult jealous of his authority to contain education. We wanted no teacher to limit a child's education whether it be to the establishment's standardized package or to his own areas of interest and understanding. We wanted our children to be free of the tyranny of any single adult, no matter how bright or benevolent.

NO TEXTBOOKS. We were also determined to end the drudgery of homework and assignments and working from textbooks. What the school feels a child is ready to learn and what the child is ready to learn are totally different. For school people, "ready to learn" is a statistical concept having to do with trafficking a standardized body of information and skills over a period of thirteen years from kindergarten to college. However, though a child of thirteen may indeed be capable of mastering basic algebra, her real interests may be in learning to purchase her own clothes or indulging in some sex play in the girls' room. But sex education is scheduled for next year and consumer purchasing has no place in the curriculum. The very process of systematizing learning dehumanizes education and forces each individual to suppress his natural curiosities and interests in order to achieve some statistical goal.

Our countereducative approach was to reverse the process so that the system became the servant of each child, supplying him as needed with what he wanted and was ready to learn. In La Herradura there were no more assigned readings or textbooks to plow through chapter by chapter. Each child discovered his own interests and started reaching out for resources to satisfy them. It could be a drawing pad, a trip into the marketplace, or a book on World War II. But whatever the resource, it was sought out and used to satisfy the student's goals and not the system's.

NO SCHOOL HOURS. So, too, with *when* children learned. It is, no doubt, convenient for the system to schedule whole blocks of time so that facilities and teachers can be efficiently employed. But the result has been the institution of learning by assembly line, a belt system uniformly paced to bring the student each day through the same five subject-matter disciplines where he is systematically fed packets of prescribed facts, skills, and impressions, then released home to eat, sleep, and rest up before being picked up by the belt again for another round of subject-packet feeding.

Here again our purpose was to reverse this process, to remove our children from conveyor-belt learning that made knowledge a fragmented, repetitive, mechanical process and to place them in a learning environment that was total, exciting, and their own. From the moment they awoke in the morning to the moment they drowsed off into sleep they would be learning; wherever they were would be their school; whatever they were doing would be their subject; whatever adults, objects, or resources were at hand would be their teachers. We wanted to wipe out the six-hour school day and replace it with twenty-four hours of working, playing, and learning blended indistinguishably into one full day of living.

COUNTERMEDIA

To leave the schools and the peer groups behind required simply getting on a plane and putting miles between us and them. But the mass media were not so easily dismissed. American songs, films, television programs were much in evidence wherever we visited. Of course, the density of mass media impressions was much reduced simply because we spent less time in front of television sets, listening to radio, or in the movie houses. But they were still to be reckoned with.

We were out to destroy their creatures, the anonymous listener-viewers. We wanted to free our children from the media's spell and bring them back into the world of involvement and interaction, to have them grasp opportunities for action and not accept the passive role of viewer, to show them life isn't a matter of one random dial-switched half-hour experience after another without pattern and without personal control. We wanted them to start directing their own lives on the basis of the whole gamut of possible experiences open to them, rather than the packaged offerings on six electronic circuits.

Instead of watching the television serial we took to story

telling ourselves. Some were tales we had read or heard, but more were fanciful stories created on the spot and for the occasion by each of us. There was no small excitement when one of us decided it was story time again. Frequently there was fierce competition for the privilege of telling the first tale.

Instead of news and documentaries, we had our own newsworthy experiences, our own on-the-spot investigations of interesting subjects; and though we may have discussed, declaimed, reasoned, and analyzed somewhat less cogently than Eric Sevareid, we did it with far more spirit. Music too was our own. It might be Seth intoning some mad narrative set incongruously to "God Bless America" or Ariel singing "Silent Night" on a sweltering summer day or all five of us roaring together some aria that Bea had started humming—but there was always song.

CONTINUITY OF EXPERIENCE. We not only wanted to restore a sense of self-direction, we wanted to reintroduce the idea of continuity in life. The fragmented, turn-the-dial kaleidoscope of experience and imagery offered by television has fostered the idea of discontinuity and purposelessness in life itself. To meet this attitude required not only that the children develop strong individual interests but also that each feel a continuity and cohesion in the family's rhythms of working, talking, and living together. If they were to experience something it happened in a family context, in their immediate surroundings and usually as a result of their own choice or actions. They were in La Herradura not as viewers or as part of a Nielsen TV rating. Experiences were not electronic, disassociated, predetermined. They were human.

6. DISCOVERING INDIVIDUAL INTERESTS AND THE NEED FOR SKILLS

We had managed to cut the children loose from their peer groups, their schools, and the mass media and allow them to begin creating a personal system of values. At the same time we had encouraged them to discover their own areas of interest. As a family we might all come to value privacy, openness, wit, imagination, and persistence, but each of us had to find his or her own distinctive interests in which to put these values to work.

Until now much of the children's lives had been taken up with other people's interests and objectives, so when we presented to them the idea that what most interested them was worthy of serious attention, it came as almost a comical thought. The schoolteachers, the Little League coach, the Brownie leader, the ubiquitous peer group, and even we—wrapped up in our own pursuits and jealous of our few free hours—had all been making demands on their time and insisting on their attention. It would have been downright presumptuous for a child to put forward his own concerns in the face of such formidable competition. And so they hadn't. They chose rather, like most children, to suppress their needs and curiosity, to turn a sullen or bitter face to the world, or worse, to docilely await that moment when these outside demands and their inner desires would coincide.

And so we set about unencumbering the children, freeing them of all the have-to-do, have-to-know dicta that had thickly encrusted their own inclinations. We also limited our demands on their time—having not only more time ourselves to follow up our own interests but more reason to doubt the desirability of making our interests theirs.

Bea and I were still very much available to the three of them, and we had our own favored activities like reading, writing, and participant sports that we wanted the children to discover too. However, our emphasis had changed. We recognized that the children had to discover the satisfactions on their own. Of course, we may have fostered some excitement in certain activities by our own example. But generally the children's interests were shaped less by imitation than by a coalescence of family values such as the need for independent inquiry and judgment, thoroughness, and curiosity. We favored this loose approach because we were convinced that this was not only what sound education was all about but the best way of meeting the requirements of the schoolroom. For as the children pursued their own concerns, we fully expected their activities to spill over into the conventional subject areas (reading, writing, arithmetic, geography, history, science) of formal education and force on them an appreciation of the need for classroom-taught skills. The difference working to our advantage was that the skills and the need for mastery in basic subject areas would grow out of their personal interests rather than be used to produce personal interests. Our children might indeed be involved with random subject areas such as sea life, photography, or housekeeping, but we hoped their keen involvement would enthusiastically awaken them to the need for books, for writing skills, for mathematical accuracy.

So at first we went about our own business, offering the children no curriculum, prodding them into no educative activity. We simply stood by—as Adam shot a few rolls of film with his new camera or sketched out a room plan, as Seth roamed the rocky shore looking for new forms of sea life, as Ariel helped around the kitchen. But when our approval was sought, or when we chanced on them busily engaged, we would offer encouragement, guidance, and occasionally ideas. The ideas were introduced casually and never as more than just ideas. Sometimes they allowed the children to see new opportunities and better ways to follow their interests. In Adam's case his problems with focus in photography led to discussions of other problems in camera work, to further experiments, books, and a many-faceted interest in the art and science of photography.

So too with Seth and Ariel. What started as a spark of interest was sheltered and encouraged into intense activity and then allowed to spread to other areas. But the initiative was always the child's.

Ariel, for example, lacking self-motivation, had hung around her brothers back home trying either to win some part in their activities or to annoy them until they went at her screaming their hate. Like most fathers, I was around evenings only, and like most mothers, Bea was occupied with a host of adult affairs in which little girls played no part. So there were only her brothers to latch on to or, if they resisted, to fight with.

However, in La Herradura, Bea and I enjoyed lots of discretionary time and, sensing Ariel's need for companionship and involvement, we started using her shiftless approaches as occasions for long, easy conversations, for doing little household chores together, and sometimes for prodding her into some activity on her own. Once, seeking me out at my typewriter, she looked particularly forlorn. I turned from my work and she seemed almost embarrassed by my full attention. We talked desultorily about the funny vendors in the marketplace, her improvement in climbing the rugged surrounding mountains, and a letter Seth had received from a cousin in the States.

"I never receive any letters," she said, looking obliquely at me.

"You never write any," I answered.

"I can't. You know I can't write letters like Adam and Seth."

"Why not?"

"I just can't, that's all."

"You've never really tried."

"I can't! You wouldn't help me."

"Yes! Yes, I would."

"Right now?"

"Now!"

And so for the next hour Ariel, sprawled out on the bed in

my room with pencil and pad in hand, composed a letter to her cousin Stephen. This first letter was more than a joint effort. I was asked what to say, how to spell every second word, whether I liked the way a sentence sounded. But as a result, writing letters became one of Ariel's favorite activities. Two or three times each week she would pair herself off with Bea or me—and later with Adam or Seth, who after seeing us work with her were eager to do some coaching themselves—and start her latest letter.

Ariel discovered there was a lot happening that she could tell about, and she was fascinated by the idea of communicating long distances via a piece of paper. As a result she slowly became less dependent on her coaches for ideas. After laboring over a letter for an hour or two, she would bring it to one of us—ostensibly so we could pick up her spelling and punctuation errors, but really so she could study the pleasure in our eyes as we read her latest communication with America. And we were truly delighted because we found not only that her memory was astonishingly accurate, but that behind many of her bizarre misspellings were some very sophisticated words.

Like letter writing, most of Ariel's sparks of interest had to be blown into fires and then constantly nourished with approval and attention. This lot fell primarily to Bea, who shouted, cajoled, teased, and pushed Ariel along in a wide range of academic and womanly areas of concern. She had Ariel join her while she exercised in modern dance, had Ariel help in preparing dinner, in housekeeping, in gardening; she worked tirelessly with the child in arithmetic, penmanship, speech. With calculation, she developed in Ariel a sense of womanliness in dress, carriage, manner, and personal habits. And because of Bea's concentrated effort, Ariel started to feel that she too had her special strengths. Whereas before she had sat back or disengaged from anything beyond her immediate abilities, she was now enthusiastically modeling after her mother and in the process acquiring new personal skills with which to meet an expanded range of interests and experiences.

With Seth our concern was not so much in developing interests as in limiting them. Our visits to a number of impressive Dutch, Belgian, and French churches, with their dusky paintings and brilliant stained-glass story windows, stimulated a lively interest in biblical times. It was Seth who insisted that Bea each night read to the family a few stories from the Bible before the children headed for bed. And it was Seth whose curiosity about ancient times spilled over into Greek and Roman history. No less intense was his fascination with map reading. He could study a map of Europe for two hours and return to it again and again, tracing rivers, measuring distances by air and land, pronouncing the names of strange cities. When his brother gave up keeping a diary, Seth decided to start one and rarely missed a day without fully recording his and the family's adventures. He was also our best story teller and began writing fantasies based upon a series of surrealistic paintings he had cut out of an art magazine.

Perhaps more important than the range of his interests, however, was the manner in which these interests were being developed. The multitude of new experiences seemed to supercharge his senses. He observed, listened, absorbed all and then associated his impressions and let them bubble over into activities and endless talk. For in La Herradura, unlike the enforced quiet of a classroom and the limited intellectual give-and-take afforded by his peers back home, Seth was able to shout, sing, and talk endlessly and to interact with adults who wanted to stimulate and augment his thoughts and impressions.

Seth, and Adam too, were convinced that we had no devious plan or preconceived ideas about what specifically they should be interested in. As a result they were less apt to jump from one project to another, less likely to grow bored or listless. With control over their activities, they now had every reason to be involved and enthusiastic about what they were doing. Their span of concentration lengthened, their inquiries deepened, their willingness to work, plan, and practice in order to gain skills or understanding rapidly increased. Their interests were developing and being tested in a neutral environment where only their own satisfactions held them to a task.

Of course, at the beginning there was some shifting as each of them—Ariel too—experimented with art forms, academic subjects, household activities, letter writing, diaries, gymnastics, woodcraft, botany, construction. But it wasn't long before each child had centered on his own major activities and then stayed with them. During the remainder of our stay abroad, other interests cropped up and, particularly with Seth, were retained as part of their continuing activities. But it was from these first interests that the children gained a sense of separate identity. For in discovering these interests, they recognized not only their release from the standardized patterns back home but their introduction to a life in which they would be free to find their own types of fulfillments.

As their interests deepened, the need for skills became increasingly apparent to the children. Frequently they became involved in an activity only to find that a shortcoming in dexterity or lack of special skill was handicapping them. Seth, printing his thoughts word by word in a diary, was enraged by his inability to keep up with his galloping mind. Bea suggested that learning script would help him to write much faster. For two solid weeks he attacked script with the fierce energy he usually reserved for schoolyard fights. A related problem existed for Adam, who had begun writing an adventure novel. I told him I thought his work quite professional and mentioned that it would be nice if he had been able to type it. A few weeks later we found him pecking away at Bea's typewriter. Bea showed him the proper fingering for touch typing, and then off and on for the next month he laboriously worked at it. By the end of our trip abroad he was touch typing fifty words a minute.

But more than penmanship, typing, and manual skills resulted from these interests. The desire to know directed the children more and more to outside sources—not just to their parents with their increasingly visible limitations—but to other adults, community resources, newspapers, magazines, and books. Again and again the pursuit of information, of entertainment, of stimulation led finally to books, and each of the children in turn found in books one of the most convenient resources. The skill and habit of reading were acquired as readily as learning to play basketball.

Seth's interest in a pine cone led him into a general study of flowers, trees, shrubs, and seed dispersion. Adam suggested that he take notes, and before long Seth had started a journal of scientific experiments. In the process he discovered the scientific method and established his own procedure for observing, recording, and evaluating data.

So too with almost all the children's activities. Helping mommy cook required Ariel to learn how to crack and open eggs, read package labels, and scrub a skillet until it was really clean. Sketching a plan for a new city forced Adam to guess and practice until he had mastered many of the intricacies of perspective and three-dimensional drawing. Winning the job of map reader from Adam compelled Seth night after night to study maps spread out on the floor or on his bed until he could estimate kilometers between two points, identify secondary versus dirt roads, distinguish northeast from southeast, relate rivers and topography to population centers. He ended up as more than our map reader; he became our geography expert.

These were not abstract skills, classified and approached systematically by grade level with textbooks and carefully worked out methodology. These were skills discovered in the process of wanting to know or do; they were needed. Bea and I felt that if certain skills were really important, a curious and enthusiastic child would quickly discover their usefulness and set about acquiring them without the promise of some distant reward for his efforts.

III.

EXPLODING

THE OLD CURRICULUM

What we did in our separate little family community in Spain was to scatter the disciplines to the winds and end formal schooling. We broke through the walls that separated school, community, and home and allowed any activity to start and continue without limits of proper time or proper place. We thoroughly blurred the distinctions between working, learning, and playing. And then, after we had stopped worrying about whether our children were losing time, keeping up with the College Boards, or falling behind or to the side of their peers, we started to savor the exciting possibilities of educating our own children. Before we could start the process of fashioning a new education, however, we had first to destroy the old.

TO HELL WITH SUBJECT SPECIALIZATION

The presumption that our schools have somehow been able to confine within five or six subject areas all that has to be learned by a child each year had long puzzled me. Perhaps at one time it seemed a good idea to rationalize learning rather than depend on tutors or random experience. And thus was born mass education, a revolutionary system for providing desirable information, skills, and ideas. The rationale was linear and the technique easily instituted: (1) certain subjects were to be identified as important to the exclusion of all others, (2) these subjects were to be isolated and thereby treated more efficiently, and (3) the material within each subject was to be ordered and placed in sequence.

However, in 1970, for students nurtured on a turn-the-dial, fragmented TV culture, this lockstep system of subject 1—teacher 1—room 1, subject 2—teacher 2—room 2, and so on each day (with slight modification under modular scheduling), five days a week, forty weeks a year, and the whole process repeated the following year with only slight difference in subject content, seemed pointlessly limited and totally out of touch with the students' needs.

Perhaps the whole mess could be blamed on intrinsic fallacies in mass education. In the process of trying to extend education to everyone, educators may have succumbed to the false logic of first establishing uniform goals that could be incorporated into a general and duplicable routine, then systematizing the routine, and finally emphasizing the machinery of the system rather than the student who was being fed into the machinery. But wherever the blame lay, this elaborate mechanism had been allowed to creak along unaltered right through the fifties, sixties, and early seventies, while the needs of young people and the world outside continued to change rapidly.

Experimental and daring programs had been tried here and there in an affluent suburb or an inner-city neighborhood. But our concern was with the other 95 percent of schools, where education was hopelessly patterned and fixed. To tamper with basic educational premises—even more, to begin the task of creating a whole new set of premises with new goals, procedures, and structures—would have been almost incomprehensible to most school personnel. In a small country like England an unstructured educational program might quickly win acceptance in the schools, but the United States contained twenty thousand jealously autonomous school systems and the implantation of fundamental reforms on a national level was almost inconceivable. The American school system had been going about its business for decades unaffected by the birth and dominance of the TV medium, the death of God and religion, the breakup of the American family, the internationalization of life styles, and the ascendancy of peer-group values. A system that could withstand such momentous change and continue undeterred in its routine was not just intractable—it was incapable of response.

It could be argued that many centuries of thought and painstaking refinement had been required to achieve this intricately detailed, universally accepted, and physically overwhelming institution: teachers specially trained by subject and grade level, specially designed schools and classrooms, sequenced and graded learning materials, a complete set of progressive educational laws and traditions, community-sanctioned methods and curricula. To suggest scrapping the system and starting all over again with something loose, something untested could only be nihilistic and irresponsible.

And yet to do less would be to continue tinkering. For the very system of American education, so meticulously, so minutely fashioned in its functions and parts, was beyond doubt itself the factor that had to be replaced.

This was no random generalization. It was based upon what I believed to be intrinsic failings in our system of formal education. If we were ever to start anew, we had at last to recognize:

- that learning inclinations are destroyed when they are confined to a small block of time, repeated mechanically and regularly, and given the same importance as five others blocks of time with subjects selected and defined by authorities
- that information, ideas, and values are not containable in subject areas, that knowledge moves freely and should be seen as relevant to all areas of interest without boundaries
- that true teachers are to be found not in subject areas but in areas of probity, enthusiasm, resourcefulness, sympathy, warmth, ability to foster—or if that is too manipulative, to encourage—attitudes, approaches, values; that they are not information mongers with varying degrees of charm, entertainment value, or personal qualities to enhance this function
- that schoolteachers are counterfeit adults, separated as they are from the functioning community and adult occupations; they are secondhand guides, talkers rather than doers

- that the school building itself, physically isolating the children from the community, reinforces the feeling that education is unrelated to what's happening outside
- that grouping all youngsters of one age in a room with a strange adult proficient in one area of knowledge is not only unnatural but confirms the idea that people are similar and almost interchangeable integers; that learning is impersonal, mechanical, sequential; that a child can learn only through a rigidly limited adult or an isolated set of youngsters his own age
- that grouping in itself is an outgrowth of the desire to be tidy and efficient; that entrance requirements, promotions, graduation, course sequences are formal educational nuts and bolts that we have allowed to override the most basic considerations of real education.

And these were only a few of the fundamental wrongs I saw in the system. Without malice or even conscious effort, the schools had turned the formal educational machinery into a robotlike colossus and allowed it to run amok.

THE FAILURE OF SUBJECT DISCIPLINES

When I first started teaching on the high school level, I occasionally teased some of the older teachers of math, of languages, of history, and even those in my own department of English, by asking how what they were teaching on that particular day was making their students better people. I had no thought of embarrassing them; I was simply trying wryly to share my own inexperience and frustration in trying to climb on top of the routine system and do something worthwhile in the classroom. It was hard to converse with twenty-five people in a classroom at the same time. It was also disturbing to know that you were one of six adults whom these kids met regularly for a fixed time in a fixed place to discuss a fixed subject each day, each week, for ten months regardless of their inclinations, their needs, or their abilities. However, since I was trying to resolve these problems and make connections between prescribed readings, grammar, vocabulary building, and my own visions of learning, I assumed such connections had long before been made by most experienced teachers. I was looking for a restatement by the pros of their original high purposes modified by the hard facts of day-to-day experiences. I wanted to learn.

To my astonishment I met hostility, evasion, expressions of lofty platitudes, cynical admissions of lack of purpose, and only occasionally a statement of a goal outside a subject-oriented aim. The cynics spoke of satisfying the authorities—in other words, avoiding parental complaints, poor test scores, discipline problems. The earnest, totally organized types spoke of visible, measurable, and standard evidence of subject matter proficiency. The more alert and progressive subject specialists spoke of inculcating skills, imparting information, establishing tastes. The substitute mommies and daddies spoke of happy and well-adjusted children. And the civil servants simply put in their time and complained, "We're not being paid enough for it."

The most righteous were the subject specialists, but their dedication to their tasks became particularly irksome when their goals turned out to be firmly anchored in the basic good that derived from excellence in their specialized areas of interest.

But what were the objectives of the secondary school subject specialist? Why should each of these traditional subject areas warrant massive allotments of time throughout the educational process?

ENGLISH. My own colleagues in the English department included two types: the "traditionalists," who pumped the kiddies full of grammar, spelling, and vocabulary; who provided them with those surefire hits *Silas Marner, The Red Badge of Courage, David Copperfield;* and who required a composition every week; and the bold "experimentalists," who turned their classes into film-making clubs or beat poetry seminars or dazzled their students with rock lyrics and anything else that was contemporary or in vogue. When I asked either group about goals, their answers turned vague.

"We're preparing them for college. We're being relevant."

"But goals? What are you trying to accomplish in your classroom? How will your students become better people? Do you want them to *read* or to read a particular book? Do you want them to do an assignment or to learn some general principle that could be applied?"

No doubt they thought I was trying to provoke them or to tease them with lofty ideals. For some it was as if their long-range objectives were axiomatic and required no probing or further examination. For others it was clear they had lost their way among a proliferation of paths and had forgotten where they had intended to go and why.

SOCIAL STUDIES. The social studies teachers, ordering chronologically and grouping by nation everything that had happened in the past, went about their business as if they were stocking an orderly library shelf rather than preparing young minds to use ideas and events of the past to understand contemporary times. The study of the past (history) was no more than a cultural backdrop or series of paintings, first the American scene, then the ancient scene, then the European, etc. True, the student was allowed to find random contemporary associations; if he was lucky he might have a teacher who enlivened the chronological packages with clever suggestions of relevance. But why hadn't ideas and trends taken precedence (in all classrooms, not just the experimental ones) and been occasionally illuminated by references to nations, peoples, and events in the past? An ordering by chronology might on occasion help to make a point. But who save a librarian trying to organize bulk information so it could be catalogued and indexed would want all of life ordered chronologically and tagged by nation?

Information so carefully blocked and grouped obviously encourages a departmentalization in minds as well. Educators, I should think, would want to encourage just the reverse—an ability to draw from and a constant reminder of the significance of man's total experience, a sorting out of particular facts and ideas from all nations and in all times to reveal ideas and trends at issue in contemporary times. In the senior year in progressive modern high schools the humanities are supposed to be doing that— presenting a hodgepodge of art, philosophy, religion, psychology, all in a forty-five-minute class. What about the other thirteen years of education during which the students learned to stash away orderly bits and pieces of history and regurgitate them separate and intact come test time? They've really learned that the past is in fact dead and pretty much meaningless; that information is a dull commodity having limited application; that teachers have little to teach them; that useful intelligence is an ability to sort out information and make it accessible, much like a computer, rather than to associate information and develop thoughts and ideas, like a human being.

LANGUAGES. I also wondered how the language department could justify appropriating one-fifth of a student's time for three or four years in high school to learn a foreign language that would later be purposefully used by only a small fraction of the students who in an entire lifetime might take a few one- or two-week trips abroad and then use their foreign language skills to order meals and arrange for rooms and little else. When I translated this into a simple question and addressed it to language teachers—"Why is a tourist's smattering of a foreign language more important to a high school student than consumer education, than banking and the stock market, than family relations or psychology or current affairs?"—I was answered by looks of incredulity or pat rejoinders about teaching not just a skill but a culture, an appreciation for foreign lands. Yet today, as in the past, most students of French or German or Latin or Spanish "literature" spend most of their class time literally translating one word at a time or learning about a mother country's cultural life in a monthly lecture and reading assignment.

Language teachers have never accepted the fact that their students will not be teachers or translators; nor have school administrators faced up to the fact that despite college entrance requirements, the entire language study program is a colossal balloon in the curriculum, occupying much time and space but embarrassingly devoid of substance or function.

If foreign cultures are indeed important, why shouldn't they be discussed directly in a language readily understandable to the student rather than through an exercise in cryptography? If facility with language is important in commerce, why shouldn't exemplary commercial courses in language skills be provided? If tourism is to be encouraged, why shouldn't its relative importance in the overall curriculum be weighed?

MATHEMATICS. I wondered about the math teachers, who had a firm hold on another one-fifth of all education time. Mathematics is certainly a valid field in our technological world, but what genuine and general educative values continue to attach to its study as millions of students move on to advanced algebra, solid geometry, differential and integral calculus? Is abstract reasoning really being fostered? If so, why not foster it using historical, philosophical, psychological, literary, and personal subject matter as well? After all, those areas are where most of us meet our problems with abstractions. If mathematics does in fact have some other educative function, we should be told loud and clear what that function is. If math is simply a useful vocational skill, shouldn't we reevaluate this skill's importance in the lives of American citizens as opposed to the importance of all the other unsatisfied claimants for educational time and then reestablish the amount of time to be devoted to numbers? In perverse moments I've even thought that a systems analysis approach to mathematics might be the best way to shake us out of our torpor. If RAND asked the educators, "What are your goals and priorities, what are all the alternate ways of achieving each of them, which is the most efficient, the most desirable?" the result might be a type of technological matricide.

SCIENCE. I quarreled most with the sciences. Each decade they absorb more learning time, and because of their increasing bulk they affect the rest of the formal system of education with their methods. Yet little attempt has been made to integrate the sciences into some kind of general learning scheme. No educational goals seems to exist for science except to familiarize the student with the subject material, which, ipso facto, is important.

And so science displaces ever more learning time and leaves in its wake more specialization and more unassociated knowledge. We are told that at the end the interrelation of all knowledge becomes manifest. But in Franklin Middle School the science teacher has his pupils memorizing technical names for the parts of a frog or discussing speed and propulsion systems. Interrelationships or human factors play no part in the curriculum. The student is taught science for the sake of science.

Certainly the teacher must provide each student with a basic foundation of information so that he can function in a society so deeply dependent on science and technology. But what of the relationship of these achievements and systems to other social or human goals? Who adds this to the mix?

NOT FACTS BUT ASSOCIATIONS. In their efforts to organize information so that it can be digested, educators have bogged down in the business of presenting the facts and allowed themselves to assume that the connections between the facts will somehow be recognized by the student in his own way, at his own time. Teachers have neglected to show him how this connecting is done, why it is valuable, and how it is an essential ingredient in learning. They've simply assumed he would manage it.

And so when Bea and I removed our children from school, we willfully removed them from a fixed curriculum. We wanted them to be free to pick and choose from everything about them. It is this story to which we now turn.

7. READING—

THE NURTURING OF

BOOKWORMS

"The books! The books!"

"Mommy! The books are here! The books are here!"

"Yay! Yay! Yay! Yay!"

The car became a shambles, our market load of oranges, lettuce, cabbage spilled all over the back seat as the children scrambled to get at the cartons of books I had just picked up from the Almuñécar post office.

"Oh! I read this one already," groaned Seth as we drove home. "Why did Aunt Jean send it? It wasn't on the list."

The children dumped the groceries, the newspaper-wrapped fish, and the loose fruit and vegetables all over the kitchen. But the books? They were carefully cradled and brought to the living room, where they were spread out and sorted on the floor—as was done back home with candy and other treats on Halloween night. Eventually three piles were formed, one for each child. Then the children brought in their other books and separated their piles into smaller groupings of books read and books as yet unread and placed those that hadn't been read into a tentative reading order. Before Bea shooed them off to wash for dinner, Seth had begun calculating how long it would be before each of them had nothing more to read.

One at a time, the books were entered into. And once started a book went everywhere with the child. Seth often embarrassed visitors as they opened the bathroom door and discovered him on the toilet seat, pants pulled down, deeply engrossed in "his" book. It was a favorite spot. Adam's light burned late into the night sometimes. "No one reminded me to go to bed," he explained, looking up at us with reddened eyes. Ariel, too, with all her limitations, frequently sprawled out on the beach staring fixedly at a page in a book. And if asked what she was thinking, she would puff indignantly, "I'm reading, can't you see!" (It was through this desire to be reading like everyone else in the family that Ariel developed the persistence and ability to concentrate that allowed her later to make real progress.)

They had become bookworms. They were still rough-and-tumble kids—a dangerous sandlot football tackle, a "highest"-tree climber, a butter-fat but tireless wrestler, three little brawlers bursting with energy. Yet there they were, two months away from home and already wild about books, excited by printed words.

That they had become readers was not all luck. It was the result of a conviction I had nursed through nine years of teaching high school English. I believed that most of our well-established methods of teaching reading were fragmented and problem oriented. The schools had made reading a mechanical skill—identifying words and sounds, systematically expanding vocabulary, testing for comprehension, bludgeoning students with reading exercises and pitiless repetition. The whole process was self-defeating. Even the clever approaches were in the long run only temporary relief—like the comic scenes in a Shakespearean tragedy—from the busywork and the continuing process of systematically destroying a child's wonder at the printed word.

Our approach—except in Ariel's special circumstance—was to allow reading habits and skills to evolve as naturally as speech. Given a healthy desire to learn or be entertained, access and frequent exposure to printed material, and a minimal amount of interference by methodologists, we felt almost any child could become an enthusiastic reader. It was simply a matter of dissociating reading from classrooms, teachers, textbooks, and assignments.

We all know how the schools have tooled up for teaching

reading: providing specialized teachers, carefully graded story material, workbooks, exercises, and special allotments of time for reading and discussion. And we all know of their success. In La Herradura Bea and I provided virtually nothing: no methods, no forms, no teachers. Still, within a few months our children were readers. We had allowed reading to become again what it traditionally had been—a source of pleasure and diversion, a way of reaching out beyond family and neighborhood and schools to all kinds of new resources, new people, and ideas.

Sure enough, problems of vocabulary, spelling, sentence structure, cropped up, but oddly, as the children continued to read and write, these problems started disappearing on their own. Also the children's reading speeds—without a tachistoscope or an Evelyn Wood to help—progressively increased; their comprehension and their ability to absorb new words and complex ideas leapt forward. But most important they assumed an attitude toward reading that was just as natural as their attitude toward tasting or touching. It was an easy way to find out, to extend their experience.

FOSTERING THE DESIRE TO READ

I think a good part of our success in developing three readers came from our unwillingness to *teach* reading. If we had tried to promote reading and good reading habits, we would have selected their books, periodically checked up on their reading ("What are you reading? How many chapters have you read?"), conducted pointed discussions on content, had them write papers summarizing plots, discussing characters, commenting critically on what was said. And we would have slowly, irreversibly soured what should have been an easy and enjoyable activity. We would have treated reading as if it were a duty, a dreary but necessary skill to be drilled into a child's head for use in tests and recitations.

THE PARENTAL ROLE

No small part in the children's initial gravitation toward reading was their involvement with two real, honest-to-goodness adult readers whom they respected. From our first night abroad, wherever we stopped, at an inn or home that took guests, Bea and I always had books at hand, and often as soon as we were settled we were reading. Perhaps the children felt excluded at these times, because being in a car one on top of another the entire day, they had become accustomed to family conversations, family activities, and our immediate availability. When we turned to our books before they were asleep, we may have seemed to be closing a door in their faces. Perhaps the fact that we had torn them free of friends, of routine school and home chores, of games and toys and phonograph records, of television and *Mad* magazine made us more important to them and left them little else to turn to. It may even have pushed them toward reading as one of the few diversions open to the traveler. No doubt they were also influenced by the protracted family socialization and lack of privacy, by their sheer exhaustion from so many rootless wandering hours. But in any case, they came to appreciate those quiet moments when there was finally no talk, no new places to see, just the lazy hour or two before going to sleep.

They often started these evenings jumping on one another in wild bursts of pent-up energy. But they shortly turned inward, flopping out on their beds, looking up at the ceiling, and collecting the loose ends of their sensibilities. Later, one by one, first Adam, then Seth, and finally Ariel, began asking for books, and before long each was absorbed outside the family. Within a few weeks it became our routine procedure, before taking luggage into our lodging for the night, to see to it that each of us had a book for the evening. The books weren't always read, but they were always readily available.

Once in Perpignan, when we stopped to shop for a bottle of wine and some picnic food, Adam demurred and stayed behind to read in the car. Next time we stopped to make some purchases, all three of them decided they'd rather sit in the car, quite happy to read while we went off about our adult business.

THE BENEFITS OF A BOOK SHORTAGE

Before leaving the States we had taken the precaution of mailing ahead five cartons of books, and so we carried with us only a few books for each. However, with the children quickly developing an interest in reading, it wasn't long before there was a shortage of reading material. When I picked up an English newspaper or magazine I had to hold the publication in hand; otherwise Adam was likely to steal it away to his room or Seth would manage to disappear with it—of course—into the bathroom.

If the children had had an extensive library, our results might well have been different. Then they could have easily tossed a book aside, picked up another one, and another one, until something unusual turned up or until it was time to do something else. But their small horde of books allowed little to spare, and each piece of reading matter became valuable, difficult to discard. They didn't want to skim; they wanted to extend and protract the life within each of their books. Whatever was read was read, to the extent possible, thoroughly; there was reason to savor each word. Seth, for example, without any prompting and before he had run out of other reading matter, reread *Bambi* and then *Black Beauty* and was enraptured again by both.

Each child would discuss his books with the others, deciding which could be read by another or to another. Adam was frequently the one who read aloud, but later Seth too began reading to Ariel. And no matter who finished a book, a regular sequel to completion was for the reader to retell the story to the rest of the family. It was this treasuring of limited resources that made our trip to Barcelona in search of a fresh supply of books such a memorable visit.

Bea and I had run through most of our light reading and as we reminisced about another book-hungry stop ten years before at a little English bookshop in Barcelona, we suddenly decided to make a special detour to that city and that very store in order to restock. From these few romantic references, the children caught our excitement and despite other talk of Barcelona's bullfights, its bizarre cathedral that quickly dizzied you if you tried climbing one of the soaring steeples, of crisp churro and calamary snacks, broad boulevards, soccer games, parks—the one feature the city came to signify for all of us was a well-stocked English bookstore.

A week later as we reentered the very store, it was like playing back an old family film. However, the nostalgia lasted only a few minutes. Bea and I quickly discovered that the stock had been drastically reduced and emphasis had shifted to Pelican paperbacks. Nonfiction and hoary classics seemed to predominate.

There were no books on contemporary Spain, only two European histories—and these included just a few pages on Spain—only a few children's level classics, no books on sea life, birds, or flowers. We were all disappointed. After purchasing a few paperbacks, the five of us left the store silently. Bea, myself, and each of the children was experiencing separately the sensation of book deprivation. I see it now as a positive influence on the children's reading habits. But at the time and throughout our stay abroad, the prospect of running short of reading matter became an ever-present fear.

Even after the five cartons of books arrived, we worried about having enough to read. Three times we sent home for books. They were not casual requests; it was an imposition on friends or relatives to find, purchase, and send these books to us, so we made careful selections. Each child had his quota and all of us conferred and agreed on each choice. Then when the books finally did arrive, they were opened one at a time with a miser's delight and fear. We all knew that this supply might be the last for weeks, perhaps months, to come.

THE RIGHT TO READ WHAT YOU WANT TO READ

One result of this sense of scarcity was that the children began reading whatever was at hand. Seth sampled Adam's collection; Ariel read package labels, recipes, and all family correspondence; Adam took to reading *Newsweek* and the *Herald Tribune* regularly and browsing through our library. Our children were hooked not only on words but on ideas and information generally. Whatever Bea and I discussed, the children eagerly tried to follow. And though we were often concerned more with making a thought clear to one another than with adjusting our vocabulary or simplifying our ideas to accommodate the children, we were frequently surprised to find them keenly attentive. As a consequence, many strange words and adult ideas that they would not have seen in a school reader or heard from a child-oriented teacher for years became familiar and often usable to them. The schools may still believe that children should be fed two or three words and one idea at a time. We found the sponge-like minds of children were hard to saturate.

Of course, if the book they picked up or the conversation

they eavesdropped on proved too murky—the work of the Jung Institute or Hayakawa's semantics versus his actions at San Francisco College—they quickly lost interest and moved on to their own activities. But the result was usually the reverse, so that the children often read materials—and sometimes heard ideas—far beyond their apparent level of comprehension.

THE NEED FOR STRAIN IN LEARNING

Again, this was not carelessness on our part. We felt that the most rapid learning took place when comprehension required a little straining on the student's part. The momentary discomfort occasioned by a strange word, the need to associate seemingly disparate elements, the stretching of existing powers into new areas of skill, ability, and understanding—these were the stresses that led to learning.

However, difficult reading could not be imposed, we felt, from the outside, as the schools do when they assign *Return of the Native* and *Silas Marner*. The child had to want to read and choose what he wanted to read. Then even with an advanced book, comprehension would be sufficient to carry the child's running interest over those complex thoughts and sentences, over those strange words, while giving enough discomfort during the moments of incomprehension to force the child to go beyond where he now was, to take a guess, to probe a little more daringly, to see an association. The difficulties, as long as they didn't become too obtrusive, could actually add to a child's enjoyment by continuously providing new insights or a larger view.

It was only when the mind-stretching words, thoughts, and language came to dominate the matter, or overwhelm the child's initial interest, that reading became a chore. And from this our children were protected by their freedom to choose and discard their reading materials. No book had to be read. What we wanted to do was establish reading as a diversified resource that could meet almost any need or taste. Then as the children pursued their interests and as their family, friends, and environment continued to stimulate and expand their needs, they would naturally turn to books because books were their most convenient resource. Once this process was set in motion, the children would reach out a little further each month, each year, and increasingly find less strain in more complex language and thoughts.

LEARNING TO REJECT BOOKS

Essential, however, to this growth pattern in reading was the child's total freedom in the rejection as well as selection of his books. True, Bea and I often made book suggestions at the children's request. But they knew we believed any book that confused or bored them should be dropped. And even with our continuing book shortages there were just too many other good books to read or reread. We had driven home the idea that there were good and bad books and furthermore that each child had his own peculiar tastes in literature just as in sports, food, and playmates. We didn't want the children to bunch all books together as a category of experience, as so many students do who remark, "I like reading" or, "I don't like books." We wanted reading to become so multipurpose and commonplace—like sight itself—as to fall outside any overall attitude toward the process. You might like or dislike some specific thing that you read or saw but this had no bearing at all on the usefulness of reading or sight. That books could be rejected, was, we felt, an essential lesson to be learned.

Adam had a friend, an American boy his own age, who like himself read a good deal. The boy was enrolled in a correspondence school for children living abroad and had to mix his private tastes in reading with a daily measured dose of assigned reading. These assigned books, to be read one chapter a day with questions on content to be answered after each chapter, included *Gulliver's Travels*, *Penrod*, *Robinson Crusoe*, and some Washington Irving tales. Adam and the boy occasionally exchanged books, and for his own reasons Adam decided to read *Robinson Crusoe*. Perhaps Adam felt guilty about his enjoyment of reading without any of the penalties the kids back home suffered when they had to read assigned books. Or perhaps he feared that without having read some school-assigned books he would fall behind his classmates. Whatever the case, he borrowed *Robinson Crusoe* and started reading. Before long we noticed that he seemed to be spending more and more time with other activities: photography, writing, architecture, horseplay—anything but reading. In the morning he was restless and noisy; in the evenings he would immerse himself in plans for a new city or tease the other children until one cried. Only when Ariel and Seth were told to go to sleep did Adam finally turn to reading, and then he was often too sleepy to continue for long. It was far different from those previous nights when we had to threaten him before his light went off.

Almost a week had passed when I noticed the book lying open and face down in the middle of his desk. He had read about one hundred pages. Later that morning I asked him about the book. He was very critical, particularly about the language. He ran to his room to get the book and show me a few passages in which sentences ran on for a third of a page. And they *were* difficult to follow. It was little wonder he was putting off reading it. I had a sudden picture of millions upon millions of youngsters in school being required to read books they were unprepared for or uncomfortable with and being steadily turned away from reading. With *Romeo and Juliet, A Tale of Two Cities, The Red Badge of Courage,* and so forth, the secondary schools were methodically going about the business of wiping out whatever good feeling for reading may have escaped the machinery of the elementary schools. Even in La Herradura, thousands of miles from his school, my son was feeling the assigned book's lethal influence.

"Forget about it," I said. "Just drop it. The books you've been picking are a helluva lot better. Just forget about it." Fortunately Bea, who had overheard us, had read and enjoyed *Robinson Crusoe* as a girl. She took the book from Adam and flipping through the pages discovered in the back a verbatim account by the ship's captain who had first discovered the young man, cast away on the island. It appeared that Defoe's story was based on a real-life adventure; there actually was a Robinson Crusoe. At this point I was interested and so was Adam. We listened as Bea read the account of the actual marooning of the young man, his initial struggles for survival, how he rapidly learned to outclimb and catch mountain goats, how he slept surrounded by hundreds of dozing cats that he had bred to protect him from the rats that swarmed over the island, how he had forgotten how to speak after his years of isolation. By this time Seth and Ariel were listening too. When Bea stopped in the middle of her reading to fix lunch, Adam was eager to resume reading the book. But Bea dissuaded him. Though the material was intrinsically exciting, the language was, after all, difficult. However, *Robinson Crusoe* was now a book he wanted to read and probably would in a few years.

A similar incident, with Seth this time, took place as a result of a visit to a bookstore in Torremolinos that specialized in English-language books. We were never casual about book buying because books were expensive and there were five of us. However, Seth was an indiscriminate reader. When he read, it was all wonder and anticipation, it was new and exciting.

On this day he picked up a science fiction book, the kind his brother was reading. It had a dazzling cover, *Warlord of Mars.* On his arrival home, it was the first book he started. After two days, however, he had stopped reading it and picked up another book. When he finished the new book, he returned to *Warlord of Mars.* But again, after an hour or so, he left it for another book. Finally he came to me and said, "Daddy, do I have to finish this?" He waved the book at me like a dirty rag.

Of course, I told him he didn't. "You aren't angry? I know it cost a lot of money," he said. I laughed and he seemed immediately relieved. He ran into his room, eagerly examined his other books and picked one to read. He was busy with it the rest of the morning and that evening too. A few days later Bea remarked that he had transferred *Warlord of Mars* to Adam's collection.

I don't think it was the money so much that bothered Seth. Probably he was astonished to find that a book that was quite readable simply did not interest him. He had picked a bad book and as a result learned an essential reading lesson—that not all books are worth reading, that not everything is of equal interest or value.

ARIEL—A SPECIAL READING PROBLEM

In Ariel's case, as I've mentioned, our problem was different. When we started our trip Ariel simply could not read. Pointing with her index finger she mouthed each syllable separately, a mechanical meaningless sound game. She had difficulty pronouncing most words and her patience was such that she accepted any approximation in sound or meaning as adequate. Words were isolate, never seen as part of a flow, much less an idea. Given a simple primer of fifty basic words, she would puzzle through it, painfully building letters into sounds like *nice* or *play* and then go on to the next group of letters to try to find the next word, and then the next word. There was no phrasing, no recognition of commas or periods. It was a form of phonics that produced agony and no comprehension. To ask her what a sentence meant would be like asking someone to say what page 97 in the dictionary meant. She would remember individual words but make no connections between them. And to go beyond fifty or one hundred of these words into an expanded vocabulary was an occasion for such tears and distress that it was little wonder the teacher in her school had her read little and then in the most basic primers.

We really didn't know how to go about correcting all the mechanical difficulties Ariel faced: learning to look at letters and combinations of letters and sounding them out, learning to stress syllables, trying to put words into phrases, inflecting her voice for a question or at the end of a sentence, or emphasizing a word. As for comprehension, she could read the same small paragraph four or five times and each time come up with some totally new idea, frequently unrelated to the reading. The only hopeful sign was that when the same material was read to her, her understanding was quite good.

So we let things drift.

Ariel was, of course, aware that the boys, Bea, and I were all doing a lot of reading, and this made her eager to read herself, to be part of the family. She insisted on her own collection of books, her own time set apart for reading. She pretended to read page after page of any book close at hand. Each time one of the boys finished a book she would respond by saying she had just finished hers too, no matter what page she was turned to. We tried to encourage her to understand what she was reading, sounding out the words with her, but the process was too painful and, we feared, perhaps hopeless.

In the meantime Seth's level of comprehension was rising all the time as he went racing through his books. By the end of our trip he had read most of Adam's early story selections and was even dabbling in Adam's more difficult novels. As for science, history, and geography, he was now reading much of the same material that Adam did. Ariel saw her younger brother's progress and wanted desperately to advance too, not only to read more books—her simple quantitative view of the gap—but to read the same books as Seth.

Clearly we could not continue to ignore her feeling of being outdistanced. She saw how central reading was to the rest of us. She knew it was important. Something had to be done.

One day while the four of us were busily reading, spread out on the lawn, sun-dappled by an overhanging Scotch pine, I noticed Ariel cuddled up on a stiff wrought-iron chair, legs folded under her, slowly mouthing the words of a book that was resting on her knees. She was not pretending for our benefit this time. It was as if she were performing some ritual act of obeisance. She seemed no longer to question or try to understand. It was blind devotion. If she continued looking at these lines of words, some relief was bound to follow. Her whole family went through this ceremony and clearly found it pleasurable. All she had to do was keep her attention focused on these lines, one after another, and it would happen to her too. So there she sat, paying her worried devotions to a cold, thus far unyielding god.

I moved my chair over to Ariel and asked, "Would you like to read to me?" She smiled, embarrassed and pleased at the attention, because she knew I was interrupting something I enjoyed. "Do you really want me to?" she questioned, clearly concerned that this attention, like so many others, might lead to mistakes, corrections, more mistakes, an unguarded harsh word, and those inevitable tears of failure. So though delighted at the attention, she was plainly frightened. She began, her voice barely audible.

It was appalling.

Clearly she thought reading was the enunciation of a series of separate unassociated words. She didn't understand that written words had meaning as they did when spoken.

Softly I tried to match my voice to hers. It soon sounded as if the two of us were conspiring in whispered secrets. Whenever she made a mistake I would whisper the sound or word correctly. But there were so many that I quickly changed tactics. I started reading slightly behind her. To make her feel a little less tight and sense that I was enjoying myself, I put my emphasis not on pronunciation but on exaggerated meaning. I blocked out phrases with gasps and popping eyes, I meticulously articulated each word, mouthing and grotesquely shaping difficult ones, until Ariel herself giggled and laughed and caught the spirit of the game. It was illustrated reading. Before long we were disturbing the others so we moved to the other side of the house and just the two of us, in this intimate way, continued the game of reading.

When Ariel's perception of printed words was matched to the sounds of spoken words—most of which she knew and used, since her speech was relatively sophisticated for a slow child—she was able to make connections far more quickly and extract meaning for the first time from what she read. She had the sense of reading even though my support, particularly in the beginning, was overwhelming. The tortuous, fragmented mechanics of phonics, words, and phrases were all now forgotten and merged into one imitative and funny game. It was no longer methods and tools and unrelated meaningless exercises—it was reading. She was reading. She knew what these words were saying.

Of course, she still couldn't really read. I had given her the illusion of reading by carrying her along with me, as an airplane passenger gains a sense of power when his jet takes off. But like that passenger, Ariel was actually moving. She had not supplied the power, but she was experiencing the process.

The more we read on that afternoon and succeeding ones, the more quickly she seemed to pick up words and, far more important, phrasing. I was particularly happy about the phrasing because I knew if she once started understanding word groupings then many of the separate words she still groped for and writhed over would be suddenly recognizable. She could start converting her fairly broad command of spoken language into reading associations, and she would be well on her way toward independent and self-correcting reading. That's what had to be done. She had to hear the printed words in the same spoken patterns that she herself used: it had to be intelligible speech, not phonics, that she worked with.

In succeeding days the exaggerated emphasis in my readings tapered off and I fell further and further behind Ariel, an echo of her voice, correcting pronunciation, rhythm, phrasing. I raised my voice and caught up to her only when she faltered or hesitated too long. She would automatically imitate my inflection or pronunciation but then quickly reestablish her lead. By reading with me her diction, too, improved. Word endings that she had slurred were now clearly enunciated. She became conscious of an exactness in speech as she became more conscious of the exactness of words on the printed page.

A few times I tried having Ariel read the same sentence after me. But the method proved too imitative, without any carryover effect. There was clearly too much guidance, no strain required to keep up. It was copycat stuff. Far more effective was a method of alternate reading that Ariel suggested. I read one sentence, then she read the next, then me. She tried to match my attempts to express meaning through inflection, emphasis, and phrasing. It was excellent practice for her, and the give-and-take made it fun.

As time went by she became much better at picking out factual material but still didn't grasp more abstract ideas (such as, "Why did the boy want the dog?") unless she could repeat specific words in the reading. Nor could she relate two separate bits of information (comparisons, for example) and come to a conclusion. But her phrasing, her pronunciation, her recognition of words improved rapidly. Questions and sentences with exclamation-point endings were now identified with a sharp upswing in inflection and firm emphasis. Difficult words were linked to phrases and rolled and searched—not only on the tongue but in the mind—for meaning. Ariel was beginning to know what was being said on those printed pages.

Ariel is still not a reader. Her comprehension is not at all what I would like it to be. But neither is her aural comprehension what I would like. The difference is that now she has a basic skill with which to accelerate the process of learning, and she is more than ever eager to use it.

SUMMARY OF OBJECTIVES

If I had to make a by-the-numbers presentation of what exactly our approach to reading in La Herradura was, I might suggest three objectives. First, we wanted the children to see the printed word as a neutral medium of exciting variety. Second, we wanted the children to see books as a prime source of insights and values. Third, we wanted the children to experience the quiet pleasure that reading could provide.

READING AS A MEDIUM. Both Bea and I believed that the most significant attraction of reading was its function as a medium, one more versatile than any other. If the children could be brought to use reading, not as a thing in itself but as a means for obtaining information, extending their experiences, or sparking their imaginations, then books would become no more threatening than TV or radio and far more useful.

Seth, for example, read the Dr. Doolittle books, *Bambi,* and *Heidi,* intermixed with science, history, and current affairs. He wasn't exercising in the discipline of reading, he was studying science, learning about Romans, enjoying fantasy and adventure tales, keeping up with happenings back home. There were so many things he wanted to do and learn, and reading matter was the most useful medium at hand in these areas, just as automobiles and radios were good in others.

In Ariel's case we encouraged friends and relatives in the United States to write to her not only to prod her into writing in return, but to make her want to read. When a member of the family received a letter, he usually read the nonpersonal parts aloud to the rest of us. It became embarrassing for Ariel to have mommy or daddy always read her letters aloud for her.

As for Adam, frequently a particular activity, such as tree grafting or studying a fruit fly's life cycle, required some research in a reference book. In seeking out information on water currents, the Greeks, pollution, religious holidays, he might start with our large Random House dictionary, then browse through his and our collections of books, ask if we had any other suggestions on sources where he could find more information or if he could send away for a book—all this before asking us directly what we knew about the subject.

He was using printed matter not only as a source of pleasure and information but as a way of establishing an independent point of view. Both he and Seth were developing a sense of pride in their own self-reliance, their own stores of information and experience. They had come quickly to appreciate that books allowed them to move beyond the limitations of the family and offered them a way to contribute something new to the family. Each was building an individual frame of reference and point of view. This was no small matter to us. We had specifically wanted a desire to share something of their own, some new idea or piece of information, to become part of their adult attitude toward life. So we were delighted to see them using reading as a vehicle for pursuing an independent course.

READING AS A SOURCE OF INSIGHTS AND VALUES. A more traditional view of reading, though nonetheless important, is as a source of new insights and values. In La Herradura it was no different. Though the children were using books for a variety of purposes, they often found themselves puzzled or prodded by new ideas and unexpected behavior. For example, as a result of their readings, they were constantly evaluating their own family relations.

I remember Adam being deeply moved by Steinbeck's *Of Mice and Men.* He couldn't understand what George gained from the relationship with Lenny, the moron, and no doubt he related it to his own relationship with Ariel. He started writing a one-act play about a mouse and a giant in which he tried to depict the interdependence of all creatures no matter how disparate they might seem. And the one ingredient that linked them all together was love. The same concern was later triggered by another book, *Flowers for Algernon,* the story of a retarded man who through miracle drugs is changed to a genius. In a letter to his grandmother Adam wrote:

> *I've never before had anything to do with the science or area of retardation, handicaps and deformities or as some call it (a word that I don't particularly care for) freaks. Now for the first or second time I was given these "sicknesses" to think about. I came up* [sic] *with a great pity for retarded people; or should I envy them for being able to take what is given and stay young in reaction with few worrys* [sic]. *No, I should not envy them. They probably wish for a day to come when they are as smart as every else* [sic]. *Why isn't there a cure for the slow like Charles?*

We had purposely avoided any attempt to analyze or dissect what Seth had read. However, the fallout from his readings was no less in evidence. One time Bea and I were wrapped up in some inane conversation about social protocol, and Seth, as he lost interest in the talk and started walking away, deflated us with a twinkling smile and a very appropriate quote from Saint Exupéry's *The Little Prince,* which he had just finished reading, "Matters of consequence, of course."

READING AS A PLEASURABLE EXPERIENCE. And, of course, the children were encouraged to view reading as an easy and pleasurable experience. Each read what he wanted to. There was never a feeling of obligation or duty regarding reading. No book was mandatory. Unless you were searching out information unavailable anyplace else, there was never any reason to continue reading a book that was dull or too difficult.

As a result, reading was always associated with enjoyable experiences. For example, Seth had started a fairly lengthy book (sixty-eight large pages with small print and few illustrations) that tersely presented the life and adventures of Christopher Columbus. It was a detailed treatment and therefore appealed to Seth, who commented, all bright eyed, after the first few pages, "I really like it. It tells about all the voyages, not just the famous ones." An hour later, when he was more than halfway through the book, he shuffled into the kitchen sadly, with the book held behind his back, and said to Bea, "I'd better put this away—till tomorrow."

"But why?" Bea asked, surprised. "Don't you like it? You seemed so involved with it."

"Oh, yeah! I want to finish it," Seth answered earnestly. "But I don't want to finish it all in one day."

He wanted to extend the treat.

It wasn't unusual for their absorption in a story to be so intense as to bring tears to their eyes. One afternoon, Adam approached me while I was at work, and holding *Johnny Tremaine* out to catch my eye, he announced, "I'm done." Then before I could comment, he blurted out angrily, "Why can't they . . ." but stopped midsentence abruptly and left the room. Later in a letter to his Aunt Alayne he condemned the schools for teaching history as if it had no relevance. He wanted to know why they couldn't use books like *Johnny Tremaine* to make the revolutionary war really come alive. "A beautiful book," he wrote, "lost somewhere between history, love, companionship and compatriotism [*sic*]. . . . You can feel pity, gladness, relief or sorrow, but whatever it is you feel it strongly."

CARRY-OVER TO WRITING AND OTHER SKILLS. By the end of our trip all three children had become not only habitual readers but enthusiastic writers, too. I believe much of their interest and increasing facility in writing was directly linked to their reading. The two boys were reading book after book and simultaneously writing letters, stories, diary entries—all without a carefully graduated program to develop reading or writing skills.

In our year away from schools both these skills improved dramatically. Samples of the children's writing during early, middle, and later periods of our stay abroad reveal their remarkable increase in vocabulary, their progressively smaller number of spelling errors, their rapid elimination of incorrect usage, their increasing sophistication in sentence structure, coherence, and organization. And most of these skills seemed to be attributable primarily to their increased involvement with the printed word—though their extensive work in writing itself, discussed next, certainly reinforced these capabilities.

8. WRITING—

BIG THOUGHTS AND

LITTLE WORDS

Before children can write, we have been told, they must practice penmanship; learn spelling; know grammar, usage, and punctuation; understand sentence structure and paragraph formation. Then they'll be ready.

But by that time most children have been thoroughly discouraged from any natural inclination they might have had to express themselves. They have become casualties of the process of learning how.

The pot of gold at the end of the rainbow—in this case simply writing what you want to say—has been each year put further and further away and new how-to barriers interposed. When the teacher finally starts diagraming sentences, most children may well have forgotten what relationship this diagramed, punctuated, calligraphed process has with anything they might have wanted to say.

There has long been a tendency to analyze complex processes such as effective writing by breaking them down into parts and then studying and working with the pieces. We shouldn't be surprised that a mass school system first turned to and then institutionalized mass production techniques to teach writing and reading. But just as mass production turned out model-T Fords, it also developed workers who were equipped to do only one thing, workers who could never alone produce an entire car. Modern man's craftsmanship was permanently fragmented and mechanized.

Under this same theory of fragmentation the schools have gone about breaking down language into parts so that children can be taught how to recognize and reassemble the parts. For this purpose the schools have prescribed a ten-year dose of grammar. Next the business of building a child's vocabulary has been systematically approached with vocabulary lists, books with sifted and graded lists of words, dictionary games, techniques of memorizing words, special books for vocabulary. And still—after all this —the usable vocabulary of many children has shown negligible growth. Spelling too has been attacked—repeatedly, year after year, with lists of commonly misspelled words and periodic assignments to memorize bunches of them, bright red circles around the child's mistakes, punishments such as writing each misspelled word fifty times. And each year publishers and school systems have developed more and more specialized techniques and private enthusiasms for usage, vocabulary, grammar, or spelling. In this mechanically irreproachable manner major areas of the school curriculum have evolved as fragments of a larger emphasis—the teaching of writing.

By making it such a fragmented and skill-laden affair, schools have made most students' writing cumbersome and halting, barely coherent, never fluent. Writing is no longer a flexible and more precise alternative to speech. Only once every week or two is any correlation attempted between the skills and actual writing —and that's when the weekly composition is assigned. Even then, the emphasis remains on mechanics rather than meaning. The outcome has been—with the help of the telephone and Hallmark —a nation of nonwriters.

It didn't seem terribly daring to us to want to try something else, and we did. Within four months our children were writing naturally and easily *and* were many years ahead of their class levels in spelling, vocabulary, and grammar. Because they read a great deal, they readily picked up words, effects, spellings, and grammatical patterns that were unconsciously transferred to their writing. For example, we were convinced that a child's vocabulary could not be built up by memorizing definitions. Our plan was simply to have the children, as readers or as listeners to literate conversations, confront many new words in context and thus be forced to puzzle out meanings and carefully note contexts. In this way they would learn how to utilize new words to express their own thoughts in similar contexts. How many English teachers have witnessed the ready and faultless feedback of definitions on vocabulary tests and then seen the strained and ludicrous attempts to utilize the same words in compositions? This type of vocabulary work didn't build up language—it provided a vocabulary of fancy substitutes to dress up plain thoughts.

So too with grammar. We believed that knowing how sentences were grammatically constructed was not the same as being able to write what you wanted to say. It might be helpful once the child felt comfortable with a pen in his hand to know the nomenclature of grammar in order to identify specific problems and refine writing style. But at the start the young writer could gain his best experience from continuous reading, and, as I shall discuss shortly, frequent, uncorrected writing.

SETH

As a student I had suffered through ten years of writing compositions and book reports; as an English teacher I had taught writing because it was a needed skill; and as a researcher and educational columnist I had used writing to make a living. Yet not until, as a father, I observed my own children using writing as easily as they used speech did I realize that writing more than anything else could be a remarkably versatile and effective instrument for educating oneself.

As Seth made entries in his diary, as Adam completed a new installment in his adventure novel, as Ariel composed still another letter to the family back home—I could observe their awareness of reality expanding. Their senses were becoming more alert, their imaginations more wide ranging, their abilities to define their ideas and meanings more certain, their associations of thoughts and facts more diversified and complex. They were using writing as a mental sharpener. What they saw and heard, what they read, were brought tightly and pointedly into use under the influence of writing. Unlike their spoken words, their written words were not accidental or happy constructions of speech. When they set about writing they were attempting to discover themselves and get a handle on the world about them.

How different it had been in the schools. Seth had been losing his enchantment with words. He was drilled in writing exercises that required him and two million other first graders to form sentences around a standardized list of words. "Use the words *circus* and *blow*, the instructions read, and he dutifully penciled on the broad lined paper: "I see the circus." "See the wind blow." Occasionally a word triggered a small spark:

> *Once Tommy waved so hard that he broke his arm.*
> *I suppose that at one time I lived in mommy's body.*

But generally the writing was built around an isolated word rather than what the child wanted to say. And even these word-oriented sentences were not discussed for meaning, but for spelling, penmanship, and correct usage, with checks and crosses and grades. The teacher rarely commented on what the child had said.

The results were immediately discernible. Seth had been impatient with writing because his thoughts came faster than he could write them down and he was always forgetting things. But with the emphasis on the handwriting process, the writing down became even slower. And because of all the erasures resulting from his efforts to improve his penmanship, his papers were dog chewed and slovenly. The emphasis on spelling compounded these cares. He used only words he could surely spell, and the result was a simplistic schoolroom vocabulary. Small wonder that his growing oral vocabulary found little expression in his writing. The two processes had almost nothing in common. Talking was really saying something, but writing, he quickly came to understand, was an exercise in spelling and penmanship.

Seth told us about one of the few creative assignments. The teacher handed each child the first part of a story printed on a mimeographed sheet and asked each class member to write an appropriate ending on the three blank lines provided at the bottom of the sheet. Seth eagerly started to write, but soon ran out of space. He walked up to the teacher and asked for another piece of paper. She said, "Try to squeeze your ending into the lines on the paper." He returned to his desk, started to erase the last line, then stopped and just stared aimlessly out the window for the rest of the assigned time.

I remember a few months later, after we had whisked him off to Spain, seeing him again looking out the window. But then suddenly his attention riveted back to the large well-used notebook in his hand, and his pencil started moving furiously across the page. He had already written five full pages of a story and had simply paused a moment to collect some new thoughts. He wrote many stories and long entries in his diary, and once he started he often continued writing page after page uninterrupted for two or three hours at a stretch.

Bea had started Seth writing as soon as we landed in Amsterdam. We wanted each of the children to maintain a running correspondence with family and friends back home so each could not only keep in touch but also have a practical reason for doing lots of writing.

Every few nights as we traveled south, Bea would lug our portable typewriter into our hotel room and begin taking dictation—from Seth. Because of all his hang-ups on writing, Bea had started off by having him talk out loud as if he were directly addressing the person he wanted to write to, and she took down what he said on the typewriter. He spoke and then the keys started clicking, recording what he had to say.

Seth was delighted and impressed with his own fluency when his letter was read back to him. It convinced him that he could write and that all he had to do was get his skills in order. He began writing his own letters, printing out each word laboriously, but he often lost his train of thought and with it his fluency. It was then that Bea decided to try some conventional writing techniques. She felt that Seth—unlike Adam who needed a continuing assurance of freedom to express himself—was still unskilled in the fundamentals of writing and required lots of exercise and guidance. She first suggested ordering his impressions before writing his letters: making a list and then an outline of what he wanted to say. But the results were a dull account of how a peasant woman made bread, a room-by-room description of a house, and an endlessly detailed chronology of a shark hunt. She then tried descriptions: "Describe the garden surrounding our house." Book reports: "Write a few sentences telling what has happened so far to Dr. Doolittle." Outlining: "Write an outline for a letter about how life is different here than back home." And lots of word exercises: homonymns, synonyms, rhyming. The results were dismally familiar:

> *I am in Spain. It is beautiful. The water at our beach is the same as the water at Croton dam.*

The stilted simplistic thought and phrasing, the stunted, disconnected sentences—it was as if Seth had never left school. She even tried some exercises to give him a sense of individuality and creativity. For example, she had Seth create a series of similes and metaphors built around an emotion. The results showed a rich feeling for language and sound:

> *Laughter is the fire sizzling.*
> *Anger is as loud as the tigers roar.*
> *Sorrow is a crinkled flower which you*
>   *love and take care of.*
> *Laughter looks like the palm trees*
>   *leaves blowing in the wind.*

But despite these samples of apparent success, it was clear that Seth was simply performing for Bea, just as he might for an inventive or personable teacher back home. He wasn't involved, curious, running on his own. It was the same imposed learning structure, and he, little gentleman, was dutifully producing. So too with phonics exercises. Seth could produce to a teacher's delight:

> *The bear is all bare except for his hair.*
> *Every time I go down the stairs*
>   *everybody stares at me in amazement.*
> *I might eat a mite.*

Cute stuff, clever, inventive. It was exactly the sort of isolated-component learning we had condemned back home. True, Bea was having more success with it. But it was far from the new, free, and total education we had wanted for the children. Bea had hoped Seth would start to discover an excitement in learning and not simply delight in her approval. That wasn't happening. She decided to try another approach—to concentrate on his senses

and thoughts. At first she had him jot down notes on a subject
—"How do you prepare for a day of fishing?"—and then put
them in order. Later she had him observe something carefully
and then record a series of impressions before writing it up. One
of these observations turned out to be a little quarrel between his
mommy and daddy. Seth wrote:

> Dad said I want my coffee hot. Mommy said It is hot. Dad said I
> want mine boiling.

(It was curious the way he had changed my "I like my coffee hot"
to a much more abrasive "I want my coffee hot." He wouldn't
allow my temperate words to obscure what Bea called "my nasty
tone.")

Bea complimented Seth on the accuracy of his ear and encouraged him to write down more conversations, instructing him
briefly in correct dialogue form. He wrote a few humorous little
stories purely of conversations:

> Bow said, "I want a hot dog."
> Bob said, "Here it is."
> Bow said, "That isn't a hot dog."
> Bob said, "This is the only thing that tastes like a hot dog."
> Bow said, "Well then get me a real hot dog."
> Bob said, "There aren't any."
> Bow said, "Are there any hamburgers? Get me 40 hamburgers."

But Bea was looking for more solid stuff. She decided to try
a game. She extracted from Seth a large number of separate
words for objects, types, persons, adjectives, and emotions, all
the while writing each word down on a separate small piece of
paper. The pieces were then tossed in a bowl and Seth told to
pick out five or six and build a story around the random words.
It was cute educational methodology, and like all such stuff it had
a first-time appeal and then became tiresome. Seth wrote a factual story about an anemone and a periwinkle, appending at the
bottom of the page, "Seth wrote this story." He was already
proud of his writing. But the second dip into the bowl was no
longer fun. The five or six words were too restricting. The whole
thing was work, and Seth stubbornly resisted even starting this
one.

He asked whether he could do what Ariel was doing, cutting out interesting photos from picture magazines and then writing what she saw in the photos. Bea had used this idea to force Ariel to observe carefully and then order her observations. Seth didn't need this. But Bea felt that it might give him something tangible to keep on relating back to as he wrote his story—because that's what he saw. It might also give him a sense of freedom because there were no restrictions in choice of pictures or approach. Yet the picture would provide him with something to hang on to.

His first story, "Dreamland," was based upon an abstract painting of a blue man running in space through a field of stars. He spoke of a man who had just died and was traveling a rainbow to heaven and referred to the "glorious times we had together." (Death is a recurrent theme with Seth.) He ended the piece with, "Remember, the next falling star you see because it will be me."

When he showed Bea the story later, he said that while he was writing it, "I cried at the sadness of my story."

Both Bea and I were impressed with his genuine eagerness to express himself. And it was then that we agreed it might be a good time to return to our laissez-faire attitude, and again assure him that we had little concern with handwriting, spelling, erasures, and grammatical errors. Seth was at first skeptical. But as the weeks progressed and Bea in fact provided no help in these areas, but commented only on his ideas, imagination, and rich use of language, Seth began to loosen up. His ideas started flowing more easily and we were surprised to find how complex a little boy's mind could be when it was unfettered by spelling and grammar rules. He quickly lost any feelings of inferiority about his writing ability, and as he did we found his control of his pen increasing, the size of his script becoming smaller, and even his spelling—since he was doing more reading—correcting itself.*
All the skills so laboriously analyzed and worried over and then repeatedly pounded into the frail heads of these youngsters were simply picked up as a matter of course—like learning correct speech patterns.

*Months later, when writing had become an integral part of many of Seth's activities, Bea did make occasional spelling or grammatical corrections, but only when something couldn't be puzzled out. Meaning was always the first consideration. Under these conditions a correction was not a question of satisfying spelling or grammatical rules but of ensuring intelligibility. And we discovered that that sort of correction had a good chance of sticking.

In his subsequent stories Seth's choice of photos continued to be fanciful, surreal, or exotic—unusual countrysides, modern ballet sets, pieces of sculpture—far different from Ariel's advertisements or photos of people in contemporary scenes. He seemed intoxicated with this escape outlet from the mundane world.

His first stories, only a hundred or two hundred words long, stayed quite close to the elements within the picture. But his later stories, running as long as seven hundred words, used the photo primarily as a springboard from which he ranged free and wide as his dreamlike imagination followed its own demands.

In his "Land of Love" story, he saw ". . . a kind hearted lady sitting in her nowhereland waiting for someone to kiss her. No one came for decades. . . ." All the original picture showed was a pop art version of a nymph sitting on a sea rock.

Seth was closest to self-discovery when he cut out a caricature of a spectacled professor carrying a book and, pointing proudly at himself, titled his story "Little Old Professor." He had been called that by his first-grade teacher back home because of a retentive mind and an ability to use any stray piece of information. The other kids had never let him forget it. Now here he was looking at himself ("Everyone calls me the smartest kid in class") and proceeding to disclaim his responsibility. Nevertheless, at the end of the story, which told of his adventures in La Herradura, he couldn't resist a "smart kid" remark: "I bet that in the next few years that the beach that La Herradura is on will be covered with apartment buildings."

Apart from the rich exploration of his mind and feelings, we could start to sense that the stories were accomplishing a much more concrete purpose. Seth's written vocabulary virtually leaped ahead from story to story, other bits of learning were artlessly woven into the pieces: much use of dialogue, references to discussions with Adam on science ("The Brain of Life" dealt with a dissection of a magical brain, but the language and procedure were modeled after an actual dissection of a chicken we had performed as a family project). My favorite piece was based on a fifteenth-century primitive painting of the Adoration.

Seth was writing two stories a week, but they were getting more and more fantastic and dreamlike, lacking in coherence, fragmented, silly. When Bea suggested that he might stop writing stories and instead keep a diary, Seth seemed almost relieved. It worried him at first that Adam had tried keeping a diary for a few weeks and given it up. But after thousands of words of fantasy, he apparently welcomed a return to concrete, clearly utilitarian things. The diary, which quickly became Seth's dominant mode of writing, was so much apart from the regular school routine that I have reserved discussion of it for a later section where all the clearly nonacademic elements, which became the real foundation of the children's total education, are pulled together.

After a few months of keeping a diary, writing well-organized letters, and doing lots of reading, Seth at his own wish returned to magazine-picture-inspired story writing. These turned out to be his most enchanting pieces. They still showed imagination and whimsy, but because of his extensive reading he had gained a better feeling for what a story could be. Although the silliness evidenced in his earlier tales was not lost, it was now given form and direction.

He was becoming aware now of the craft of writing. He still used the photos as a jumping-off spot, but now Seth knew that a story often assumed a direction of its own. We had had no discussion about such a sophisticated topic as the craft of short story writing. Yet Seth was now thinking about what he was doing in a remarkably professional manner:

- Explaining his scrawled notes on the margins of his story, Seth remarked: "I started out thinking of two things I wanted to write but when I wrote of only one then it [*the story*] *went on its own way.*"
- He was discussing with Bea an image he had used in "Wine and Music": "It no longer tasted like wine, but the very soft, delicate kiss of your mother." He said, "Do you know when I talk about the wine like a mother's delicate kiss—to feel that, someone reading it would have to like their mother very much. If they didn't, could they understand how delicate a mother's kisses are?" He looked off to the side for a moment, then concluded, "I guess they would have to use a lot of imagination."
- And again in a conversation with Bea: "Do you know, in a diary all you need is memory. In a book [*to write a story such as his magazine-photo-inspired stories*] *you have to think; it's a challenge. You have an idea, you combine two ideas—it's not only what happens. I haven't put any ideas in my diary.*"

These were the sort of observations on writing that, dressed up in more sophisticated language, were the stock-in-trade of high school and even college level creative writing classes. Learning of this kind was a question not of retention but of insight and understanding. The more such progress we saw in his writing as a result of the magazine photos, the more we were convinced that freedom and lots of exercise were the crucial ingredients in learning to write. It required little imagination on our parts to involve Seth in other forms. They were all about us, once the writing became a usable tool rather than a homework assignment.

Seth had been keeping a notebook for work in arithmetic, history, reading, science, and other more formal learning assignments. As he lost his fear of writing, it was easy for Bea to interest him in taking notes on his scientific observations and experiments, in recording his thoughts on life styles in Sparta and Athens in comparison with life in Peekskill, New York, in putting into words a justification of why God was so cruel to the Egyptians when he visited them with seven plagues, in recording his impressions of our one- or two-day journeys into the surrounding countryside.

We were clearly on the right track now. In story telling we had found our first usable device for making writing exciting and purposeful to Seth, and now he was expanding his new tool of expression from a story-telling medium to a medium of multiple uses. It was becoming an integral part of many of his personal interests, including letter writing and diary keeping. This type of writing was no longer related to what was happening in schools back home. Almost every aspect of the school curriculum—spelling, handwriting, vocabulary, book reports, reading comprehension paragraphs, synonym and simile exercises, all the neat school disciplines that cripple a child's interest in writing—by this time had been discarded. We were now engaged in improvising a new curriculum.

ARIEL

Ariel's progress in writing was so slow, almost imperceptible to us who worked day by day with her, that it wasn't until we returned to the States and placed early and late samples of her work side by side that we realized the extraordinary advances she had made for a slow child. During our year abroad, Ariel's writing ability had lurched forward by three full years. That's what the schools finally judged her progress to have been, and they were looking more at how she wrote things than at what she wrote.

We had decided to avoid teaching skills, and even in Ariel's extreme case—her skills were close to zero when we started—we tried at first to stick to our decision. After all, spelling, punctuation, conventional structure, and a strong legible handwriting are simply parts of the etiquette of writing and not its substance. We encouraged her to approximate in writing—with her big, shaky, laboriously tooled block letters—what she would normally say out loud. Not only was her verbal ability, like most young children's, far in advance of her writing ability, but she had the added advantages of much adult discussion and full-day involvement with articulate brothers—quite a change from the sluggish environment of slow learners we had removed her from.

So our plan was to get her—like Seth—to write as freely and fluently as she spoke. If it could be managed, she could take a big jump forward, perhaps even catch up to her peers. Then we could backtrack and start setting her skills in order for parade performance.

For us, improving her writing was a means to improving her reasoning. No doubt a third-grade teacher would have found our early results grotesque (Ariel's thoughts were thickly encrusted with errors in spelling, punctuation, and ellipsis) and missed the impressive progress in basic thinking processes taking place.

We were making a sneak advance on the existing system. If we were successful, Ariel would gain a sense of the simplicity—rather than the awesome complexity—of writing. And a feeling of success might make her more inclined to sharpen this tool, to sit tight for skills exercises. Bea had already put together a list of Ariel's writing shortcomings, and some of them were reflections of much more general problems that Bea had wanted to work with in any case:

> *No evidence of contemplation, association or ability to concentrate; lack of organization: no sense of beginning, middle and end; fragmented thoughts, choppy sentences—no connection between ideas; few references to past happenings or information.*

Ariel was a little girl with active senses and sluggish thoughts. By allowing her to make good use of her senses, Bea hoped to make writing—the putting of things on paper—a simple translation of sight into word images. She hoped to demonstrate to Ariel that order could be imposed on what her nose, eyes, and ears brought to her attention. Bea's first attempts were to get Ariel to write brief essays on what she saw on a mountain, what she heard in town—to establish the easy transfer of sights and sounds to words; then to have her focus on a single object.

When asked to describe a sea plum she had found in a tide pool, Ariel wrote:

> *The sea plum is all red. The sea plums body feels soft. The sea plum moves under the sea weed.*

About an ordinary household object, she wrote:

> *The Rocking Chair. The legs are curved. The legs and arms are brown. Even it has a hand [arm] rest arm to lie on it. The rocking chair has a seit [seat] on it [made of] straw. Then it has a cuchon [cushion] on it. The legs [are used] to make it rock. It skweeks.*

Bea also felt that Ariel needed an awareness of continuity, a feeling for sequence. So she had her start doing descriptions of household chores and activities. These subjects were often tied in with other activities important in Ariel's general education:

> *First you crak [crack] the egg. Then you put the buder [butter] into the pan. Then you pour the yoke into the pan. Then you put the chez [cheese] into the pan. When there is some white on the end and when it starts bubbling you turn it over. Then you are ready to srefe [serve].*

Compared with our laissez-faire approach with the boys, this initial work with Ariel seems contradictory in its studied goals. But as I've indicated before, our goals with Ariel were far more conventional. These little assigned essays were intended to make writing a comprehensible tool to Ariel. Later when she started writing magazine-picture-inspired stories and letters back home she would begin seeing it as a useful tool as well.

MAGAZINE-PICTURE STORIES. Bea had Ariel look through some old picture magazines we had found in a storage bin and cut out anything that interested her. Unlike Seth, who picked fanciful, exotic, or abstract photos and paintings, Ariel selected realistic advertisements and news photos, usually featuring people or a familiar scene (beaches, people in summer apparel).

Ariel was then asked to create a story, anything at all, based upon one of the photos she had selected. Bea wanted her to go beyond her senses—to turn inward into her own mind, to draw on other experiences, make new associations, start using the reserves of her brain and not just the nerve endings. If Ariel could be moved from literal statements to associative ideas in her writing, she would take a giant step not just in her approach to writing but in her approach to the world. Ariel at first missed the point of the stories. As she had done in the essays, she began by listing details of the picture, often misinterpreting even the literal scene and going off on some completely unrelated lead.

Bea didn't mind if Ariel noted some details, but she wanted more of Ariel's attention to be focused on explanations of who the people were, what they were doing—explanations that went beyond the picture and identified relationships between people and things, people and people. This sort of understanding would also help Ariel in recognizing the details.

Her description of "A Spanish Prison" shows the process at work. She had cut out a color photo of a somber prison exterior—no guards in view—surrounded by a beautiful formal garden in which tourists were strolling. She wrote:

> This is a big prison and all brick outside. There is a bell on top of the building outside. There is a garden green, yellow and dark green and a blue sky. The people do bad things. Just the good people could visit [them]. The prison is open at 2:00 p.m. It is closed at 4 p.m. [Bea's clock training]. There are lots of windows. They [there] are no hall ways in it. It is chilly in the prison. The guards watch the people so they don't escape. The guards stay there all night to watch the prisoners. The prisoners if they know what they have done wrong they can get out.

After the initial description she had begun to create the interior and imagine what was happening inside. She had even worried through how the prisoners could earn their release.

In a later piece based on a photo of a nude woman seated in a sauna looking down pensively, Ariel turned to real story telling:

BY ARIEL—A GIRL ALL BAIR [BARE]. *The girl has long hair. But she doesn't talk to any one because shes mad at pepole [people]. Her hands are on her knees. She combs her hair everyday. She took a shower that way. Shes all bair . . . Her name is Dieanner [Diana]. Dieanner is mayrie [married]. Her husbeen is nice. She does shopping a lot. Her husbeen is sick and he is in bed . . . until he dies. Do you want me to tell you what he has. He has a flew. . . . They have 3 children. Everybody serves him in bed. He is about 80 years old.*

After writing each story Ariel would try it out on Bea or me, make some corrections, and often ceremoniously read it to the assembled and attentive family at dinnertime. It was then proudly added to her growing pile of stories. "Someday," Bea had said, "we'll collect them into a book of Ariel's stories." Gestures of recognition like this provided Ariel with reasons for wanting to polish up her skills. As a matter of fact Ariel was so eager to complete her book that shortly after the talk about making a book, she cut and stapled her papers together and almost ruined her entire collection. Whether it was the result of this incident or Ariel's increasing interest in other forms of writing, particularly the letter, the magazine-picture-based story became less important to her. During a two-month period she had written twelve stories—some three and four pages long—and she seemed now to be tiring of the creative regimen. Bea thought she was ready for something closer to her immediate life and its real needs.

LETTERS. Ariel's first letters had been fun even though Bea required two and three revisions before she would allow them to be sent out. Ariel too didn't want her grandpa and her grandmas, her aunts, cousins, friends, or teacher to see any of her "silly mistakes" so she dutifully worked along with Bea. Bea's method was to have Ariel read her letters aloud so that Ariel heard when a sentence didn't make sense or where a period was needed. For a misspelled word, Bea would ask her to sound it out—frequently it was her pronunciation that was at fault—till she discovered the correct spelling. The major emphasis was still on meaning—what Ariel wanted to say—but writing skills were being brought in more frequently as ways to clarify the meaning. At the same time, many of the processes Bea had tried to encourage in the essays and picture-based stories were now being naturally called into play.

Ariel's early letters had been short, staccato bits and pieces, a virtual chaos of consciousness:

TO GRANDMA MATTY, FEB. *Your letter is fine. It is cold in Spain. There was a big shark in the water. There was lots of workers in our house. They were watching the shark. My father is fussy about eggs. And we went to Bacas house and we saw her make bread. Theire is flowers in our garden. Love Ariel.*

But only a week later, during which Bea had had Ariel start to write essays based upon her own detailed observations, Ariel wrote this letter to a friend back home:

TO KAREN, FEBRUARY 25. *I hope you are fine. Are you having a nice time in school. We have a new house. The living room is big. The fireplace is in the living room. The house has a window with a seat under it. My mother could serve the food out of a window from the kitchen.*
     The garden has some flowers and trees. It is a big garden with grass. We have catis [cactus] and a fruit tree in our garden. A farmer owns a field behind our garden. We went to the fiesta. We saw the soccer game and had rides on the merrygrond with Adam and I and Seth. Then we saw the band and the fire works in our town. After it was over we went home.

And a month later there was evidence of still further improvement. This was written after a trip to a Spanish seamstress's house, which we had reached by way of a treacherous dirt road winding up into the coastal hills:

TO GRANDMA LILLY, MARCH 25. *The road to the seamstress is bumbby [bumpy] and rocks [rocky] and drity [dirty]. Her house has a waiting room to measure us. No light comes in her house. Dolores measure[s] everything on us. She basted the arms and pants on [me]. They have a house and a pig and rusters and goates. . . . I will build a house in New york for my family.*

Bea's efforts to bring a sense of order and sequence into Ariel's writing also seemed to be working:

TO MARK, APRIL 29. *We went to a circus last night at 10 o'clock. I liked when the bull made on the table yesterday and the lady gave the banana to the man. The man did not take it. The people were in the costumes. They were wearing different clothes. Some of the people were playing instruments and the audience was laughing it was shouting out. The girls were not doing any triks on the rope just the boys. Then two animals came out and the man was smacking them. The audience was saying more. Everybody liked the circus very much. The children was good on the triks. The horse jumped verey high. Then the girls came out and danced. Than all walking in a circle. Then everybody went home. My father and mother said to go to sleep. The children fell fast asleep. Today when we were eating breakfast we saw them packing up. Nobody said goodby to them or said thank you.*

You can see in the last few lines of this letter the mind of a little girl emerging, wistful and considerate. We had a long way to go, but we had clearly made a start. As for the skills, they were still a bother, but at least they were now being utilized to further Ariel's own interests.

SCRIPT. Since handwriting is a matter of manual dexterity and practice, Bea did give Ariel much exercise once she was ready. But she waited until Ariel wanted to learn, until Ariel actually said she wanted to write letters that looked like Adam's.

SPELLING. We really weren't terribly concerned with her spelling problem because we knew there were far more serious difficulties lurking behind it—things like poor auditory perception, sequential and ordering confusion, and inadequate reading ability. If we could bolster these other areas, we felt her spelling would improve automatically and she could be spared a regimen of spelling exercises. Bea did have Ariel keep a list of words she misspelled in her letters (Ariel also used the list for practicing her script). But these were words already in Ariel's vocabulary, which she hadn't been able as yet to translate into written form.

VOCABULARY. The spelling list was soon turned into "Ariel's dictionary." Bea had Ariel add to her dictionary any new word she tried to use and had trouble with. We both agreed that the school's method of putting together age-level vocabulary lists with definitions didn't work. We wanted Ariel's writing to reach her oral level of articulation and the number of words at her disposal in speech to be the number available to her in writing. In addition we hoped her oral vocabulary would continuously expand through contact with us and her brothers and through her reading. And if she did become an interested reader, the automatic process of word assimilation would carry her even further along. After all, most of us reading newspapers and listening to TV are exposed to hundreds of strange words each year and manage to survive without vocabulary lists and without consulting a dictionary.

To move Ariel along in these separate skill areas while keeping in mind her ability to say something meaningful turned out to require more planning and formal teaching than we had expected and clearly contradicted some of our ideas on education. But in Ariel's unique case a regimen turned out to be necessary. When Bea first summarized Ariel's writing problems, she had these as her major goals:

> *To establish writing as comfortable form of communication. To have Ariel first learn to write what she is seeing and doing, then later what she is thinking and feeling.*

The second stage has not yet been reached. We have brought Ariel a little closer, but she is still a long way from being able to use or express what she thinks or feels. It's been terribly hard work for Bea, but it's been no less exacting for Ariel:

> TO GRANDMA MATTY, MAY *14. Then all the children got into percharmers and went to sleep. The next morning we woked up and the two boys took a bath and got dheresde [dressed]. Then my brother asked my mother can I make breakfast and she said yes.*
> *Then Adam said frist egg is here s[e]cond egg is here 3 egg is here, froth egg is here, fith egg is here. Then we all ate our eggs. The breakfast was over and Seth clerd [cleared] the table off. Then we went to work. And me and Seth worked on a letter to you. And my mother tipeing and my father reading . . . the Wether was cold. Everybody workes so hard on working. But after workes over we could play anything we want.*

ADAM

There is nothing more irritating in a child's writing than pretension or fake scholarship. Often this is not the student's failing so much as his attempt to meet a teacher's standards with a false face. Adam's writing was phony. He had the sentiments, he had the big words, he had the ideas that schools find acceptable, but he had nothing of himself in what he wrote. It wasn't just the teachers* who were at fault. The problem was with the system.

If a child is to learn how to speak and write, he needs constant exposure to richer language, more complex ideas, broader subject matter than his own peers can provide. Yet in our schools his social contacts are rigidly limited to his own peers, his educational contacts are restricted primarily to one adult (a pedagogue who speaks down to the student's age level), and even his contact with reading matter is confined to grade-level books with grade-level vocabularies and ideas. This isn't educational exposure. This is educational isolation, an organized effort to deny children access to the real adult world. Is it any wonder that a student like Adam, who managed to dress up his writing with a few out-of-classroom ideas and pretty phrases, would be applauded?

We had thought we'd be able to disentangle him from his slick classroom writing style pretty quickly once we had him out of school. He'd have no more weekly compositions,** book reports, or vocabulary-building exercises, and we hoped he'd soon find his own more natural uses for writing. Well, it took a little more time to free him from school influences than we thought it would, but once the job was accomplished the creative power and the intellectual curiosity released were astonishing.

During our first month abroad, Adam, like the other children, started by writing letters back home and even began keeping a diary—the idea for the diary was his own after visiting the Anne Frank house. And we started to feel that he was indeed finding his way. But after a month or so we could see that neither

---

*Most teachers don't know what to work with in student writings. They've been trained to look for skill problems—spelling, punctuation, usage—the safely objective grounds on which a teacher can hold his own. Convenient grounds, also. A teacher can correct thirty papers in half an hour if all he has to do is pick up such errors.

**One of the most damaging of the schools' practices in teaching composition is the teacher's arbitrary selection of a single topic for an entire class to write on. It's a naked admission that what a student is thinking and ready to express is not what writing is all about. Writing is concerned with how he says what he's supposed to say. Ironically, when a less restrictive teacher insists that each student find his own subject to write on, the majority of students balk. They want the teacher to decide for them, so that they'll know what he's looking for and have some control over how he'll grade their papers. Writing in school is not treated as a mode of communication. It is "composition," the formal presentation of classroom skills.

the letter writing nor the diary keeping was making any appreciable difference in his stuffy style or his basically wary attitude toward expressing himself on paper. Whereas letter writing was becoming a marvelously effective writing tool for Ariel and diary keeping an equally effective one for Seth, for Adam both activities were proving duds.

His diary lasted about thirty days. Bea surmised that he was too aware that what he was writing might—and no doubt hopefully would—be read by others (after all, Anne Frank's diary was read by millions!), and so he dressed up his own feelings and the diary became a self-conscious presentation of himself rather than a personal account. After a few weeks, in any case, it was just another dull exercise without prospect of immediate reward. His interest waned, his entries became shorter and more fragmented and finally stopped.

His letters proved no more beneficial. Initially he wrote them only on command and in a style stiff, earnest, and painfully self-aware. When they received no answers or only brief notes in return, his hurt feelings made further correspondence even more distasteful to him. Most of these early letters were dreary affairs, solemn or down-your-nose pieces. It wasn't until he had been thoroughly loosened up in his fun essays and particularly once he was engaged in writing his adventure novel that his letters began to show the flair of individuality and openness that we had looked for from the start.

Our efforts were complicated, as I've indicated, by his success in school. He'd been following school directives and meeting school standards for so long that he felt we were unfair to expect him to improve his writing through letters and a diary and with no formal instruction. When Bea asked him to write a paragraph on a subject of his own choice, he grew flustered and demanded *her* suggestions. When she asked him to present fresh ideas stemming from his own experiences, he tried, but discovered he couldn't manage it. When she had him set his own schedule for writing, he couldn't deliver until a deadline had been set. As a result, Bea decided that the first step would have to be a return to the familiar environment of specific assignments and specific expectations. But there would be one change. Adam would be measured by the substance of what he said.

The first few assigned paragraphs turned out to be sterile pieces stripped of any personality, clearly defensive. Adam was hiding behind facts and impersonal observations. Bea was harsh in her criticism. Adam had been safe in school, presenting a front of impeccable spelling, standard usage, and dazzling phrasing. But Bea was now questioning how he thought and the logic and depth of what he said. The emphasis had radically shifted from how he wrote to what he was trying to say. He was being listened to. And he suddenly realized he didn't have anything important to talk about. Bea's insistence on integrity in his writing had brought him up short.

She moved on to establishing a firm base for such integrity. She focused Adam's attentions on his raw senses. She had him, as she had had Seth and Ariel, start reporting on what he saw, what he smelled and tasted, what he heard and touched. The first pieces he wrote were still in his old puffed-up style of lush words and familiar expressions:

> *The quiet breeze hovers over this quiet, sweet and tender location on the Mediterranean. . . .*

But as he began to loosen up under Bea's gentle prodding, the highfalutin phrases were cut down to size, the imagery was extruded with less strain:

> *The seagulls swarm over the rippling water in great clusters; one or two taking occasional dives toward the water.*

And he even began, tentatively, to extend out again into the world of ideas:

> *Fog is a carpet on which heaven is held, the cause of a lost ship, of a scream; it's an enclosure, a blindness, a mournful spirit, the coming of death.*

Bea had written in her own notes:

> *My theory is that life for most people becomes a blur of impressions. But the writer isolates certain of the impressions that come pouring into his mind—he bothers to stop and reflect. And once he stops, he "sees."*

Adam did begin to see for himself. When Bea asked him to write about a rhinoceros that he had at first dismissed as just "ugly," he described the rough skin, the huge snout, and the wallowing in mud. But he also noted that his view wasn't objective but human after all and added:

> *We are probably equally strange and ugly to a rhinoceros [and the real truth no doubt is] relative or arbitrary.*

In an essay about the area in which we lived, Adam started with a description of the terrain and people but then went on to discuss how tourism, farming, and fishing affected the area. Here's a small section from the essay:

> *If tourism is allowed to grow, the few patches of farmland left now would probably completely disappear. That would result in foods being canned or frozen more often. Factories would be built not only to can the food but to fill in the needs of the tourists. After a while it would come to . . . be very similar to New York: factories throwing off huge amounts of waste, a modern port to receive tourists from the cruisers, an airport . . . the sounds of drilling on new paved roads, sky scrapers puffing their way up through the clouds, the sound of bull dozers wearing down huge mountainsides to a flat piece of land and more, much more.*

In addition to the keen use of his senses and a growing ability to think critically, an element of speculation, of intellectual curiosity was emerging. We had much evidence of this in our discussions, and we were now starting to see it surfacing in his writings.

One evening after dinner Adam suddenly started talking about how miraculous man was, what a phenomenon. After a few minutes of fumbling with his ideas, he was visibly upset by his inability to articulate what he was thinking.* Bea said, "Why don't you write it out?" The essay he did write skimmed over what he had tried to verbalize and didn't really cover the whole jumble of ideas, but it was still a unique piece of writing:

> FROM "THE PHENOMENON OF MAN". *Yesterday I had a peculiar sensation. I suddenly realized that I don't think I could call myself*

---

*One of the affectations of youth in the seventies is their studied inarticulateness as consciously worn as their patched jeans. To speak clearly and precisely makes them seem adult and rigid, lacking the sloppy naturalness that bespeaks unaffected youth. Adam learned to play this game and, like so many others, played it so consistently that it became his natural manner. He was indeed halting and almost inarticulate in speech and that's why having him write pieces such as his "Phenomenon of Man" was our way of getting him around a verbal blockage.

me. My body is like a worker as a wheel chair is to a crippled person. I should really consider myself as a brain. As I talk of myself right now I can imagine me as a brain telling my slaves to make me walk, talk, feel, smell, touch, taste, etc.

Any human would be afraid of anything that looked like a brain. Yet most humans never notice that they are a "brain" and that their brains happened to have a form of a disguise or mask so that the ugliness of the brain is not exposed.

It was about this time that he wrote a four-page letter to his cousin Darien discussing some of his speculations on relativity in relation to light, sound, and touch. For an eleven-year-old, this was solid and original thinking and writing, but it was also a little too solemnly intellectual. So Bea decided it was time to leaven the intellectual mix.

After all, we weren't interested in getting him into critical thinking and introspective reflections. There would be time enough for that.* We did want him to feel comfortable in expressing himself without school or even parental standards to meet. We wanted him to take delight in himself, in his body and feelings as well as his mind, and we wanted him to feel free to express all of them. Bea wrote down some zany titles ("What's a Shoe For?" "The Origin of Oranges," "Lazybones") for which she offered Adam no guidelines or form and no set of relevant facts. He would be forced to create his own scheme. The first of his writings were indeed forced, awkward attempts at style and humor—the sorts of things a child inflicts on adults when he is first discovering how to tell a joke. Bea wisely forbore and laughed at his puns and foolish dialogue. Here's an excerpt from one of them:

WHAT'S A SHOE FOR? . . . *For a place where only cockroaches abide, shoes are made with pointed fronts to make it possible to stamp on them even when they're in corners.*

For girls in love or almost in love: The best shoe in the world, fantastic, fabulous, guaranteed instant forever love. A press of a button and a little needle (not painful, no after pain, no scars) is injected into your foot. Instantly you will faint into your love's arms.

. . . There are many, many others such as roller shoes, computer shoes,

*A youngster with a good attitude toward himself and those around him needn't be pushed into these areas. When he's ready he'll suddenly do it. However, if you're looking for evidence of intellectual perception, you can elicit it from your children in the same way that a rote teacher gets rote answers from his pupils.

telephone shoes, TV shoes, skating shoes, fathom shoes and growing shoes, and the miraculous "Everything or All in One Shoes."

Through these nonsense essays Adam was testing out a few of his guarded inclinations—no small matter. But he was also discovering his private views, views that were no longer extensions of a curriculum. This was his de-academized and de-matured real self—and he could see that we, the only authorities in sight, clearly liked what we saw. And he was no less impressed with what was happening to him since leaving school.

In an essay on education he concluded:

> *A child has a need for these things: personal attention, reward, praise, and compliment; and excitement in his before-dreaded, now disliked and hopefully later, loved education. A child should enjoy education, respect it and greet it with happiness.*

In those first few months Adam and the other children had their full share of attention and praise—two functions parents are uniquely qualified to offer. But they also had the firm guidance of concerned and purposeful adults. Adam was fully aware of our close involvement in what he was doing, and after an initial confrontation with Bea on his inability to organize his own time and pursue his own interests, he welcomed our participation. He wrote:

> *The "Do It Yourself" policy is excellent as long as it is accompanied with a learned participator, the teacher, but in a new form, a participator, part of the group, capable of as many mistakes as anyone else, just a person trying to help us have a good future.* *

I remember one time taking the children to see their first bullfight. Adam, camera in hand, started shooting the initial stages of the corrida, but soon looked at me in disgust and turned away. Bea saw an opportunity in the situation and suggested that he continue to shoot and try to capture his disgust on film. He did. Later when the shots were developed he placed them in a

---

*One of our most notable features as the children's "teachers" was our fallibility. Time and again the children mentioned it, and usually with pride. They seemed delighted with the fact that though we knew so much we were after all just like them—we too made mistakes.

sequence and wrote an accompanying narrative for the series. A few days later he returned to the subject and created a dramatic scene in which he personified the bull in a Kafkaesque trial of innocence in a court of evil:

> *The judges marched into the court, their servants holding the judges'*
> *cloaks high. One by one the indifferent judges go up to the victim and*
> *overlook [sic] it making stabs at the guiltless victim's weak spot. The*
> *victim answers in a baffled way. So much bustling voices. More*
> *questions and more. The heart of the victim pumps harder and harder,*
> *faster and faster, trying to pump the remaining faith in innocence*
> *against the coming death sentence. Every stab weakens the victim*
> *more. And the victim's fear grows, he attacks feverishly with the last*
> *source of strength. He breathes hard coughing, hopelessly looking*
> *about for a friend to help fight the battle with him, but there are none*
> *of his kind—he is in a strange society with different laws of life and*
> *death. He is sentenced to death; his heart pounding like mad to supply*
> *the remainders [sic] of his strength. He now quite sincerely believes*
> *that he is guilty—he is accused and condemned, sentenced to death.*
> *One last frantic call for help to relieve the victim of the pain of death*
> *and he dies.*

My contribution was not always simply to demonstrate that parents were fallible. Once Bea was having trouble making Adam understand how his dry, factual notes on a subject in history could have incorporated a distinct point of view. I happened to be reading *Newsweek* at the time and, overhearing the conversation, called Adam over. Together we examined world reports, sports stories, and business articles in the magazine, picking out the bias or the point of view of each writer. Adam was delighted with the detective work and his ability to discover the writer's values. He also became keenly aware of the special powers he could enjoy as a writer.

He started to experiment with forms totally new to him. His tone and approach were often distinct for each piece, as if he were hopping through a range of possibilities that offered themselves to him now that no one was prescribing what he should do.

He read *Of Mice and Men* and instead of a book report, wrote his own playlet—a form in which he had never read, much less written, before—on a similar theme. He had been preparing exact graphic designs of his ideas for new cities and one afternoon sat down and wrote out a comprehensive rationale for one of them, an underwater housing complex. He had been living closely with simple, hardworking people in La Herradura and reading about the common man in ancient Greek and Roman civilizations, so he turned inward in his notebook and in a long angry entry spilled out his ideas on a historical pattern of abuse of the common man that he attributed to the uncommon man's lust for power and money.

One of his finest pieces was written after a dissection of a chicken. Instead of writing a blow-by-blow reenactment—as he had done for experiments on crossbreeding and on a visit to a Spanish photographer's darkroom—he chose to piquantly dramatize the scene:

ADAM—"DISSECTION TIME," APRIL 24. *C'mon! Everybody gather round. Dissection Time. Bring out the chicken. Where are the tools?*

There was much bustling and shoving as Howard S. Rowland and his three children manned their places around a small table by a large window in their vacation house in Spain. They were all soon quiet though as they waited excitedly for the chicken to arrive; the children (one 11 year old boy, one 7 year old boy, and one 9 year old girl) with hands on their laps, eyes toward the kitchen where the chicken would appear from; and the father high in a chair, tools spread before him which included needle, tweezers, throng [?] and knife.

And there—wait a minute—yes—yes, it was—and there was the dead patient being carried by the proud Rowland mother into the living room to the window. The patient was plucked of feathers. It was lying in a bowl, its head dangling over the side. The mother put it down and left us alone to "do whatever we wanted to do with it just as long as she didn't see."

The neck of the bird was attacked first. A slit was run down through the length of the neck revealing the throat (the larger of two tubes) and the windpipe.

Triumphant of their first observation they went on to the next. This project was to look at the wing muscle. And for the first time the 3 children found that the meat we eat is all muscle. And they also found out there must be a lot of muscle.

After a little discussion, the father dug down and cleared the muscle from the rib cage. In the process they stumbled over some tendons which held the muscle firmly on either side of the joint. The so-called "wishing bone" which served as a collar bone and had a floating joint was also examined. They saw the way the chicken's rib cage differed from ours; how on the front part of the rib cage two seperate [sic] *layers of bone overlapped each other and how one was hinged. They opened one side of the rib cage and all crowded around to see the heart, lungs, intestines and so on. The lungs were looked at first. There was a thin diaphram covering them. The diaphram was cleared revealing a red and black sensitive surface. One part of the lung (which had been cut into) was lifted up revealing some air sacs. The wind pipe was seen branching off to the lungs.*

Then a look was taken at the digestive system. The throat was followed down to the stomach (which was shaped very much like ours). Then from the stomach to the intestines and then to where the waste was let out.

The heart was seen next. It was imbedded between the stomach and lungs with a thick layer of fat around. * *After it was looked at it was taken out of the body. The older boy took over then [Adam himself] and cleared the heart of the fat tissues. He cut a cross section right through the deep red heart and 2 of the four blood sacks were seen and their connections also.*

The kidney was not seen. There was one "unidentified object" —a dark brown ball near the intestines.

At the end they cross-sectioned the throat, but there was nothing much to see.

When the family dissection was over the mess was handed over to mother "for her to clean up."

An essay like this reveals not just a schoolish familiarity with the details of an experiment, but, more important, an easy and highly personalized interest in learning and people. This was the direction we had wanted his education to take. And it wasn't an isolated bit of whimsy. The tone of his letters was also changing dramatically. No more was there a careful literary posturing. He could now speak directly and with ease to those he corresponded with back home.

So it was no surprise when one day Adam said he hadn't been able to make much progress with a topic Bea had suggested, "The Origin of Oranges" and wondered whether he could "sort of write a story to explain the origin." After two days he mentioned with a grin that he thought he had drifted a little bit from the original subject. On the third day he turned over a fifteen-page closely written manuscript, which Bea had him read to all of us that night. It was the first installment of a two hundred-page

*The whole aorta was seen with its 4 arteries coming out. The blue veins were also seen coming out.

adventure story he was to write over the next two months. Some days he would write for three- and four-hour stretches, totally absorbed in his own creation. It was during this period that we saw the most rapid growth in his writing. And as we suspected, from this point on he had no need of teachers or assignments.

WRITING CONCLUSIONS

What conclusions can be drawn from these family anecdotes?

WRITING SHOULD GROW OUT OF THE NEEDS OF A YOUNGSTER. It should not be introduced as an abstract skill. The promise of a future payoff is not comprehensible to a seven-year-old, nor will it be later after years of spelling, grammar, and handwriting drudgery. Writing should be associated with individual interests of the student and should be seen as a convenient tool for pursuing these interests.

The very word *work* in connection with schoolwork, written work, homework may be symptomatic of a work ethic that intrudes too early on the pleasures of learning. School should be a place for playing, doing, and learning, not just working.

WRITING SHOULD OFFER STUDENTS AN IMMEDIATE SENSE OF ACCOMPLISHMENT. The mystery of saying things and having them permanently available should be made much of. Writing should be seen as a way of extending one's range of communications. Nothing should interfere at first with getting each student to sense that being able to write makes it possible for him to do all kinds of significant and pleasurable things that he couldn't do before. Thus writing could start with dictation, to supply a sense of what happens when the ephemeral spoken word is put on paper, the wonder of having a thought or a fact made permanently and readily available. This could be followed by a minimal amount of assistance with handwriting—though I would prefer having children start to hunt and peck on a child-size typewriter and thus avoid another mechanical obstacle to getting on with what they want to say. Then as quickly as possible engage the child in real writing tasks rather than exercises, in letter writing to grandma, telling a story, keeping a diary. Scant attention should be given to spelling, punctuation, or handwriting. The full emphasis must be on what is being said. We know too well the stilted style of the student subjected to five years of "the cat eats the rat" exercises.

WRITING SHOULD BE SEEN AS A MORE EFFECTIVE TOOL FOR SAYING SOMETHING. Writing should perhaps start by approximating speech, but then it should go far beyond speech since, in fact, it enables greater control of thought. However, in our schools writing is approached as an occult skill. As a result a student's writing is rarely as effective as his ordinary speech. What should be a tool to overreach the limitations of speech is turned into a stilted or halting parody of communication.

WRITING SHOULD BE A CENTRAL MEDIUM FOR ALL FORMS OF LEARNING. It should be used as a tool for expanding reality, for making the senses more alert, the imagination more ranging expressions more exact, associations more diversified and complex. It should be a mental sharpener that functions best when supported by experiences—real or acquired through reading. For too many of us, good writing is a happy accident of expression; it should be a tooling of truth, an approach to perfect communication. There is good reason why whenever something important is to be spoken, it is almost always carefully written beforehand.

WRITING SHOULD BE DIRECTLY RELATED TO READING. A person who writes will have a better feeling toward and more interest in reading, just as a schoolyard basketball player going to see a Knicks' game will enjoy and learn more from the game than his girlfriend will. Conversely, the student who enjoys reading will have a better opportunity of picking up professional writing techniques and skills in a spillover process that is effortless.

9. SCIENCE—

"JIM AND I" AND

"LIO THE LINE"

As a biology student in college I had to memorize every part of the anatomy of a crustacean. I was compelled to remember the phyla, orders, families, classes, genera, and species of animals and plants. And slowly I grew, with my classmates, to hate the subject. I often wondered why the professor, a witty, personable man with an obvious wealth of knowledge in the field, was wasting his time and ours on nomenclature. But I never asked him. Perhaps if I had, it would have made me feel a little more honest about my own attitudes toward learning.

In La Herradura, Adam, Ariel, and Seth had no similar inhibitions. When they didn't understand what we wanted or thought it foolish, they let us know. Some people might think that in such a loose educational framework scientific disciplines could find no place. After all, the schools make science inaccessible to a student until he reaches a specified age and in some cases until he demonstrates real academic potential. It's a preserve of knowledge guarded by educators and doled out according to formula.

In high school, most students study earth science, but then only those who show college potential go on to biology. From this group an even smaller number is permitted to advance to chemistry. When finally a student is allowed to move on to physics, you can be sure he has proved his intellectual credentials.

However, the Rowland children needed no credentials and had no set learning sequences to follow, and so a few months into our trip abroad all three of them were happily involved in astronomy, comparative biology, botany, geology, ecology, and even physics.

Bea had made some initial attempts in science, as she had in reading and writing, to control the children's activities. She had provided each of them with some printed material or a school text and had had them read a few chapters and do some follow-up assignments. But as in the other fields, she quickly sensed that these carefully directed assignments were producing only false flashes of interest to please us, the surrogate teachers.

The real excitement in learning always seemed to stem from the children's everyday lives—activities that often had to do not with what a textbook writer said but with a hill, a stream, a flock of goats—things right at hand, things interesting or puzzling enough to one of the children to provoke a question. The children were not being questioned. They were initiating the questions and seeking answers. And if answers or suggestions were forthcoming from us to make this everyday world more manageable or understandable, then what we said was usually given keen attention.

The children saw Bea and me as neither their teachers nor their passive, doting parents. We were simply wiser, older people available to them as resources. They could expect us to chide them when we thought them undisciplined, perfunctory, or careless. But, equally important, they could confidently turn to us when they needed encouragement.

Because we were living in an undeveloped area, the sea, the land, and the sky—what they looked like, what they contained, how they were used—became ready material for learning.* For example, one night as I was tucking Ariel into bed, I noticed tears

---

*A city-bound child would have even richer materials to deal with if he were permitted to question and discover his surroundings instead of being isolated in a schoolroom.

in her eyes. I inquired what was wrong and she protested that she was being put to bed earlier and earlier. I tried to explain that each day simply had more daylight. But I could see she thought I was trying to fool her. So I called the other children into her room and using two oranges with lines drawn on one to represent the equator offered a brief explanation of seasons and daylight, time zones, and why we expected southern Spain to be warmer and sunnier than the Netherlands where we had started our trip. But Ariel remained unconvinced. So I said I would show her how the earth moved that very night.

Two hours later when it was dark, we woke her up along with the two boys, bundled up against the cold, and went outside to the open field fronting on the sea. Fortunately there was no moon. We all stared up at the heavens and were able to identify the Big Dipper and Orion, the only constellations I could recognize. Bea explained that the constellations would seem to move if we continued to observe them. But neither of us could figure out a quick way of showing how the heavens seemed to move without keeping everyone awake for an hour or so. There was much interest in the few bits of information we were able to dredge up on constellations and stories behind them, but general disappointment with our lack of more detailed knowledge. A promise to send for a book on astronomy saved the situation, and we all returned to the house.

On another day Seth questioned me about what caused the color in the sea. I made some guesses about color intensity according to depth and reflection and the changing texture of the surface of calm large bodies of water. This was accepted practice in the family because Bea and I were not teachers who knew it all. We were simply daddy and mommy, who knew a great deal but who also could be very plausible and wrong. So Seth and the others listened and walked away seemingly satisfied. They all knew that their parents believed theories, logic, and personal observation to be tantamount to knowledge, that harder information simply meant someone else had observed the same thing even more closely or was being more logical. As a result authority for them too became a relative commodity. Whoever or whatever was best informed on the subject at a specific time or place became the authority. Therefore Bea and I, who frequently could claim such authority, on a number of occasions had been found, understandably, to be wrong. However, because our record was pretty good—we made use of disclaimers about being expert—our information was accepted, though it was also frequently challenged and whenever possible checked with books or people who might know better.

When we received some books on the sea and the children started reading about ocean currents, temperature patterns, tides, and sea life, it wasn't long before Adam collected the family together to straighten us all out on color variations in water. It appeared that "daddy was only partly right." Adam proceeded to explain his findings on sea color.

Seth then suggested that my theorizing regarding surface texture might also be less than complete. Under pressure for some explanation of the smooth lines running through the generally even roughness of the sea's surface, I had speculated that the surface texture of the sea represented a homogeneous interplay of current, tide, and prevailing wind conditions. Whenever these were disturbed by passing boats, sudden gusts of wind, or local currents, the uniformity of the surface so patiently built up by the usual forces was broken and permanently scarred until new forces were brought into play. It sounded good. But of course I had no basis for my conjectures, and at the time I had admitted as much to the children.

Neither Seth nor Adam was able to find any specific information on surface patterns in any of the sea books we received—though they did use what they read to develop some theories of their own. Some day, however, I'm sure they will chance on the information, and when they do, their earlier speculations will help to make this new knowledge memorable.

THE SEA

The children often adventured along the rugged shore, jumping from rock to rock, scaling cliffs, climbing down into almost inaccessible coves, discovering hidden tidal pools. Occasionally we accompanied them—a sea book in hand—pointing out limpets and periwinkles, sea urchins and oysters. But it wasn't long before Adam and Seth were both checking in the book—*Life in the Sea* (Hamlyn Books, London)—and doing their own observations and reading while we looked on or went about our own business. They became expert at identifying the different sea creatures that abounded on these shores and began studying each animal minutely.

They built an aquarium of sea animals in a hollow of a large rock down at the shore, but soon discovered that the animals died unless the tide reached the area. Then they reestablished the aquarium in a tidal area and found that the animals disappeared at high tide, either escaping to habitats of their own choosing or losing out, under Darwin's laws, to unfamiliar surroundings. Their last attempt was to place a collection of sea creatures—clam, oyster, sea urchin, chiton, periwinkle, green and red sea anemones, *Murex* mollusk, hermit crab, limpet, barnacle, and assorted algae and water worms—in a large bucket and to replenish each day the foul water, the algae, the attached plankton and sea worms that served the animals as food. But the periwinkle and mollusk seemed determined to escape from the pail and in the process went catapulting over the side cracking their shells.

A combination of pity for the imprisoned and self-destructing animals and boredom with the daily chore of refitting the aquarium caused the children, finally, to return to observing nature naturally. They needed only to wait for low tide and any number of sea animals could be observed alive, functioning normally in a natural environment. The lesson of not possessing, of living and letting live, was clearly presented to them.

Seth wrote about an adventure bearing on the same point in a letter to his grandma Matty:

> *After lunch me and Carmen [a friend] went to the rocks. There we started to colect sea urchens. We wanted colored sea urchens that were not black. Then we moved to another pool. There I saw all different colored sea urchens. I tried to get a yellowish-green sea urchen but my hand slipped and some of the sea urchen's spikes got stuck in my hand. I quickly plucked the spikes out and ran across the whole beach crying. When I got to the blanket my whole left pointer [index finger] was filled with blood. Mommy first squeezed the blood. Second mommy tore a cloth and made a bandade. Mommy told me to rest and I did.*

But the experience was not wasted. A few days later his notebook revealed he was observing the sea urchin even more closely:

> *A sea urchen has these feeler like things which have caps on them . . . they use their quills to walk with.*

And his interest quickly spread to other sea animals:

> *It [the hermit crab] has a very soft rear. It has two small pinchers*
> *[two pages of minute descriptions of legs, feelers, colors, sizes].*
> *. . . Do you know why the hermit crab wears his shell? To protect his*
> *rear. He lives in rock shores in a bunch of sea weed. He's right on*
> *the splash zone in tide pools. Do you know how the crab knows when*
> *his shell is to small for him? Because of instinked* [sic]. *That's*
> *how.*

Later Seth felt so familiar with the sea animals and their habits that he wrote a story titled "The Sea Tiddle Pool," featuring three humorous characters: Mr. Sea Plum, Mr. Sea Anemone, and Mr. Periwinkle. He used the characteristics he had observed of each to embellish their dialogue and develop separate comical personalities.

It wasn't just Seth who was drawn to the sea as a learning environment. Seeing her brother record his notes on sea life, Ariel sought to write down her observations too:

> *The sea nemonee has lots of toobs. He gets his food from the sea.*
> *It goes in his mothe [mouth]. He lives under the rocks. He clinks*
> *[clings] to rockes.*

We had no desire to keep Ariel abreast of the boys—she had her own special interests—but we did feel she had something to gain from learning to use her senses purposefully. By encouraging her to focus her attention and record her observations as the boys were doing, we were gradually able to get her to understand what differentiating and generalizing were all about. She became fairly skilled at grouping and distinguishing things according to properties—color, texture, function (things that grow in the earth, things to build with, bodies of water)—and these were major steps forward for Ariel.

Only Adam seemed reluctant to make more than casual observations on his own, though he actively participated in family science activities. However, when he made fun of Seth's methodical approach in keeping a science notebook, Bea lashed out at him for his own lack of scientific curiosity and his inability to stay with a project. His answer was to grudgingly read a few chapters in a science textbook and begin taking some tentative notes on his own observations. His notebook entries were at first mechanical and cursory. But as Bea and I continued discussing with him his notes on personal observations, thus lending them some importance, we found his descriptions growing more complex and detailed and his use of illustrations and legends increasing. Our adult concern and curiosity seemed to be important factors in exciting his interest and often resulted in a more responsible attitude on his part in activities that might otherwise have degenerated into nonsense or mischief. However, if his interest in an activity started to wane—as, for example, when his enthusiasm for dissecting sea urchins was replaced by an equal enthusiasm for photographing them—we let it happen rather than insist that a subject be adhered to until it was exhausted.

This didn't lead the children to jump haphazardly from one fleeting interest to another. On the contrary, because we were readily available and our involvement in their activities was often intense, the children learned that maintaining our interest often required serious involvement on their part as well.

During our stay abroad Adam methodically catalogued every sea creature he could find. He would study each animal in its natural habitat, then bring it home for more detailed studies, and finally dissect it. His findings were then fully detailed in his notebooks: description (external and internal), eating habits, locomotion, protection, and reproduction (some wild guesses here).

No doubt studying sea life turned out to be fun because Adam was now able to involve Ariel and Seth in his work in science. At first he comically imitated his schoolteachers back home. He might spend a good part of a day preparing a lesson for Ariel and Seth. I remember one of these lessons on food chains. Adam read a textbook, took notes, drew diagrams, organized a presentation, and then formally lectured the two children who sat goggle eyed at his manner more than his expertise.*

Later he became much more casual. He would take Ariel and Seth for walks along the shore, carrying a book on sea life as reference, and as he discerned a sea anemone (a red, plumlike creature that clung to shore rocks) or a cluster of barnacles, he would point them out to his two wide-eyed companions. He was

---

*Another time he set up a series of light experiments, and for two days the children as well as Bea and I were called periodically into his room for demonstrations of reflection, refraction, diffusion, inversion. Much of this technical knowledge he later used in his experiments in photography.

not just teaching, he was reinforcing his own learning. In her notes Bea described one such scene:

> *Adam is explaining to Ariel how muscles are attached to bones. The two are squashed together on an arm chair, book spread across their laps and both very intent. Ariel is obviously delighted and absorbed in real listening, but Adam is no less delighted with his demonstrated mastery in the subject.*

THE LAND AND THE SKY

Just as Adam clambered with the children along the shore, so he climbed with them through the surrounding hills, a geology book in hand, pointing out signs of erosion or earth stratification. Often Bea and I were by his side learning too. Together we discovered how to differentiate herbs and spices; to recognize by sight, by smell, by taste, and by touch the olive, the almond, and the fig tree; to observe sea currents and tides; to distinguish the types and causes of erosion on the hills and cliffs and the sedimentary buildup of the rich delta below.

Moving from fertile valley to barren and parched mountainsides, we closely examined the plants, animals, herbs, and trees and speculated about the process of natural selection. We wondered at the mountain goats suckling their young, scampering up cliffsides, copulating. We studied what was underfoot: ant colonies, soil composition, vegetation, and root structure; and what was overhead: the blue color of the sky, the different cloud formations, the wind currents as evidenced by the effortless flights of swallows and terns. Seth recorded in his diary:

> *Birds like hawks can soar in the wind, turning and doing other stuff for hours without flapping their wings. They fly on the curints of the wind.*

Many subjects first introduced at random as part of a discussion became regular features of our family activities. At least once each week, after that first midnight outing with Ariel to study the stars, we would wait until dark and then, with a map of the heavens and a flashlight to illuminate it in hand, study the constellations. Ariel became so familiar with star formations that her drawings—and even her zany spelling—proved more accurate than either of the boys'!

She was able to identify:

> Jim and I [Gemini], Roriger [Auriga], Lio the line, canser, ursa miner, Leber [Libra], liter deeper [Little Dipper], big deeper, hercles [Hercules], Torse [Taurus], Sbcer [Spica], Noth [North Star], closder of stars [cluster of stars], Pleandes [Pleiades], Viego [Virgo], Serpens [Serpent].

DISCUSSIONS

The range of discussion and inquiry in the sciences was broad: bird migrations, heredity, geology, magnetism, centrifugal forces, leverage, the characteristics of light, agriculture. For example, a trip to Málaga became an occasion to discuss problems of agronomy. We were passing through a dry and rocky coastal area south of Almuñécar where the only vegetation seen was olive, fig, and almond trees sparsely covering the mountainsides. Suddenly we came upon Nerja, a rich delta area flat and green, lush with oranges, lemons, sugar cane, tomatoes, and other vegetables and fruits. Through the middle of this vast garden, in a broad, flat, slightly depressed rock-strewn band, rushed a torrent of muddied water that quickly emptied into the sea.

We stopped beside a field of sugar cane, and breaking a stalk I peeled off the tough outer skin as I had seen the local people do and began sucking the juicy inner fibers. The stalk was passed from one to another, and Seth, tearing at the strands with delight, asked, "Why can't we grow this at home?" We talked generally about soil, temperature, and rainfall; how deltas were formed; and how these and other factors determined what could or could not grow in an area. Adam was first to point out that the United States used fertilizers and irrigation as ways to improve on natural conditions. But Bea reminded him that many ancient peoples and specifically the Moors in Spain had made good use of irrigation long before us. However, she couldn't understand why Nerja, an old Moorish settlement, would in the 1970s allow so much water to escape while land not more than a quarter of a mile away was dry and barren. Then the conversation branched out to the need for forests to hold soil and water, the problems of erosion on mountainsides, the lack of money to build dams and reservoirs, the use of reservoir dams for water and power, the Aswan Dam and Hoover Dam, desalination schemes—Adam managed to interject a short lecture on photosynthesis—the use of atomic energy.

This was only one discussion stemming from farming. Others dealt with terracing, contour plowing, crop rotation, hybrids, breeding, grafting, seeding, the making of soil, the agricultural economy. For example, as we were returning from an afternoon's visit with a local farmer, Seth asked why there was so little variety in the crops grown along the coastal areas of Spain. We talked about soil and climate restrictions and contour plowing but then, as so often happened in our rambling, the subject broadened out to Russian experiments in developing their tablelands for winter wheat, the rise and fall of Lysenko, Mendel and his laws of heredity (we later started playing arithmetic games predicting family eye and hair color characteristics), Khrushchev's trips to America to study our corn crops, the use of hybrid forms in developing better vegetables, fruit, and livestock.

Later, as had happened before, we found that the discussion had triggered some follow-up activity—in this case intensive experimentation in plant cultivation and breeding. Adam worked with fruit flies, fashioning an enclosed environment with a plastic bowl; Seth tried a succession of experiments with potatoes, pine cones, and tomatoes.

> *Next day after breakfast we started an experiment . . . we first cut a tomatoe in 4's. Then we got a planting pot of dirt and water. I was in charge. I waited till the water had soaked threw the dirt.*

Each of his experiments failed, but Seth was left nonetheless fascinated with the scientific method. For the pine-cone experiment he set up a special notebook carefully divided into two sections: "What I think" and "What it is—the Truth." The idea was his own, though Adam suggested a control group. Seth wanted to see how seeds were dispersed. Each day he dutifully recorded his observations: "Cut slit—did not open a bit the third day. . . . [The control] No slit—did not change." And through fifteen days he made his entries—unfortunately, without observing any change.

When Bea, in an effort to give him some success, tried to

involve Seth in a more formal experiment, borrowed from a science book, that concerned measuring water before and after freezing in a glass, he was not nearly so eager. After dutifully writing up each of the steps he had taken, he added:

> *Then you take the glass out and see how much it expanded. How much does it? I don't know, don't ask me. You find out. Goodbye.*

Far different was his tone when he wasn't in a formal learning situation. His comments frequently had elements of science, history, geography, aesthetics woven through them. After a trip to Granada he wrote in his diary:

> *We saw places where big rivers were. We saw how far in the sea went when I think a tidle [tidal] wave came in. We saw Almunecars aqueduct. Adam took a picture of it. We were soon on a flat plain 4,000 feet above sea level. The plain was like a rainbow. It was beautiful. We could see Granada from there.*

Such entries clearly indicated we were on the right track in opening up the sciences and all other subject areas to the children.

THE FIRST DISSECTION

The children were tightly gathered about me, intense and expectant, as scalpel in hand I made my first incision.

We had taken my first-year biology dissecting kit abroad because it contained a number of instruments we always found useful at home—for removing splinters, for cutting ingrown toenails, for probing electrical wiring, for realigning torn screening or strands pulled from sweaters. Besides, I had often promised to dissect a frog with the children, yet somehow had never gotten around to the bloody business.

As they looked on watching me cut through the chest of the chicken, I could sense the children's faint repulsion. All of us had been critical of the local townspeople's custom of caging, outside their homes, song birds that provided occasional and very brief flurries of music when the streets were quiet. The cages were frequently so small as to permit the birds—usually dove-size— barely room to turn. Yet free-flying flocks of swallows and song sparrows were forever flitting and twittering and darting through the same village streets, nesting in every outside wall cornice or crevice, finding their own food, and endlessly singing their excitement. The caging seemed redundant and cruel. Yet here we were tearing apart a bird on the grounds of intellectual inquiry.

The idea of mangling a vertebrate out of curiosity or simply to make use of my dissecting kit—bloodless these twenty-two years—was difficult to defend. In many of our discussions we had touched on human anatomy—breathing, digestion, reproduction—and we had mentioned the similarity of other animals to humans. But the idea of a dissection not only conflicted with the children's Bambi-oriented background but also suggested a ritualistic blood ceremony. No matter how factual and scientific the approach, mystery and revulsion always attach to the business of cutting open a living or freshly slaughtered animal simply to examine its body.*

Nevertheless, our children had not been won over to the ideas of the vegetarian or the antivivisectionist. We had managed to keep separate their interest in science and their children's sentimentality regarding animal life. So when Bea suggested dissecting a chicken—jumping from where we were with the mollusk through eons of evolutionary time—since she didn't enjoy removing the innards in the first place, all three of the children endorsed the idea. I would have quietly forgotten the whole thing if Bea, a few days later, hadn't followed it up on her return from the marketplace by ceremoniously handing me, by its twisted neck, the full, plump, totally intact body of a chicken. The children were overjoyed. Adam ran for the dissecting kit, Seth brought in a chopping block, and with a false show of bravado, I resumed where I had left off twenty-two years ago in Room 202 at N.Y.U. The dissection lasted two hours. With Adam's help (see his description on page 104), I probed muscles, bones, and diges-

---

*The eating of flesh in advanced industrial countries—where meat is never seen except in neatly prepackaged and weighed identical cuts, sorted and stacked like any other mass-produced factory item—is an act difficult to associate with a ripped and bloody animal carcass. In Spain you play with and enjoy the birds and the animals as they graze and cavort, as they slither through the muck of an alley pigpen, as they leap from ledge to ledge of precipitous cliffs, as they feed their young or scurry behind the crowing rooster. You watch them, meek and docile, being led to market. You see them hanging whole in butcher shops with their necks twisted and eyes glazed, flayed and skinned bodies with bulging eyes and bared skulls. In Spain the scene has not been simplified to a row of frozen-food cases in a brilliantly lit, air-conditioned supermarket.

tive, nervous, circulatory, and reproductive systems. We discovered the kidneys, cracked through a cross section of the neck to reveal the spinal column, studied the pliability of the vertebrae. Only when Seth started poking into the beak to examine the tongue and spoke of breaking the skull to probe the brain did I find myself losing interest. Providentially, Bea announced dinner at this point.

In a few days Bea would cut up the chicken into its familiar A&P-style sections and cook it. When we ate it, it would no longer be a complex creature with respiratory, circulatory, digestive, excretory, and nervous systems; it would simply be white and dark meat, a drumstick or a wing. The children could still see the animal as a part of nature, unique and inviolate. They could see it as an early model of life, worthy of study in understanding man and all animal forms. And finally, they could accept its slaughter without sentimentality, as necessary for man's carnivorous diet. The balancing act required to hold aloft these three concepts simultaneously was something I did not call attention to at that time. But I know that Bea, Adam, and myself were aware of conflicting values, and it was tacitly understood that their resolution would be put off for another time.

Fortunately not all issues are pressed to the wall for immediate resolution. We all knew that there were no textbook or curricular dogma in these areas. We were feeling our way. And even if we had an answer, it would be tentative. Adam knew—and Seth, too—that he would be hearing and learning more about many of the things we discussed and observed. It was all insight, logic, previous experience, guesswork—and all subject to change and clarification later. We were on safe ground. Nobody was conning anyone with absolutes or final statements. We were all obviously learning.

Within the next few weeks the boys dissected everything in sight: fish, shrimp, seeds, acorns, even flowers. I can imagine the astonishment with which my mother received this description from her seven-year-old grandson in an otherwise casual letter about the fun he was having in Spain:

TO GRANDMA MATTY, MAY *12. Just two days ago we were dissecting some flowers. We saw the seeds of the morning glory. They were black. As black as this [black ink spot]. The morning glory has eight pistils. We saw the pistils in the white daisy. There were 10 or 11 pistils.*

The pistils are higher than the stamens which held the pollen which was brought to the pistils by bees. It is the same in all other flowers but the places are different.

Do you know why flowers are so beautiful? To attract bees. They try to make them selfs more beautiful than others and to attract more bees than others. In the yellow daisy the pistils are lower than the stamens. There are 11 or 12 pistils in the yellow daisy. The pistils in all flowers are in the midle of the flower.

The thing that covers the bud is call[ed] the sepal and as you know then come[s] the stem.

Did you know that all the fruit you eat in a pear is part of the ovary which protects the seed insinde [inside] which we call a pit. It is the same in all fruits.

If you took off all the petals, stamens and pistils off a succulent plant you would see something that was green and looked like a green apricot cut in half. We saw the eggs of the seeds in every single flower we looked at.

Near the end we started grabing for the twissors [tweezers—we had all picked up bristles in our fingers from the stems of flowers]— except Ariel who had no splinters.

10.

MATHEMATICS—SNEAKING

UP ON THE ABSTRACT

One afternoon the family was lolling in a field, Bea and I reading, Seth working on his diary, Ariel humming quietly to herself, Adam casually observing the Spanish farmer across the valley from us slowly working his donkey and plow along the contours of a closely terraced hillside. Adam turned to me and said, "You know, if you purchased an acre of sloping land you'd get more land for your money than you would with a flat piece."

It was an interesting idea, and before long we had borrowed Seth's diary and started drawing diagrams to see the difference between the surface of a flat piece of land versus a sloped piece. We quickly arrived at the difference between a side and the hypotenuse of a triangle and the fact that the more acute the angle the more land you would get. But, Adam noted, there would be more likelihood of erosion too because of the steeper slope, which was why the slopes were terraced. Then he suddenly realized his original error. It was an optical illusion. All the advantage of the slope was lost when you terraced because the bases of all triangles (the flat terraced portions) added up to the exact equivalent of flat acreage. When I mentioned the formula $a^2 + b^2 = c^2$ as a way of checking this out, Adam asked, "Where did you get that from?" I remembered my own distrust of teachers who had fallen back on, "It's an axiom" as a way of dismissing a student's query. And so for the next hour I set about discovering out loud something I had never attempted before. I ran through lots of false starts—with Adam peering over my shoulder suggesting new approaches—but finally when I finished multiplying $(a-b) \times (a-b)$ and arrived back at the original formula, there was triumph in the family. We had discovered a process to get at a truth. A method of logic, not just a theorem, had come alive. It was an unplanned, intense moment in which mathematics suddenly took center stage because it was needed.

Although Bea started each child initially with workbooks at their grade levels, the emphasis in math, as in so many other subjects, shifted progressively during the first few months to less ordered learning. Math, like speech and writing, became a tool for clarifying complex ideas, for dealing with ordinary problems of living. Ariel paid vendors in the marketplace and anticipated the change she should receive. Seth discussed the advantages of putting our reserve of money in a Spanish savings bank as opposed to a business bank and then figured out the difference in interest. I used property values and taxes to compare the sums available for education back home and in La Herradura; a trip to Tangiers, where we were approached by black marketeers, became an occasion to discuss the relative values of money and the reasons for smuggling; the need to convert kilograms to pounds, kilometers to miles, liters to quarts, and meters to feet were ready opportunities for calculations and for reinforcement of measurement skills.

Once we calculated the height of the village church by measuring its shadow and relating it to the shadow of a stick; another time we averaged the depth and surface area of a large cup-shaped depression in a rock to estimate the amount of water it held because we were considering making an artificial sea pool and wanted to know how much water we would have to lug to the rock. Math was removed from the workbook and allowed to function freely as one of our ways of seeing and understanding things. It hadn't started that way. As I've indicated, Bea had taken special pains to assemble math workbooks and study materials for each of the children because we had assumed there were clearly defined skills and subject areas to be covered in math and the idea of loosening up this particular discipline seemed a little too ambitious.

SETH

Seth had a natural feeling for math. He could add and subtract in his head long before the schools taught him how to work out addition and subtraction problems on paper. When he was working out a problem in his head, his light green eyes would shift dreamily to some distant object, and you could almost see playful numbers streaking back and forth across his mind.

Concepts like averaging, using decimals, relating miles to speed were barely suggested before Seth was putting them to use. But if he were asked to recapitulate the steps by which he arrived at his accurate answers, he would balk. He liked the mental leap to an answer and seemed to want no part of a step-by-step procedure to discipline his bit of magic.

For a child like this, second-grade arithmetic exercises would have shorn the mystery from the numbers game. Bea realized this, but she also recognized that putting things on paper would be necessary if Seth were to continue moving ahead in math. So she started showing him what some of the things he had worked out in his head looked like on paper and before losing his interest introduced him to similar but more complex problems that he simply couldn't handle in his head.

Bea had taken along a math skills test and outlines of the formal sequences in math covered from second through eighth grades. According to these Seth was more than proficient in third-grade math. So she introduced him to more advanced work. At first she used a workbook, but after a new concept had been exercised four or five times, one could almost see Seth's shoulders go slack as he shifted gears to a mechanical routine. It seemed pointless to have him do one or two hundred similar problems after he showed no trace of difficulty dealing with the first five. And when he asked, "Why do I have to keep doing the same thing over and over again?" we really had no answer. It was then that we first seriously considered the whole idea of reinforcement and decided we weren't going to hold Seth back any-more.*

Bea started with addition, and within a few hours Seth had mastered carry-over and was adding eight and ten five-digit numbers. During the next few days she went on to multiplication and found Seth able to grasp the basic concepts and then move rapidly to multiplication of three-digit numbers by four-digit numbers. Then on to division, to problem solving, to concepts of time, down payments, fractions. He gobbled it all up.

During one session on adding fractions, Bea used a round loaf of bread she was cutting up for dinner, then gave Seth a similar problem to be worked out on paper. When he had finished, he cut a few more slices of bread to demonstrate the accuracy of his answer and then giggling at his success said, "Give me more. I love arithmetic."

True, he made careless errors in addition and division, but there was no question that he thoroughly understood what he was trying to do. And no question of his perky confidence in his own judgment. One day when he returned one of the math problems Bea had created on the spot, she was surprised to find a neatly written statement at the bottom of a page covered with unfinished calculations: "This problem is not unnerstanable." He was certainly not afraid of his teacher. Besides, he was right. An essential fact *had* been omitted.

The work he did was taken less and less from his workbook during those early months. Just as she had used a loaf of bread to illustrate a point on fractions, Bea now used the everyday problems of running a house or understanding what was happening around us to tease Seth's imagination and start him off on new problems. Once we gave up the abstract and uninviting environment of the workbook and turned to the infinitely rich world of objects and happenings around us, we found there was no end of raw material for learning.

---

*We didn't know enough about the new math to use it, but it certainly sounds close to what we had in mind. The old math is based upon a drop of conceptual understanding and a bucket of sheer drill. It is a Pavlovian regimen designed to produce automatic reflex and mechanical response.

Mechanical aptitude with numbers—fixed methods and consistent accuracy —may well result in efficiency in calculations as some new math debunkers claim; but it surely doesn't promote conceptual or logical thinking, which are the ostensible functions of math. As a matter of fact, reinforcement through exercises in accuracy almost certainly has an aversive effect in that it smothers any inclination to think freshly or logically.

When Bea wondered how much it was costing us to eat meat and fish each week, she turned to Seth and had him figure our average daily cost; when we bought a few unfamiliar brands of sardines to compare their tastes, it became Seth's job to determine which was the best buy by figuring the cost per ounce for each package. When Seth spent an afternoon talking to and helping four laborers who were building a drainage ditch and returned saying they would probably take ten more days to complete it, Bea asked him to figure out how long it would have taken if he were a man helping them or if he were alone doing the whole job. One time Seth figured out that he was about one-fourth the age of his mother and about two-thirds the age of Adam. Bea asked him to get an approximate fraction fifty years from then, and Seth was fascinated with the way age differentials became increasingly less significant over time. He said, "In a hundred years there'd hardly be any difference between you and me, mommy. We'll be like brother and sister."

We found ourselves using mathematics as a convenient aid in our discussions and everyday activities. For example, after Seth had told us which can of sardines was the best buy, Adam pointed out that the contents—like the cans of anchovies we had previously examined—seemed to belie the weight labeling. The largest can was again loosely packed, while the smallest can (labeled to be half the weight of the largest) was packed to the top. Adam improvised a scale to check his point, and the conversation shifted to fair labeling and the need for a bureau of weights and measures. Bea noted that the fully packed can had both English and Spanish print on it, meaning that the packager was exporting to British or American markets and had to meet their standards. She surmised that the other packagers were probably taking advantage of their domestic customers because there was a minimal or perhaps collusive government presence, and we started discussing imports and exports, balance of trade, attitudes of governments toward their own people. It wasn't a math lesson, a social studies lesson, or a lesson in home economics. It was rather another experience in which math played a natural and integral part.

Within two months Bea had not only taken Seth through four years of school math, she had made math a working tool. We were elated at his progress. But we were also fearful that having allowed him to advance at his own pace, we had put him too far ahead of his classmates back home. He could not expect to learn anything new in math now until he reached junior high, and here he was only a second grader. So we stopped. No more formal math for Seth—he'd have to concentrate in other areas.

ADAM

Adam started with a sixth-grade workbook and dutifully completed three or four pages each day. He seemed comfortable with the routine and rarely made a mistake except through carelessness. We were so pleased with his other interests—photography, city planning, writing—that we paid little attention to what he was learning in math. He had to cover the grade-level material, and if he mastered the workbooks that took care of that. Adam had been well trained by his seven years of formal schooling so that at first he felt it was important to keep up with the kids back home, and though he was finding most excitement in activities that had nothing to do with school, each day on his own he allotted time for the standard subjects like math and history and science.

In a few months he had finished the math workbook—something we hadn't anticipated—and thus he had no materials for algebra or geometry. Bea, flaunting her distaste for math, decided to turn him over to me. Adam had to wait two weeks before I agreed to become his math tutor, but when I did we started working intensely for one- and two-hour stretches. We covered only those areas of algebra that I could still recall, and as soon as Adam had mastered a principle or approach we moved on. No doubt I was impatient; sometimes in these early sessions Adam would end up crying in frustration at not being able to keep pace. My constant insistence on reasons and logic rather than method probably annoyed the hell out of him. The schools had made Adam comfortable following a pattern, whereas I was bored with methodology and more concerned with mental agility.

Every three or four days we would have a long session and were able to move rapidly through random chunks of algebra and geometry. Adam at first was troubled by the fact that there was no clear sequence in what we discussed and that I was never certain myself of the answers because I created the problems on the spot. Then to check his answers I found it convenient to have him review with me what he had done to solve each problem by explaining why he had taken each step. As a result the reasons for doing what he did became more important than the eventual accuracy of his answer.

I recall once asking him to discover four different methods of constructing parallel lines using a string and a pencil. He did figure out three after about a half hour of drawing—he had started with a line and then used a point, a bisecting line, and a perpendicular line—but for the next hour no matter what he tried he could not devise another method. We must have spent two more hours together—holding up Bea and the other two children, who were eager to get down to the beach—trying to find· other approaches to the problem. We finally tried using a circle and an isosceles triangle and were pleased with our success. Adam then asked about solid forms because in designing his plans for buildings and cities he often had to draw three-dimensional objects. We constructed a perfect cylinder, a cube, and a pyramid in two dimensions. However, Adam objected because we had not allowed for perspective. He wanted to know how to calculate accurately the distortion caused by perspective in objects he drew. I took a swing at it but after fifteen minutes was unable to find a satisfactory formula. By this time the others had angrily left for the beach, so we hurried down to join them.

This sort of groping for answers was really, I felt, the key to learning. We may not have found the right answers always, but we were going about the business of thinking logically and creatively in finding solutions to our questions. For Adam, seeing my lack of knowledge and indifference to rote methods or formulas, math became a challenging field for fresh thinking, for logic and sudden insights.

ARIEL

Ariel and arithmetic simply didn't get along. When we took her abroad she could confidently add one plus one and one plus two. Anything beyond that was chancy. If she didn't use her fingers she was helpless, and even counting on her fingers she would run into trouble. Conceptual thinking could be taught to her, but the price was so high in tears and failures that we thought it more important in her case to shift our emphasis to Ariel's needs. She had to learn to function in society as effortlessly as possible.

A rote ability to add and subtract, to count change, to tell time, to distinguish measurements and weights—these were crucial tools that would allow Ariel to go about her business simply and independently. Without them she could be labeled and judged different; with them she could move through a normal day's activity without any noticeable handicap. Certainly, most adults used nothing more than basic arithmetic once they were out of school.

Bea found that Ariel enjoyed drill if she felt confident in her ability. She would sit alone for an hour doing simple arithmetic exercises in an area that Bea had thoroughly reviewed. The anticipation of success was her strongest motivation. Every time a new type of problem or procedure was introduced, Ariel was visibly delighted. She thrilled at the idea of progressing like her brothers, but she was also acutely sensitive to her own shortcomings. At the slightest suspicion that she wasn't following an idea all her confidence was shattered. She stared blankly at the pad or meekly into your eyes and inwardly she seemed to shrivel. Bea and I often talked about what to do about her slow pace in arithmetic. She would drill for hours on adding five to other numbers and solve problem after problem correctly. But two days later she had totally forgotten how to add. Once she was taught how to carry over in addition and completed almost perfectly fifty problems that got progressively harder. There was jubilation in the house, and Ariel was toasted by each of us at dinnertime. But after a few days of studying subtraction, she had no memory of how to do carry-over, and we had to start all over again.

She took one step forward and one step back, two steps forward and two steps back, three steps forward and three steps back. She progressed to more difficult levels, but the problem of keeping her there remained. Occasionally there were moments that made the whole tedious process seem remarkably worthwhile. For example, one morning down at the beach Bea was badgering the children about not doing more real swimming. They had recently gotten some snorkeling equipment and spent almost their entire time in the water floating face down or swimming listlessly underwater. Finally, Bea said, "That's all. Everybody has to do one hundred strokes of Australian crawl before any playing with equipment." The one hundred strokes had to be reduced for Seth and Ariel, but all the children did begin to swim again. By the next day Ariel, who never swam more than six strokes at a time, was able to cover about ten yards and even tried to turn around and swim back to where she had started. Here are Bea's notes on what happened:

> *"How many strokes did I swim to there?" Ariel asked me pointing in her first direction.*
> *"Thirty strokes one way. That's pretty good," I answered.*
> *"Thirty and thirty, that makes sixty strokes altogether," crowed Ariel without a moment's hesitation.*
> *I was just as impressed with her instant ability to add the two-place numbers as with the swimming.*
> *I heard no more of the matter when we came home, but two days later in helping Ariel clean out her papers, I came across the attached paper. Contrary to her usual ostentation in showing off anything she has done she seems to have written this to set a private goal for herself. Again this is more evidence of her beginning to think of and for herself. At the top of the page was a whole series of additions:*

$$
\begin{array}{cccc}
60 & 90 & 70 & 101 \\
\underline{60} & \underline{90} & \underline{70} & \underline{101} \\
120 & 180 & 140 & 202
\end{array}
$$

> *and under it she had written:*
> *"Swimming on stroke. 30 Strokes bothways to day 60 altogether. tomorral 60 strokes bothways is 120. The next day 70 strokes bothways is 140. 90 strokes after this day makes 180. After this day 100 strokes bothways wich makes 200. 101 the next day to town, both ways is 202."*
> *The biggest number Ariel could think of was one more than a hundred, and with this grand number she anticipated swimming all the way into town.*

Objects and physical things were never more demonstrably useful. Bea used real money in a game of going shopping that continued through the year and that was later exercised in the marketplace itself. Ariel would make a list of things she wanted to buy, estimate the cost of each, then add up the total and calculate the change she should get. There were side benefits in spelling, handwriting, and an awareness of relative costs. Bea used pebbles, leaves, tomatoes, the sounds of woodpeckers, pile drivers, foghorns, the varying tastes of coffee, food recipes to create arithmetic problems.

However, no matter what she was learning, Ariel remained quietly anxious about the fact that her younger brother was outstripping her. She wanted to do whatever Seth was doing. Because he was learning multiplication, Ariel insisted that Bea teach her the tables too. She would spend endless hours repeating those tables and at one point she could actually rattle off an answer automatically for any combination through the number eight. Yet at this high-water mark in her arithmetic prowess, she would still have to use her fingers before she could work out the sum of three plus six. The use of paper seemed to anchor her thoughts.

The fact that Ariel had two bright brothers proved both good and bad. Seth often helped her. One of the entries in his diary read:

> *While I was writing my diary Ariel cam in and ask* [sic] *me to check her multapication* [sic]. *To my surprise Ariel got everthing right except one. Then she left and I finished my diary.*

Adam erratically assumed a teacher's role too. He would drill Ariel pitilessly for an hour—my influence?—and then bring her to us in triumph with her hard-earned new ability. He was enraged the next day when she had forgotten everything, and it might be another week before he started again.

Nevertheless, Ariel seemed to be making significant progress in her tentative grasps at arithmetic, progress that carried her far beyond where she would have been in a school for slow learners. Her improvement was real. But the boys' more rapid strides meant that Ariel would fall further and further behind and lose all prospect of the equal status she so desperately sought.

She needed her own areas of excellence, areas not open to comparison with the boys' abilities, areas that would give her a sense of her own separate identity. And so we continued her arithmetic instruction, with limited success, but we also turned with more concentration to those activities through which Ariel could start to build a special set of interests in which she could enjoy a full measure of competence.

11.

HISTORY—DIGGING

INTO THE PRESENT

History, we are told, is significant because it offers us a way of understanding and coping with the present and of planning for the future. And no doubt this is true. At first glance, then, the problem in school-taught history would seem to be that the subject's connection with the present and future is so infrequently explained. However, I believe the fault is much more fundamental. Children must be involved in things that immediately concern them. Only from things at hand can lessons in history be drawn. What I am suggesting is a complete reversal of sequence. Not some facts and people, remote and abstract, linked randomly to the contemporary scene, but the immediate and concrete present illustrated pointedly with events and ideas of the past.

Some of the popular methods of making history tolerable are story telling about bold or wicked men, wars, and adventurous discoveries (one of the reasons, no doubt, that so much emphasis is placed on characters and exciting happenings in history texts and courses); the use of media (the latest tool for making exposure to the past palatable); the exploitation of the novelty element in past events (the exact reverse of history's function).

But if we want students to learn from the past, not merely be entertained by it, we must reorder the school's premises. We must start with those areas of knowledge that will immediately and clearly help young people in coping with or understanding what is happening around them. We must elicit questions important to the children and ask more of our own that are pertinent to them. Why do they have to go to school for twelve years? Why is there smog in the city? Why is a family moving to another state? Why is there no public transportation to town? Why are the schools closed each summer? Why can't they work? Why was a brother drafted? Why did a racial incident or a strike occur at their father's factory? These are the types of questions that concern the youngsters and for which a wealth of antecedents can be used to make the present understandable by reference to the past. Questions like these have no pat textbook answers, no preset direction. They're wide open and call forth a freedom of inquiry and a need for fresh, pertinent answers.

They were the sort of questions that Bea and I found ourselves answering time and time again on the trip. And our recourse to history was constant and demanding. Most often it was only our inability to carry the subject further that ended an inquiry. I remember one night Bea's being surrounded by the children as she read a book by de Tocqueville on the French Revolution. We had picked it up because we had been unable to answer a flood of questions on the Reign of Terror when we had seen a guillotine on display while passing through France. The children were teasing Bea about what she had learned so far, whereupon she launched into a discussion that ranged from pre-Revolution, Revolution, and Napoleonic eras to comparisons with the Russian Revolution, the American Revolution, and the Spanish Civil War. They were beaming with delight at their mommy's sudden ability to discourse so knowledgeably and were impressed by the ease with which information could be found in a book. Bea wasn't a teacher telling them from some hidden resource of knowledge, she was a learner just a few steps ahead of them. Discussions like these were often rooted in something important that the children were already involved in, and most discussions spilled over easily from one period or place in history to another.

After our visit to the Anne Frank house, where Seth, visibly affected, closely studied the photographs of Nazi concentration camps ("What are they doing?") and of a little girl being led to a gas chamber ("Where are they taking her?"), we had many talks about the Nazis, the ghettoes, and assimilation; about the origin of European anti-Semitism and the structure of medieval society with the Jew forced into the role of moneylender; about the Inquisition; about cultural continuity; about the scapegoats of different societies; about pogroms, lynchings, and genocide; about the motivations for war (economic, power, religious); about World War I and World War II and Vietnam. And just as a single incident led to Adam's reading *The Diary of Anne Frank* and his subsequent attempt to keep a diary himself, these follow-up discussions often opened new avenues of inquiry and activity in the months to come.

Israel's history was a case in point. One day I read that Israeli agents had stolen two gunboats promised to Israel but later held back by the French. For the next few days we intermittently kept lookout to see if we could discover the gunboats as they passed through the narrow section of the Mediterranean where we were living. During this period we discussed the French and their self-interest, the use of the Mediterranean by all the big powers, the Russian involvement with Arab nations, the American position (at the time ambivalent), the lack of international support when the Arabs threatened Israel, the three clashes with the Arabs, Arab and Jewish relations prior to Israel's declaration of nationhood, the biblical relations of Jews with indigenous people of the Middle East, the promise of the promised land, the Diaspora, and the promised land brought to reality.

The best of our trip abroad, I believe, was in these conversations. They not only provided a free atmosphere of inquiry and strengthened the separate identity of each child, but they supplied a rich background of ideas and an awareness of the past from which each child could start to reach out into private areas of interest.

History constantly underlay our discussions when abroad. An environment of new people, values, and conditions seemed intelligible only in terms of a knowledge of the past. "Why are the people so fearful of the carabineros?" asked Seth. "Why are farmers using horses?" asked Ariel. "Why are the resort towns so new and modern and the villages so impoverished and why is everyone Catholic?" asked Adam. The questions poured out. We answered some, we reasoned through others, and many we put off until we could get more information. And as a fabric of knowledge started covering this new environment for the children, they began searching out their own answers to their own questions. They reasoned, they guessed, they brought old knowledge to bear upon new observations, and they started using the past themselves to explain their curious present.

On our occasional marketing trips to Almuñécar, the nearest town to La Herradura, we often discussed the alien presence of West European tourists, expatriates, and retired people, the way they formed European enclaves and insulated themselves from their Spanish hosts, and the limited advantage they derived from being abroad. We discussed how tourist centers were all alike, the imposition of foreign tastes and habits that eventually overwhelmed the local scene, the glut of fellow tourists until only that familiar breed of hotel and service people was visible to falsely represent a culture. On one occasion, when we were shopping in the town's only supermarket—no bigger than a neighborhood delicatessen, but after weeks of real marketplace shopping strikingly foreign to us with its rows of cans and bright packages—Adam started talking about the homogenization of cultures, of fashions, and of tastes; and when we climbed into the car and started for home, Seth commented on the advantages of modern city versus our remote village living. Then Adam linked this to suburban versus rural living back home. I remarked on the corruption and variety in the city, on the peasants who tilled infertile lands and lived without running water and electricity, and the slow transition to a modern economy as the young drifted off to cities and the barren but scenic land was bought up by absentee vacationers, on garden-belt cities and the New Deal. Then Adam took off on the need for city planning and his own plans for new cities.

Our children were caught up in the excitement of history because their parents were excited about it—not because they were lucky enough to travel and see historical sights. Some of their dullest hours abroad were spent in the places of history that tourists flock to when they seek culture and education by going abroad. Listen to our children reporting on some of these visits:

ARIEL. *We went to Granada and sooer* [*saw*] *the casel* [*castle*] *and sooer a musime* [*museum*]. *Then we went home and went to bed.*

ADAM [*Part of a three-page letter to Grandma Matty minutely describing everything he saw, including . . .*] *the ugly cathedral . . . huge columns as big as redwoods supported the ceiling and on display were beautiful robes and silver cups ornamented with rubies and large diamonds.*

SETH [*After visiting the Hofburg, tells how disappointed he was with the guide and why we left the tour.*] *We didn't even understand him because he switched from language to language. We saw a dinning room with all different glasses and plates and silver ware. If you took the wrong glass you would get a slap.* [*Bea had dramatized table etiquette*]. *We went to see a crown of gold and a flower of gold. It wasn't so shiny and beautiful. The only reason they had it was because it was so rare.* [*He went on to describe in detail all the finery and how unimpressed he was with it.*]

The sightseeing was of minimal interest, and the guided tours mechanical and sterile, similar to some of the worst moments back home at school. But always interesting was a question evoked by something privately observed or a suddenly enthusiastic dialogue between Bea and me on a point of interest. And most important were the free-wheeling discussions that often became the central feature of our visits to historic places and that even more often cropped up in the most ordinary and unhistoric places. Children are concerned with social experiences, with spontaneous and alive people, with what is really happening at that very moment. They aren't easily taken in—and won't, like their elders, pretend to be—by the stalely repeated accounts of a tour guide.

ADAM

Back in Lakeland Junior High Adam had had his full share of guided tours through history. Like other youngsters he thought of history as dates and names and battles and dreary textbooks. Perhaps that was why he turned sullen when, during our first weeks of settling down, with little occasion for thinking or spending time together, Bea carelessly asked him to read a few chapters in a book on ancient civilizations that we had picked up. Reading a book on history was altogether different from dealing with an idea or a story in which history played a central role. Adam was not turned off by the subject of history, he was turned off by an organized but unrelated presentation of it. Where his particular interests were piqued, there was always ready response. Any hint of social injustice always won Adam's attention. For example, when Bea was preparing to celebrate Passover and inventively made her own matzos—they were not readily available in La Herradura—she asked each of the children to create something special for the occasion. Adam wrote an essay on slavery and the Jews under the Egyptian pharaohs in which he waxed philosophical about "reason" and how it can be misused —in this case to enslave men. He outlined how men may have started as equals but inevitably they "pick out differences among themselves and arrange differences" until there are rich and poor and "the rich felt they were special and should be honored. In this way exploitation starts and the end of exploitation time and again is slavery followed by revolt."

Even during his tepid reading of ancient civilizations, Adam was outraged by the equal tax on rich and poor in Rome—thus further impoverishing the poor—and wrote:

> *Did they like having the people poor. Maybe the nobles wanted the people to work as slaves. Maybe they like the idea of having the people come and beg for bread or have the people sell them their votes—which the people did. Maybe the nobles liked the idea of power and being richer than others.*

But the things that most concerned him were those directly at hand, and these he observed closely:

> *The Spanish are hard laborers. Their work is most all manual labor. . . . Day in and day out they sweat over their tedious work, plucking the fruits and vegetables from the field, building a house, collecting mussels, pulling in a net . . . and all their time and labor gives them is barely enough to survive. As the people work in the sun their eyes squint, they grin in reply to their friends jokes, they wrinkle their faces in the glare of the sun . . . [and before long] they look 20 years older than they are.*

In a letter to his grandfather Adam described the exquisite view from our house and then added:

> *There's another view though, a different kind. To the right a farmer works. He doesn't farm on a regular flat American style surface. He*

farms on a terraced hill, for this is a mountainous and rocky land. It's hard labor: the farmer has to use a hand plow with a horse and throw the seed himself. . . . Life is different here. Instead of going to a nearby grocery, the people go to the market place. There everything is sold—fresh meat, fish, vegetables, etc. People here don't have as many coverniences as we do back home. Taking the farmer's family across the way for instance. Every day the mother and daughter go down and collect the water for drinking in clay jars. Many times I see her washing clothes at the stream. Every night a fire is built to warm and light the place. And to cook. And instead of a machine to plow the farmer plows with a horse. Many times I see a mule passing loaded with whatever goods that have to be transported from one place to another. That's Spain for you.

SETH

Seth was quite different. Like so many other fields, history for Seth was fascinating even in the abstract. He could read a biography of Columbus and find himself in Queen Isabella's court pleading along with Columbus for a chance to reach India and the Spice islands. A book on Lincoln transformed his little room into a log cabin, where he continued his reading late at night studying for the law. When Bea handed him a book on Greek myths, he was enchanted with the all-powerful and playful gods. He startled us with his sudden applications of dry unassimilated information to the most exciting immediate experiences.

Discovering a cave one afternoon, Bea and the children decided they would recreate the art of the indians. Seth wrote to his Grandma Matty how "mommy and the three of us" found a piece of driftwood and chiseled out and painted a totem pole and then "using our own paint" how he had painted on the wall a minotaur "which is half man and half bull and comes from the story of Theseus, and that story comes from The Myths and Legends."

On the other hand, he too resisted formal exercises of his competence. When Bea tried to get him to compare ancient and present times in an essay, his mind virtually froze. He stuck to a few facts on each side and seemed unable to comprehend what comparative evaluations or judgments were all about. Bea was noticeably disappointed, and Seth in turn felt humiliated by his failure to please her. When she questioned him, however, she found him quite discerning and articulate for a seven-year-old. She asked him to tell her what he thought about Rome and how it was different from the way we lived in the United States, and she wrote down what he said. His words at first were hesitant and disjointed because the situation was so theatrical. But Bea was in no hurry and after a while Seth started talking freely. She put it all down and after a while he watched her and seemed to savor each word. When Bea read what he said back to the family at night, we were all quite impressed; and Seth was, too. His confidence in his judgment and his delight with history were restored by simply bypassing a school-made obstacle—the written assignment.

Driving near Nerja one day we passed the neglected ruins of what Bea thought was a Roman aqueduct. Seth asked Bea what the Romans were doing in Spain, "Don't they live in Italy?" It was a good question and Bea took off on it: What the Romans stood for, the growth of Roman power, far-ranging colonization, evidence of modern-day imperialism; the spread of Roman technical culture, dispersal of cultures through war and trade, Coca Cola in Europe; the portable Roman culture—government, baths, emphasis on good transportation, entertainment, gladiators and Christians; our bloodthirsty sports—boxing and football; the role of conqueror—taxation without representation; the cost of wars, Roman warfare methods, Leonardo da Vinci, medieval warfare, medieval architecture; the plight of the Christians as a growing minority, the Crusades; overextension of interests, Roman Empire, Ottoman Empire, downfall of Roman Empire.

The discussion lasted a full hour and occupied almost our entire trip to Granada. On our return home that same night, Seth searched out the book Adam had grown sullen over, on Roman civilization, and began methodically reading it through, chapter by chapter.

ARIEL

For Ariel, who had trouble enough understanding her immediate environment, envisioning other times and places was almost impossible. If we presented her with facts or people from other times, they elicited such comments as, "That's funny" or, "Is he dead?"

Our emphasis with Ariel, therefore, rarely left the here and now. The most notable attempt I can recall in any area bordering on the social sciences was Bea's attempts to have the child understand the different functions performed by people in a community—part of a larger effort to fill in some of Ariel's glaring gaps in areas of everyday knowledge. Ariel learned about the job of a policeman ("He stops cars"), the restaurant owner ("He serves dinner"), the garbage man, the farmer, the teacher. But any attempt to show differences between Spain and the United States were met with incomprehension. As Rudy Vallee used to sing, "There's no time like our time, and no place like home."

12

GEOGRAPHY—A MAGIC

CARPET OF ROAD MAPS

SETH'S DIARY, JUNE *30. After I finished [writing a short story] I spread all the maps out. I looked at the main map of Europe and found the seperatens between countrys. That was a real chalenge to me. When I had got all the maps out . . . I took a pencil and an araser and told Ariel how to tell the shortes routes to citys.*

When we were driving down toward Spain from Amsterdam, I would usually have some idea of the roads we would be taking, and then as we drove Bea would refer to the road maps and check out specific details. One day, when she was busy preparing sand-wiches on her lap in the car, I asked Adam to find a town on the map. He tried but was unable to, and I had to stop the car and look myself. Of course, he had a big cry. That evening I had an obligatory task of discussing map reading with him, while Seth and Ariel leaned over our shoulders. We covered national boundaries, terrain, railroad lines, major and secondary roads, air and land distances, and time estimates. Then the conversation spread to the interrelation of roads, communications, and the economy; topographical differences and natural borders between countries; differences in language and the relation of natural barriers to the development of distinctive cultures; the migrations of peoples, the origin of American Indians; *Kon Tiki* and ocean currents.

As in so many of our discussions, the children found themselves plunged deep into a subject with only minimal concessions made to their ages. Since there were no tests or classroom protocol to keep them listening, it was soon apparent if they were bored. In this instance, there was an unmistakable result, for Adam quickly arrogated to himself the role of official map reader, and Ariel and Seth before long were pouring over the maps with him, evidently intent on not being left out of a new family activity.*

We had a basic collection of European maps from the AAA, which we used in combination with a few world maps contained in a book on the sea. In addition, Adam had his own map, an excellent topographical rendering of Europe, which he had found on a restaurant table (evidently forgotten by a traveler) and promptly appropriated as his own; and Seth had his, a stained and torn affair that he had meticulously Scotch taped and salvaged.

At first they used their maps simply to follow our journey, eliciting frequent comments from Bea and me on the provinces and countries we passed through. When we settled on the Costa del Sol, occasionally we would all study the maps together, focusing our attention not only on things we could see but on the entire Mediterranean area. Gradually these conversations too moved afield, to land and sea routes throughout the world, to underwater mountain ranges and continental shelves. Soon references to geography began cropping up in many of our conversations, whether the subject was politics, food, housing, or the arts. Often the discussion would be interrupted while one of the children ran to get a map. Then spreading it out on the floor with all of us gathered around, Adam or Seth would proceed to theorize about, illustrate, or prove some point.

I recall a two-hour discussion immediately after a trip to

*By the end of our trip Seth had become, through persistence and ability, the official map reader.

Tangiers on the northernmost tip of Africa, opposite Gibraltar. The Ceuta tourist-guide map, the AAA map of Spain, and Adam's and Seth's maps of Europe were all spread out on the bed, and the five of us, our heads bobbing from one map to the other, noted the protected bays and boat basins, wondered at the importance of Gibraltar and discussed who had better claim to it, Spain or England. We remarked on the change in the color of the water from the Atlantic to the Mediterranean and the changes in water temperature at different points along the coast of Spain and other countries on the Mediterranean; and related these to temperatures inland. We noted the path of the Moorish invasions, discussed why Morocco had sandy beaches, why to get to Tangiers from Ceuta, which is due west of it on the African coast, we had first to go directly south for twenty-five kilometers. Then we traced and explained the thin network of roads in the country and the positioning of cities in Morocco and Spain.*

For Adam, Ariel, and Seth geography was no longer a textbook assignment of dull print and pastel-colored maps. It was rising far above the surrounding hills and mountains and suddenly gaining a giant's view of the land around them. The maps had become magical extensions of their perceptions and imaginations making vast spaces and areas of knowledge marvelously accessible.

*In other discussions we touched on why flights across the Arctic were shorter than flights further south, why and where early roads were built. We talked of air currents, mountain ranges, climate changes, seasons, rivers (old and new), the building of towns on rivers, pollution, erosion, hydroelectric power (I told a story of visiting Niagara Falls and discovering that the falls were turned off for a few hours at two o'clock on winter mornings because there were few tourists around to see that all the water was being diverted to the turbines), the Suez Canal (ships stuck in the canal, problems with Israel, Moors of Spain, great cultures of past), free trade zones, English sea power, the Gulf and Arctic streams and climate.

13

ART AND MUSIC—AND

A MOTHER'S DAY CARD

Evenings, after dinner, we would often sit on the terrace, lazily watching the cloud formations, the changing colors of the surrounding mountains, the big sun setting. The occasional storm was an event, and the five of us, sweaters and raincoats donned, would huddle together outside and marvel at the powerful bolts of lightning out at sea and the thunderous crashes that followed. We took quiet, conscious pleasure each day in the natural rhythms and beauty around us. The solitary flight of a bird, the intricately patterned ripples on the sea, the sinuous weaving of schools of fish, the distant song of a peasant woman wafting across the still valley. There was art in the ordinary sights and sounds around us—and we had bought the time to examine, to touch, and to admire little things, close at hand, things never really seen through car windows or double-paned home windows or school windows. In La Herradura there were no windows between us and the immediate reality.

We climbed along the rocky shore and peered into silent tide pools at an alien plant and animal environment; we walked along the narrow beach to the rhythmic accompaniment of pebbles tumbling in and whooshing out with each wave; we stepped carefully through mountaintop fields and kneeled to examine an exquisitely delicate weed, a mottled bug, a brilliant cactus blossom; we held our breaths to hear a cicada calling or the tinkling of a goat on a distant hill. Up close like this we sensed a richer texture in our environment, a texture of which color, design, rhythm, and sound were integral parts. Even in the marketplace the children grinned with delight at the cacophony of vendors' calls, at the rhythmic singing and hawking ("*naranjas, pescado fresco;* señora, señora, *huevos, huevos dos para una peseta, huevos, huevos,* señora"), at the bountiful display of the season's vegetables and fruits, at subtly shaded spices, at meats and nuts and luxuriant flowers.

Music too was everywhere—a solitary farm girl in the hills singing to herself, a funeral procession with the muffled sounds of trumpet and bass drum, a flamenco beat heard from a campfire on a distant hill, the jeering, raucous music of a family circus come to town, the ritual and ceremony of the bullfight, the holiday pomp of a religious festival, the fishermen silently hauling in their nets at dawn with the water lapping on the shore.

This was not the music of the classroom, with rhythm bands, music appreciation classes, and after-school band and orchestra rehearsals. Nor was it the busywork classes in art for students who couldn't manage a full academic program. This was the everyday music and art of the street, of the field, of the marketplace. Here the aesthetic dimension of life was not boxed into museums or classrooms, but existed easily in the rhythms of nature and the traditional customs of the town. It needed only ear and eye to discover. Others might see this small section of Spain in terms of the number and quality of hotels and restaurants or the man-hour productivity trends in key occupations. Our children too had an almost adult awareness of social inequities and economic and political abuses suffered in this backward community. But they also had an unsentimentalized respect for the quiet poetry of the land, of man and his work, feelings somehow accorded little attention in their lives back home. Their unaffected delight in the small treasures of art and music found in this austere environment played a large part in making them aware of the possibilities for music and art in their own lives. Before long we too were commemorating, we too entertaining, we too celebrating nature's wonders with art and poetry and music.

For example, Bea and the children admired some intricately

structured sea plants and decided to dry them out and preserve them. These natural designs suggested what was to become a favorite family activity—making collages out of natural materials like rocks and shells and weeds. The beach sand itself became our most versatile art medium, offering inspiration not just for sand castles but for face and body sculpture, abstract design, comic-strip drawings, and experiments in perspective. It was even a handy medium for Adam to try out his complex new city ideas.

Just as the beach was used, so too were the open fields. Each day Bea and Ariel—and sometimes Adam, Seth, and I—would wander through the fields picking exotic weeds, wild flowers, and green ferns for our dinner table centerpiece. The pains taken to arrange floral settings for an ordinary family dinner would have shocked a metropolitan hostess, jealous of her time. But in La Herradura each meal was a conscious effort in color and design, an almost obligatory attempt to match the exquisite natural setting that surrounded us.

When it was carnival time in town, the children noticed some of the local youngsters wearing masks and decided that they too would have them. So they set about designing their own and in the process discovered anew how to make and form papier-mâché.

Sometimes the children would surprise us with an improvisation. One rainy day when the children had been unusually occupied for about two hours, Adam suddenly shouted to us to come to their bedroom. Inside we heard muffled shrieks and grunts. When we entered, the room was darkened except for two spotlights made from tilted lamps focused on a live tableau of costumed children, objects, and mirrors. Adam had arranged a happening, and Seth and Ariel remained rigid as statues while Adam read, robotlike, through a pipe sticking out from between the beds: "Ladies and gents! Standing before you is the most modern, creative, and imaginative live sculpture in the world's time. Just gaze at it and gaze at it and you will agree that it is superb. Thank you for your attention. This is a recording, This is a . . . Beep! . . . Beep!"

Every few weeks the children would organize a family entertainment night in which they would sing, recite their own poetry, dance, or do acrobatics. Or on an afternoon you might find Bea seated with the big folk song book open on her lap and the three children crowded around her, arms locked together, singing one folk song after another.

Perhaps the most exciting art pieces came from the innumerable cards the children produced: for birthdays, Father's Day, anniversaries, religious holidays. For each, the children set out to make a distinctive card, creating unusual forms and employing a wide range of materials from charcoal, pencil, pen, crayon, watercolor, cardboard, and notebook paper to bark and homemade oil paints.

The most inventive was a Mother's Day card. On that morning the children woke up at four-thirty and got me out of bed to help. We gathered wild flowers of four varieties that grew in profusion throughout the area. The previous day we had talked of doing something different for mommy and mentioned a surprise trip, breakfast in bed, a special card. And when Seth remarked, "Mommy likes weeds and wild flowers," Adam had the idea.

We collected them in bunches, literally by the hundreds. Adam, who had sketched out a design on a piece of loosely woven straw matting about four by six feet, inserted the flowers between the straw strands until whole sections were totally covered by a single burst of color. Then we all helped fill in the six-inch border with daisies and the handsome script design of the words *Mother's Day* with orange lilies and bluebells. Finally we pushed through the stems of hundreds of purple wild flowers until the last visible patch of straw had been covered to form a brilliant background of purple.

By this time Bea had awakened and Ariel had been sent inside to keep her from coming out on the terrace where we were working. When we were done we all stood back, and Bea, smiling broadly with anticipation, was ushered out by Ariel. But when she saw the flash of color from the thousand or more flowers she blanched and simply dropped to her knees beside the mat and just stared, overwhelmed.

For the next three days we watered the mat. But the odor finally became too pungent and disagreeable, and on the fourth day all five of us on our hands and knees solemnly surrounded the mat and picked out the dying flowers. It wasn't a chore, it was a ceremonial dismemberment of a family work of art.

There were other more formal attempts to involve the children in art. Bea occasionally took them up into the surrounding hills, each with a notebook and crayon, pen, or watercolor set in hand, for an afternoon of sketching. Once she suggested that they start from scratch and make their own paints and brushes and use rocks and trees for their painting surfaces. She wanted to use primitive conditions to recreate the excitement of discovering means and uses for art. She had the children find different colored sandstone, which they pounded and pulverized into a powder for paint; at Adam's suggestion they squeezed the juices of flowers to obtain a variety of hues and derived a yellow oil from onions; brushes were made from fine, dry weed stems and bound to twigs with fresh weeds; bark was stripped from trees and both the inner surface of the bark and the naked wood were painted. Finally, Bea enthralled the children with tales of cavemen and prehistoric animals and they ended up drawing bison and painting sequential pictures of primitive man's activities.

Each child's particular artistic interests were used to support other interests. Ariel, in order to promote concentration on detail, was encouraged to draw and to be as exact as possible in representing what she saw. Her drawings of faces, landscapes, and objects in the house played, we believed, a significant part in improving her ability to perceive rather than just blandly witness. Her proudest achievement was, as with most children, a perspective rendering of a house, and it has become a recurrent feature of her art.

Like most children, Adam and Seth loved to draw. Seth's notebooks were covered with drawings. Whether he was dealing with math or history or science, drawing seemed to be a natural extension of what he saw and tried to say. Adam's drawings were much more controlled and often he used watercolor to fill in his careful pen sketches.

Music was another matter. I recall waiting for our order to be prepared at a restaurant and walking out to a large unused patio affording a sweeping view of the Mediterranean. A guitar was being played in the restaurant, and Seth, who has a sense of staging and drama—and is also something of an exhibitionist—started to dance, turning and leaping, all very athletic and not at all graceful. "My heart wants to dance," he said, "but my body doesn't know how."

Besides such impromptu happenings and our family singing on car trips, there was really no strong attempt to make music an important part of our days abroad. We did buy a portable radio so that we could hear more flamenco music, but we soon discovered that the surrounding mountains blocked off all stations but those in Morocco. Our exposure to Arabic music could have had some educational value, but I admit we failed to find any pleasure or special features in the sounds. Music, like books, became an area of deprivation. Perhaps because of it, once we returned home Adam started lessons on a clarinet, Seth on a violin, and Ariel on a flute, all without any pressure from us.

If you have gone abroad specifically to educate your children, it's hard to discuss art without mentioning museums. After all, millions of tourists each year make the long and expensive journey overseas and spend large chunks of their time visiting museums, palaces, churches, and stately homes for an in-person, close look at art treasures. Here we were abroad for a year within easy reach of these great treasures. Surely the children gained from it? I'm tempted to say no, emphatically, because I have little use for those who rarely visit their own museums, but who, when abroad, allow themselves to be shunted from one art treasure trove to another and rarely have time to watch a Punch and Judy show in Luxembourg Gardens or buy a fresh tomato in the marketplace. Bea and I are dilettantes and we did take the children with us when we sniffed out a museum in a small French town or journeyed to the Hofburg when passing through Vienna for the first and perhaps last time in our lives. Our legitimate interest in art rather than the obligatory obeisance to it obviously rubbed off on our children.

I remember spending a full half hour with the children studying and discussing two Brueguel paintings, one titled *Games* and the other depicting a wild town debauch. Seth in particular seemed fascinated by art. Here are a few excerpts from his diary:

GRENOBLE, FRANCE, MUSEUM, JULY 7. *All of us inkleuding mommy and daddy went to the Museum of Arts. . . . What I liked best of all was the modern art. I just couldn't get over it. They seemed to change color and move. Som pictures said to your mind its horrible. I can't get over it.*

MUSEUM IN VIENNA(?), A BOSCH PAINTING, JULY 18. *We saw a triplit [triptych]. We saw a picture of Adam and Eve in the Garden of Eden. We allso saw a horror picture of people in hell. A women with blood poring out of her belly. A fish with a nife coming out of his mouth and ready to kill a person. A devel squashing a man like butter, letting all the blood to come out for her to eat. A devel with a nife in somebody and only a little snip of the nife in the man. A devel cooking a man for dinner. A person with only a head and legs.*

Devels burning houses. All this time the lord sat watching this spred-
ding out his arms in kind of a sense saying, what could I do. This
is all man's falt. If he does something very wrong in his life. Well
when he dies he meight as well go to hell. We looked around a little
more and left.

THE HOFBURG, JULY *19. We saw garments of very fine gold. On it*
were all different Saints. It was so detailed. We couldn't find anything
wrong. It showed every single hair. Even the slightest rinkle they
showed.

The extent of his interest may be suggested by what happened on our first holiday in New York City after our return to
the States. We gave the children a choice between going to
F.A.O. Schwarz, one of the most fabulous toy stores in the world,
and going to the Museum of Modern Art. Adam and Ariel chose
the toy store. Seth picked the museum.

IV.

IMPROVING

A NEW CURRICULUM

If I were asked to spell out our goals in La Herradura, I'd probably produce the same platitudes that formal educators so easily dish out at parent conferences and in report card comments. We too wanted our children to become curious, alert, many-faceted people. We wanted them to be capable of independent effort and sustained concentration, to be self-reliant and self-motivated, to have individual interests and personal goals, to respond and express themselves well and freshly, to be creative, imaginative, healthy, and happy.

But beneath the familiar phrases, our paths veered off sharply. Bea and I were not married to system or method; we had no buildings to fill, no standard tests to administer, no teachers to keep busy, no buses, no clocks. We had only these same goals plus a total freedom to pursue them in our own way.

THE FAMILY AND THE IMMEDIATE ENVIRONMENT AS LEARNING BASES

However, before we could start improvising a new curriculum, we had to break down the classroom walls around the children and expose them to the real world of community, people, jobs, and institutions. From these immediate surroundings they could enjoy a broad range of experience that would be pertinent and readily available to them in developing their own interests. You will feel throughout this account the presence of this real world of the marketplace and the home; of the beach, the barren field, and the open sky; of houses and things at hand; of routine household chores. You'll also feel the presence of the family itself, a sleeping educational giant that we wanted to awaken to a critical role in the reeducation of our children. We wanted the family to be used not only as a miniature community in which to work, play, learn, and live twenty-four hours each day, but as a center for thought-provoking discussions, for impromptu adventures, for household roles, for learning events, and for planned entertainments.

UNDISCIPLINED LEARNING

Using the family and the immediate environment as springboards, the children were encouraged to pursue an idea or an interest wherever it led. We wanted no course or subject boundaries to interfere with their pursuit. Because there were many vantage points available in understanding most events, we felt that the mixing of disciplines should be a learning constant rather than an inventive possibility. If there were no teachers or textbooks to interpose parameters, a student's interest might readily involve him in facts, thoughts, and fantasies; in law, ethics, and private morality; in intellect and feeling; in social, family, and individual values. It was an undisciplined world we wanted our children to be exposed to; a world in which subjects, ideas, and feelings intermixed; a world varied, multicolored, and formless waiting for each individual to impose his own order on it.

Once you give up the idea that learning is properly channeled through five or six disciplines, a good number of subjects worth exploring pop up: sex, city versus suburban society, agriculture, consumer purchasing, comparative religion, family living, the stock market, food preparation. Almost any subject can serve as an educational vehicle. For example, take the unlikely subject of goats. In La Herradura our children saw the breeding and husbandry of goats; they saw goats copulating, carrying young, nursing young, being herded, climbing rocks, being milked; they tasted the warm milk fresh from a goat's udder; they tasted the yogurt made from the milk; they saw the goats slaughtered, limp, skinned carcasses hanging from hooks, and then butchered into usable cuts. They witnessed the whole life cycle of the goat, and woven into their sights and tastes and sounds were our family discussions of local geography, economy, history, and technology.

Phrases such as "nimble as a goat" became vividly intelligible;* biblical and romantic references to goatherds and shepherds became meaningful; the anatomy of the animal and its milk products became part of a larger reality, not just labeled illustrations in a zoology textbook or a food package in a supermarket freezer cabinet.

INDIVIDUAL INTERESTS

The children were free to incorporate new interests, mix subject matters, move up to adult resources or down to little brother or sister levels. We had no preconceived idea about the curriculum or interests each should end up with. But we were convinced that the wider their exposure the more likely they would be to find interests closer to their needs.

Often the children didn't know just how to go about developing a skill or learning more about a subject, and then they would seek our advice and welcome our suggestions: "What book should I read next?" "Teach me how to do division." "How can we build our own aquarium?" To further their own purposes they came to appreciate the need for order, for concentration, for the learning of skills.

They discovered that to learn independently they needed not just free time and a precept like, "Be creative!" but real involvement in a subject, appropriate resources, and adults who could encourage and help without controlling.

*We even saw a lone sheep with a herd of goats climbing jagged rock abutments trying desperately to be one of them—"like a sheep."

There were times when we actually did take charge, when we sought to push along specific skills with schedules and assigned work. But we found the children developed the same distaste for our system as for the formal system of education. So each child's curriculum as it developed remained pretty much his own. Work was done in the regular disciplines—science, history, writing, art. But after the first few months such work was almost always used to extend a child's existing interests or to cope with problems like Ariel's that couldn't be met any other way. There were no longer any course requirements to worry about.

The real curriculum was improvised, developing, with some prodding and encouragement from us, around each child's separate tastes and needs. Adam's education was centered in his work in photography, city planning, and adventure story writing. Ariel's curriculum concentrated on dancing, housekeeping, and corresponding. Seth, who had a voracious appetite for reading, arithmetic, and science, developed a parallel set of interests in map reading, diary keeping, and anything else he was exposed to.

Let us now turn to this improvised curriculum.

14.

FAMILY ACTIVITIES

If you were to look freshly at what education is all about, to challenge society's fundamental acceptance of professional teachers and fixed curricula, it would be hard to deny that major educational possibilities exist outside the classroom. The family in particular looms large, and the educated American family—there are twenty million American families in which one or both parents have a college education—emerges as a strangely untapped resource.

Perhaps there was a time when wealthy parents with education jealously pursued their own interests and chose to send their children to private schools or bring in tutors to educate them; when the great mass of poor, uneducated people were grateful for universal public education as a way to improve their children's prospects in life. But these times have long since passed for many families in the 1970s. I have no desire to condescend or to deny the serious need for adequate educational opportunity for tens of millions of impoverished and deprived families in the

United States. The needs of these people are more urgent than ever and must be met with greater effort and imagination by outside agencies. But at the same time, I want to emphasize this book's special focus on the needs of an American middle class of educated parents. Such parents are uniquely qualified to participate in the education of their own children. They enjoy the leisure and economic resources, the educational background and experience; they have the concern to undertake such tutelege, and to undertake it thoroughly and imaginatively. Perhaps more important, they desperately need this function if they hope to find a way out of the dilemma of stagnant family life and dulled and alienated children. That was our concern. We wanted to revitalize our family as the source of individual values and as a center for learning. We wanted to improvise a curriculum in which family activities played a significant part and in which each individual could discover and fully explore his own separate interests.

LIVING TOGETHER

The children saw Bea and me enthusiastically involved in work, and it made them see in their own work the possibilities for pleasure and absorption. But no matter how absorbed we were, they sensed our willingness to share our time with them. Much of what we did we did in twos and threes or as a family. Bible reading, marketing, swimming, fireside story telling, browsing through town, hiking and exploring the surrounding area, studying sea life, astronomy lessons under the vast Spanish night skies, discussions of Spanish politics, culture, and economy—these formed a broad base of common interest.

There was no pigeonholing of information into disciplines; no limiting function for people such as teacher, friend, or head of family; no clear distinction among learning, working, and playing; no artificial assignment of proper places for specific activities, such as home for eating and sleeping, school for learning, beach and park for playing. Any place could be used at any time for any activity. There was a looseness about our emphasis and attitude that made limitations in subject, place, or time meaningless. Education was constantly being defined each day and hour for each child. And in this way learning could be total and nonexclusive. We found that the more open the world was to the children, the more openly and enthusiastically they responded to it.

We made no categorical distinction between learners and teachers. Everyone had the capacity to teach, the need to learn. The children knew we believed this, though we were certainly offering them more knowledge and insight in our living together than they were offering us. But they also knew that we enjoyed them, weren't afraid of them, wanted to interact with them. We made no secret of the fact that we were affected by their thoughts, that we were legitimately learning from them—not necessarily geometry or spelling, but how they viewed the world, what they liked, how they reasoned. We were usually concerned and curious. And when we were not—and there were lapses—the children quickly perceived that the give-and-take quality of the relationship had disappeared, and we became in their eyes teachers just talking at them.

I know that at those moments when I was most effective in getting across a concept or introducing a new idea to the children, I was myself alive with a fresh insight or visibly delighted with my own ability to recall and use a stray piece of information. And when the children produced their insights and made use of their experiences, they were no less alive in presenting them to us or each other. Adam taught Seth, Adam and Seth taught Ariel, and all the children took particular pleasure in teaching us. And we listened—not as teachers checking out an assignment but as parents, one to one, and vitally concerned with their progress. If Seth observed a periwinkle, he would write about it, tell us, show us. If Adam planned a house, he would explain why and how he had done what. If Ariel saw an incident on the beach while fetching bread from town, she would proudly describe it as her own experience that she could share with us. We were there twenty-four hours a day to listen to the children and to try to handle their questions.

A schoolteacher knows little of a child's life or thoughts outside the classroom and limits his discussions and references to a specific discipline or a specific order within that discipline. Only if he's bold does he venture an occasional sally into current events. But we were there with our natural interest, legal responsibility, and unaffected love, and without the economic restraints that make teaching in a schoolroom on a one-to-one basis unaffordable. As parents we could easily afford the price.

There was little whining or dissatisfaction with tasks or jobs while we were in La Herradura. Perhaps this was because the children could pretty much choose their own activities each day and then switch readily from one subject to another if they lost interest or encountered discouraging problems or couldn't get help. As for household chores, so many of them were made fun and challenging that even Bea and I had difficulty distinguishing among learning, housekeeping, and having fun.

Still another advantage of living together—which some might consider a sign of vanity or a burden rather than a parental responsibility—was the opportunity to act as models for our children. If we could win their respect by being forthright and honest with them, by trying to be helpful, by never recommending values to them that we didn't hold ourselves, there was every reason to expect them to do as we did. And to a large extent it worked: we read, we talked and talked, we laughed, we enjoyed each other, we took pride in our individuality and in our separate interests. And the children read, talked and laughed, enjoyed each other, and took pride in their individuality and separate interests. It was a do-as-I-do relationship rather than a teacher's do-as-I-say one. As a result the child can become a better pupil, the parent a better person. Bea and I did a lot of growing while we were away.

Finally living together provided a texture in our lives. Though each day contained an important ingredient of chance and adventure, it also moved in a rhythm of activities. Often we would separate from a family activity and each move to a separate interest; then come late morning, after each of us had had a full share of privacy, there would be little resistance to a rousing shout, "It's beach time, beach time . . . bathing suits on!" There was a rhythm and order, a sense of belonging in our family lives, which provided a common home base for our separate lives.

LEARNING EVENTS

Some of the most exciting things we did while abroad could be looked at from a pedagogue's point of view as "learning events." For us, they were simply part of our family activities, diversions, and sudden inspirations that involved creating or organizing or working on something together as a family. The fact

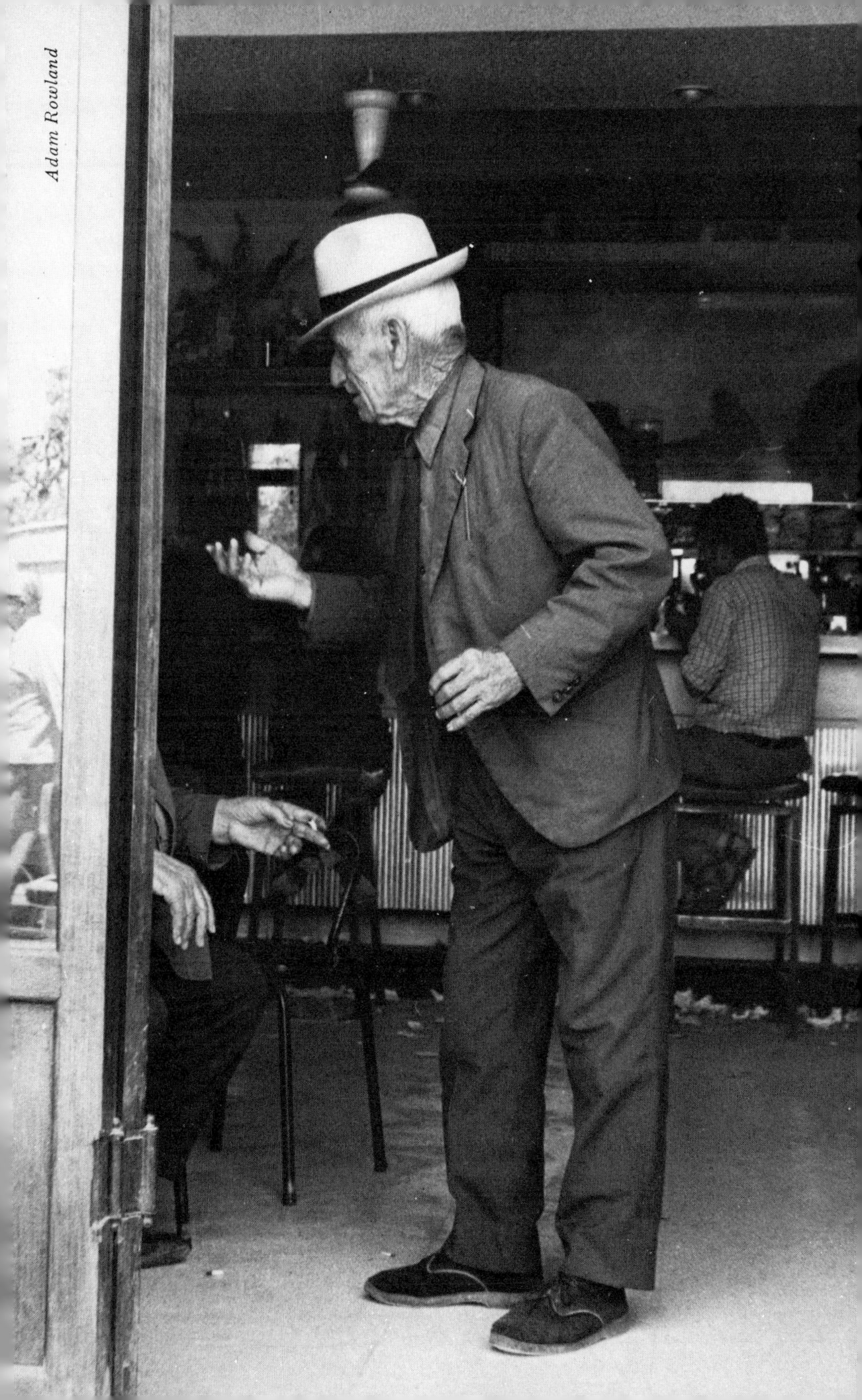

Adam Rowland

Adam Rowland

Bea Rowland

Adam Rowland

Howard S. Rowland

Howard S. Rowland

Howard S. Rowland

Howard S. Rowland

Howard S. Rowland

Adam Rowland

Adam Rowland

Adam Rowland

Howard S. Rowland

Adam Rowland

Adam Rowland

that Bea and I were not supervisors but eager participants made these experiences exciting to the children. My dissection of a chicken (see Chapter 9) with the entire family crowded around an improvised operating table led to a succession of independent experiments by the children and a surging interest in comparative biology. So too with Bea's inspiration to recreate caveman art by which she involved the children in making paints and brushes and had them simulate caveman mentalities (see Chapter 13). Or the night when the entire family lay in the fields in a star formation of our own studying the heavens, using a flashlight to match drawings in the book with the constellations above and speculating about other times and other peoples stargazing all through history (see Chapter 15). Or when traveling across Europe by car —with Bea and then Adam and then Seth and then even Ariel becoming involved in map reading (see Chapter 12)—spending an entire evening with maps spread out on the floor discussing contours, commerce, national boundaries, river basins, climates, and everything imaginable—five people, heads inches apart, studying a two-dimensional representation of a world they were experiencing first hand.

Sometimes the simplest physical need could also turn into a learning event: capturing rain for our drinking water, repairing a washed-out section of road, creating a wind baffle, using a Coca-Cola bottle as a casting reel for surf fishing. When we first moved to La Herradura there was no path down the steep incline to the beach, and together the five of us set about carrying stones, setting them, and securing them in a stepped progression down the hillside. The project took weeks of labor, and all of us were equally involved in digging, hauling, finding materials. But during this period we also learned about terracing and drainage, we examined other paths made of cement and stone slabs, and when we saw a concrete building project in progress, we studied each phase of the work so that we too might build and set stones in concrete if the occasion arose.

Sometimes the event took on a ritualistic quality, such as the weekly night of Bible reading. These were not cane-in-hand, you-better-listen-if-you-know-what's-good-for-you Bible readings, but story-telling nights, when, with candles burning (the children insisted on atmospherics) and the children all huddled about her, Bea would dramatically read about Isaac or Jacob or Joseph or Solomon or the Queen of Sheba, and the children would be transported back four thousand years. Before or after the readings there was often some mention of Bea's father, Grandpa Meyer, who lived in New York City and who in his talks with the children often made scholarly references to biblical times.

ENTERTAINMENTS

Many of the learning events originated with Bea or me, but the sudden outbursts of creative entertainment were most often the inspiration of the children alone. It is hard to conceive of an activity that children like more yet are so systematically denied in the schools. It's puzzling because through entertainments children can be introduced to a wide range of arts and skills and can quickly discover what creativity is all about. The here's-how-you-do-it cut-outs, the sun-over-the-house art classes, and the all-together-now sing-alongs in music are hardly opportunities for creative expression. But in La Herradura, entertainment burst out at the flimsiest excuse. There were rainy-day spectaculars, return-home celebrations, achievement nights, national holiday pageants, or simply art happenings. We would never know when Ariel or Seth or Adam would invite us to witness the latest spectacular. On an overcast day the children might busy themselves for hours devising costumes, setting lights, memorizing lyrics, choreographing and rehearsing a miniature variety show.

When Bea and I returned from a weekend in Tangiers—our young village maid and her mother baby-sat—the children greeted us, scrubbed and grinning, with streamers and a big bold "Welcome Home" sign on the outside wall. Inside we found an immaculately clean and tidy house, a lavishly set dinnertable, and a complete eight-course meal that they alone had prepared and kept steaming hot in the kitchen.

They also organized impromptu entertainments to celebrate a particular feat—Ariel's learning to swim underwater, my finishing the final proofs on a book, Seth's not picking his nose for one week straight. And there were more formal entertainments. We would read parts in a play together or hold an evening concert of dancing in which Ariel and Bea would perform while Adam snickered and Seth with grotesque movements of his own mocked them and in turn was mocked. And, of course, birthdays and anniversaries were most special occasions, celebrated with an inventiveness that makes me marvel now that we've returned to the suburbs and the packaged Hallmark event. Whole days were often occupied in preparation. Elaborate cards were made by each child, cornucopian meals planned with special emphasis on the favorites of the celebrant, presents created, rooms decorated, entertainment planned. For Bea's birthday, in addition to all the above, the children emerged from a darkened kitchen singing "Happy Birthday" and bearing a huge chocolate cake that they baked themselves and decorated with their own hand-crafted candles.

The emphasis in these celebrations and in the giving of gifts was always on doing something for the other person. Rarely was a present bought. The excitement came in creating with your own hands or with your own thoughts and imagination something that would please the other person. And whereas a wallet, a tie, or a new pocketbook could be valued in cost, these ingenious cards and special meals and commissioned entertainments totally lacked the commercial and venal quality of most birthday giving and taking.

If a gift was offered it was usually a promise of time or service to the other person—"I'll make your bed for one month." "I'll do the dishes." "I'll sharpen your pencils and set your clock each morning." And on those rare occasions when an object was offered as a present, it was most often handmade or discovered at some pain—a huge star fish or an elaborate bouquet of dried weeds or a meticulously carved walking stick.

Beyond these large, planned family entertainments there were countless other moments of improvised song, high jinks, imitations, and clowning. The world of La Herradura was not one of solemn, joyless workaday routine—it was designed to free the spirit and open wide the door to creativity.

ROUTINE IN FAMILY LIVING

So much of our lives was taken up with the repetitive tasks of housekeeping that it seemed important to us to try to make something worthwhile out of them. Either we could use household chores as tests of skill and efficiency so as to get through them as quickly as possible with a minimum of fuss, or we could rethink them, approach them freshly as creative challenges as well as opportunities to learn something useful. The problem back home was that everyone so automatically regarded repetitive tasks—shopping for food, setting the table, preparing food, scouring pots and pans, washing dishes, disposing of garbage—as dull and mechanical that no one really bothered to do more than grumble, "Why me?" "Do I have to do it now?" "Aww Mom, again?"

In La Herradura we tried to approach food differently. The first one out of bed each morning would walk a mile down the beach to the baker's and pick up a loaf of fresh bread. There were compensations. For Ariel there were her own things to talk about from what she had seen alone on the beach; for Seth there was the sensuous pleasure of holding the hot loaf of bread next to his skin as the cold sea wind nipped at his body; for Adam it was an opportunity to shoot some photos when the village was just coming alive. In any case the bread arrived without fuss or assignment each morning, and as each of us tore crisp, hot chunks from the beaming bread-carrier's hands it signaled the beginning of another day at La Herradura.

Setting the table for each meal was an assigned, rotated job. But a new emphasis was placed on efficiency. The children took pride in rapidly organizing a tray in the kitchen with napkins, cups, saucers, salt, sugar, cereals, silverware—everything needed —and then striding into the dining room with it and within a few minutes having the entire table set. We encouraged a sense of professionalism in carrying out the task with spirit and dispatch. There were other occasions, frequently for our evening meal, when the table setter would decide to take the time to arrange his own special atmosphere for dining. These became intense aesthetic exercises: sparkling glasses and gleaming silver, candles carefully positioned, napkins folded decoratively in cleverly devised designs and usually a centerpiece of arranged flowers or dried weeds or driftwood and shells. When the rest of us approached the table, it wasn't only to eat dinner, it was to appreciate a display of home decorative artistry.

So too with preparing meals. Bea is a superb and a creative cook; she makes the preparation of the most succulent, complicated dishes seem effortless. Yet she consistently bungles breakfast. Don't ask her to make a bowl of hot cereal (it's always lumpy) or to fry eggs (the yolks are broken) or to scramble eggs (they stick to the pan). And since, as you can see, we are finicky, it won't surprise you to learn that we were soon taking turns at showing how to fix breakfast. It became an almost daily challenge for the breakfast maker to test his abilities in preparing the meal for an increasingly critical family. We watched to see how he cracked eggs; how quickly he prepared them; whether the butter was crackling but slightly browned; if the quality, color, and texture of the finished eggs were right; whether the eggs were sizzling when deposited on our plates. We checked whether all the other elements of breakfast arrived hot and on time—the coffee, toast, french fries—whether the bacon was properly crisp, the butter hard. We were severe. But we were also generous in our appreciation when breakfast making was well handled. Adam became so proficient at scrambled, fried, and poached eggs that he went on to Spanish omelettes, eggs flamenco, cheese omelettes, and eggs Benedict. With our help, Ariel and Seth made breakfasts too. Later the children took to preparing lunches and even dinners, following Spanish recipes, preparing Jell-O and special salad dressings, making their own spaghetti sauce. Food preparation had become an expression of skill and creativity as well as of love and consideration.

Shopping was still another chore that all of us came to relish. Better than the Muzak atmosphere, the brilliant fluorescents, and the clean rows of cans and packages of the suburban supermarket were the confusion, the hawking, the pushing bodies of the open-air marketplace. Each trip was an adventure in socialization, in hard bargaining, in sudden taste surprises. Instead of the faceless checkout girls, the computer-priced packages, the same display of fruits and vegetables perpetually in season with only fluctuations in prices to suggest where they were grown, we saw the farmers, the fishermen, the shepherds themselves, or the small entrepreneurs who dealt directly between us and them. There was no great mechanism of mass distribution to depersonalize the social business of marketing. It was always fun for the children.

Not every household chore, however, was tackled with a smile. When it came to garbage removal and washing dishes, pots, and pans, we weren't able to devise a fresh approach. The family took some advantage of the fact that I enjoyed restoring rusted and blackened pots to a shiny newness. My occasional rewards were burned skillets and pots encrusted with creamed corn. Seth too, who dreamily soaped each dish and marveled at the brilliant sparkle of a detergent-cleaned glass, was given slightly more than his share of dishwashing.

Other chores were regarded each a little differently. Collecting driftwood and kindling entitled the gatherer to build a fire on chilly evenings with the whole family gathered around the fireplace and waiting expectantly to see how quickly and successfully he could get the fire to roar up the chimney. For bed making and tidying rooms, we used the old army trick of inspection, though it was only intermittently successful. Far more successful in making chores tolerable was a shared sense of being on an adventure together. If a job had to be done, it was done not for mommy or daddy or on orders from someone who could enforce a command, but because the task needed doing and each family member had one-fifth responsibility for making the adventure work. In this way the routine of family living became a civilizing device and a powerful force in welding the family together. The children weren't being threatened or bought into sullen obedience, they were accepting their responsibilities for the dull as well as the exciting tasks in life.

IMPROMPTU ADVENTURES

Distinct from the learning events and the entertainments was a more sudden or impulsive idea that one of us would suggest and the rest promptly adopt. While traveling to Almería to do some shopping, we saw a tiny village situated on a cliff at the very tip of a peninsula jutting three miles out to sea. Two days later, after exploring the village and its Moorish origins we continued on. Another time in southern France we spotted high on a hill a deserted château with moat, battlements, drawbridge, and all and decided to spend the afternoon picnicking there and telling tales of gallant knights and King Arthur's court.

There were also some unpleasant insights resulting from these impromptu adventures. Like the time we decided to follow a beautiful stream high up to its origin in the snow-covered Sierra Nevada. As we climbed higher and higher we noted the different uses made of it—drinking, irrigating, washing, bathing—and then at the very source, just below the melting snow where the rivulets converged to form the main stream we had a shock, for there was a huge fresh garbage heap, the refuse of the luxury-class parador, (a government-run hotel), spilled haphazardly over the entire width of, and a hundred feet down, this crystalline stream. Before the water had been touched, it had been wantonly, hopelessly polluted for all those people below.

However, most of these pick-up-and-go family adventures had no climax. They were simply unanticipated events or opportunities to see or learn something—a visit at dusk to a shepherd's house, an exploration of the fishermen's cemetery, a boat trip along the rugged shoreline with a deaf mute who clawed mussels free from the rocks and then insisted on cooking a batch for us over an open fire, a full day's visit with a peasant farmer and his wife. Devoting whole days or large chunks of time each week to such random unplanned adventures turned out to be one of our best approaches to exciting educational experiences. But, of course, such a careless lack of planning would be unthinkable in a well-run school.

15

ADAM—A BOY

FOR ALL SEASONS

In what school system would an eleven-year-old have a curriculum that consisted primarily of city planning, photography, and adventure story writing? Yet these were the three activities that occupied most of Adam's time abroad. I've already explained how he worked in many conventional subject areas—though with a freedom impossible in a school environment. But it was in these special activities that the most exciting educational developments started to occur and, rather than resist them, Bea and I rode with them, suggesting here, restraining there, obtaining resources, and often participating ourselves. And we discovered the obvious: that all knowledge is interrelated, that a single interest if pursued eagerly and thoroughly leads inevitably to the whole interconnected network of basic skills and knowledge. There was no need to plot out learning sequences with fixed courses and objectives and tests and allotted time. It was far more interesting and immensely more effective to join a child where he was and help him along his own stream of interest, pointing out possibilities for new explorations as you drifted along, assisting him over difficulties, encouraging his skills, and then gradually disengaging and allowing him to fend for himself as his stream widened and branched off and joined other streams.

CITY PLANNING

A number of factors can account for Adam's interest in city planning: our discussions of community living and values as we passed through cities and villages in Europe, our visits to some new towns on the coast of Spain and particularly in Torremolinos, our search for a suitable place to settle down, the fact that I had recently done some writing on cities and federal aid. But you can pick out specific incidents or people met in the past to create a plausible rationale for any new-found interest. The important thing was that Adam himself started experimenting with planning ideas and then at critical points—not because of any brillant insight but simply because we took the trouble—was given both encouragement and assistance.

His first experience centered around a barren hill not far from our house, where with the help of Seth and Ariel he was constructing an outdoor toilet pit. Since our toilet seemed to be functioning well, I inquired what they were about. In dribs and drabs I learned that Adam had planned out a half acre of hillside as a recreational facility for children. It had been lonely for the children those first few weeks in a strange environment without familiar sports and outdoor activities. So Adam had imagined his own recreation area and then, with Ariel and Seth eagerly assisting, had marked off areas for "climbing trees, an off-balance house, an upside-down room, a central mountain of caves-rocks-sand-and-darkness, a bubble house, a tennis court (for daddy), *and* a bathroom." And that's where they started, digging into the clay soil, lugging rocks, shaping a seat—building the toilet.

Seeing how pleased both Bea and I were with the concept, Adam that night set about sketching out the project. He even added two more layers in his drawings including a beach park with fountains, bridges, and walks and an upper layer for conventional sports like basketball and handball, and for swings and rope ladders and, since Seth insisted upon it, for "a castle with many rooms."

In the process of sketching out his multilevel playland Adam had sought our help on problems with drawing and perspective. However, it was a field we knew nothing about. But I remembered seeing an architect's workroom in a real estate developer's office we had visited during our search for a house, and so the following day Adam and I walked over to the office and for more than an hour he observed and talked with a draftsman who was rendering plans for new houses in our area. Adam discussed the problems of scale with the draftsman; he noted the thickness of the walls and surmised correctly, to his delight, that they would be made of stone; he questioned the emphasis on internal gardens, the position of the house in regard to wind, sun, hills, neighbors. And he came away exhilarated by the close contact with a professional in his own field of interest.

He started sketching a plan for a house on an adjoining hill, immersing himself in drafting techniques, aerial views, cross sections, cutaways, scaling. I remember losing an argument with him over the size of a bed he had sketched in a room when he showed according to his scale that it could indeed comfortably sleep *a child.* He was so fascinated with the designs he could create with a ruler and compass that it took some prodding on my part before he would try to enliven his blueprints with drawing techniques of color and shading to achieve depth and texture. He started using detail drawings to illustrate Rube Goldberg-type gadgets in his house, such as a spring-operated device for automatically remaking beds, an outside spotlight manually controlled from within the house, a built-in and *sliding* radiator to conserve heat, a bare room with three glass walls and one mirror wall that, at the touch of a button, dropped to the floor unfolding a bed, chair, side table, and lamp and revealing an entire wall of drawers, sink, and bookshelves.

In his math and science and history notebooks little drawings and bursts of color started popping up, sketches of sudden inspiration for planning ideas. Soon sections and then entire notebooks were devoted to these drawings, and microscopic notes to himself—da Vinci style—on special features were crammed into every blank space on the page.

Adam's attention then turned to apartment houses as an alternative to suburban sprawl, and fanciful drawings of apartment house complexes were soon strewn about the house: three cylinder-shaped, twenty-story buildings that tipped toward each other and met at the top forming a cathedrallike arch; residential environments completely enclosed and protected from the foul city air by geodesic globes; underwater houses "that moved along the sea bottom like squid by jet propulsion"; an all-glass arc sweeping up and back (which we were startled to see under construction the following year on Forty-second Street in New York City); and some astonishingly novel cookie cutouts of arcs and cylinders that would have made extraordinarily handsome buildings. Most of the projects were grandiose projections of his ruler and compass, thirty stories high, five blocks long; intricate geometric designs, ignoring the presence of flesh and blood people. His involvement was with novelty forms and drafting: colors, lines, beautifully rendered sketches.

After a while, I suggested that he try working with something he knew thoroughly, something he really cared about. He decided to redesign the institutional facility most familiar to him, the school. His first drawing, curiously, was of a U-shaped school building completely sunk to the roofline in a mound but open in the center as if the earth had been gouged out to permit the buried rooms to face one another across a bleak pit. There was no mistaking the imagery.

But Adam was soon caught up in more positive ideas, specifically in the idea of reforming the schools. In one classroom design he sought a more private and casual environment by furnishing it with couches and club chairs—and a few desks collapsed into a wall for use only when necessary. In another set of designs he attempted to deflate the importance of the teacher by arranging desks in circles, arcs, V shapes, irregular shapes. He finally settled on a semicircle of most of the students faced by a small arc of four or five students plus the teacher. It was the best solution, he said, "providing some leadership while giving the kids good representation."

In his last set of school drawings the classrooms were completely deemphasized—they had become little pods for intense small group activities with removable canopies that turned them into outdoor patios. Adam was making lavish use of space for library learning centers (surrounding his drawings with detailed notes on how film, TV, tape, record, and computer would be utilized services); glass-enclosed gyms; natural play areas with streams, forests, and pools; open-air cafeterias; multiple craft shops and stores. He was far beyond drafting. He was dealing with matters that directly concerned him and attempting to suggest answers.

He had filled an entire notebook with school drawings and had still not exhausted his ideas when Bea suggested that he move on to another area where she would welcome some improvements—the shopping center. The suggestion was followed by another flood of ideas, drawings, and rationales for shopping centers. From there, on his own, Adam began planning resort areas, then human complexes and transportation systems, and finally entire new cities.

Some of his ideas, no doubt, were triggered by discussions we had while abroad: blacks and minority problems; the cleavage of classes and the flight to the suburbs; the inadequacy of schools; the relocation of industry and company headquarters in the suburbs; the city's dilemma with less taxable real estate, fewer jobs, more need for services; environmental and recreational problems; the frontier attitude of despoiling and moving on and how it affected planning and design; the attempt to bring belated planning into built-up areas; the need for new cities, for mass transportation, health care, multiple-income housing, police protection; the present status of cities as residences for rich and poor, as centers for culture, finance, media, and company management. And much of this information was sifted through and utilized in Adam's fresh approaches to city problems. He was attempting in his new city master plans to integrate and rationalize education, recreation, housing, industry, agriculture, business, culture, transportation, public services, and economic and social diversity.

To encourage a mixing of classes in one city plan, he provided poor people with free land to build on and free transportation to jobs in the city. To make a green belt around his city not only aesthetically pleasing but functional, he made it primarily agricultural to provide fresh fruit and vegetables to city people "and closer contact with livestock, crops and orchards, and the growing soil." He noted it should also be "a place to develop children's work camps modeled after adult society where they could earn and spend money" and arts camps for music, drama, and writing.

To make cities places to work in again, he virtually eliminated the car and devised ingenious mass transportation systems that were safe, speedy, noiseless, and economical; that featured moving sidewalks and storage for free, public shopping carts. To control future growth and maintain the special balance of his communities, he designed inland cities as spurs and shore and mountainside cities as spreading root systems.

He became alert to the whole range of problems that a planner, not just an architect, would have to face: How does this facility relate to the surrounding environment and the needs of the community? How does it serve the people who use it? What provisions have been made for future needs and changes? The questions were complex and interwoven with many allied fields of interest, the problems to be answered were real, the opportunities for learning incredible.

Adam's interest had carried him far beyond a hobby. He was dealing with virtually every aspect of contemporary life: consumer purchasing, recycling of waste and sanitation, quality of education, the need for industry and its effect on community life, architecture and aesthetics, home design and furnishing, the nature of community culture, quality versus economy, amenities versus necessities, individual rights versus social responsibilities. And as he planned and thought through each part of his new cities, a full sweep of contemporary problems confronted and challenged him.

In addition—for we hadn't eliminated the three Rs, only displaced them from center stage—because of his interest in city planning, Adam read widely (in any number of fields related to his immediate concern: education, transportation, city planning, architecture); wrote extensively (his explanations and rationales were often voluminous and painstaking prose essays); vastly improved his knowledge and skills in photography, art, and architecture; became interested for the first time in biography and history; and exercised his skills in mathematics in any number of ways from statistical briefs that defended the economic efficiency of his transportation systems, to projections on population, land use and leisure time activities into the year 2000 to justify his emphasis on high-rise buildings.

Adam's interest in city planning had opened a door to other interests and to massive amounts of new knowledge. However, he did face problems in moving ahead: How to make up for his general lack of experience in the adult world from which he had been cut off all these years at school? How to allocate his time among these many new interests? And how to find resources to satisfy them? But these were the types of problems students should face, types that most schools would have been proud to have created.

ADVENTURE STORY WRITING

There was only Adam's voice and the quiet rhythmic breathing of the family listening in the darkened room. We were gathered around the dining room table, bare except for the two candles softly glowing on either side of the outspread manuscript from which Adam was reading. Visible through the window, far across the black expanse of the bay, were the few scattered lights of La Herradura backed by an immense blackness of rugged mountains and fronted by an even more immense expanse of black sea. Our candlelit room, a secure station within this dark setting, was a vantage point that would have prodded even a commonplace mind to wander off into exciting possibilities.

Adam had helped clear the table, placed the candles, opened the draperies so that the view of the bay was exposed, and, now that we were all attentively silent, begun his reading. It was another installment of his adventure story, an epic tale of two young brothers adventuring on the high seas. He had started writing it as a single story incident but then, entranced by his own creation, began adding to chapter after chapter. From the first reading, Ariel and Seth were goggle eyed following the episodic adventures of Adam's two young heroes. Bea and I were even more fascinated as his writing craftsmanship galloped ahead and his working language assumed more and more fluency and precision with each chapter. He was enthusiastic and involved, feeling a sense of power through the written word to create his own thoughts, his own world.

It had started, as I've indicated, when Adam decided he would write a story rather than, as Bea had suggested, a zany essay. During the first three days he had been secretive about what he was doing. But after he had completed a full adventure, a fifteen-page story, he decided to try it out on Seth. Later at dinner Seth announced with pride that Adam had written a "great" story. Of course, we all insisted that Adam read it aloud then and there. And he did. It turned out to be far from great. But it was still one of our own's creation and therefore fun and exciting. Thus began a regular after-dinner feature, the reading of another installment of the adventures of Jim and Bill Philliet.

Because we were all so enthusiastic, it took no prodding or reminding to get Adam to continue writing. Story telling allowed him to adventure in a world without discipline or clear academic function, in a boundless and uncharted world in which a curious child could wander and tarry without restriction or direction. As his characters tried to cope with new situations, Adam himself began seeking information and understanding in areas previously unexplored; as he fleshed out his people and scenes with his own thoughts and insights, he began reaching out for effective images, freshly examining relationships between people, rethinking his own values. Story telling was a natural extension of a curious boy's world, a way of going exploring.

In all, during a two-month period, Adam wrote thirty thousand words in his neat, unfaltering script. There was rarely a correction or an insertion. His words seemed to flow across the page without strain or hesitation, as if he were quietly but intensely talking to someone. His first writing sessions were short half-hour bursts of energy, but as the weeks progressed and his own pleasure in writing soared, the sessions lengthened until he was sometimes busy for three-hour stretches without interruption. Usually when he emerged from his room and joined us again, he was vibrant and alive, for he was returning from a private adventure and was clearly delighted and puffed up with a sense of accomplishment.

When he read his pieces aloud to us or when we read them privately, we never made corrections and rarely even suggestions. It was as if we were onlookers watching a runner jog along the beach and admiring his developing grace and speed. It wasn't that he was learning—though clearly he was—but that he was doing. And if, as a result of doing, he actually learned some things, these would clearly be things that would stick in his mind, not be forgotten after the next test.

Even in traditional classroom terms, however, the benefits were real and measurable. From his first to his last adventure, any critical reader would see the steady improvement and control in Adam's writing. The language, at first stiff and standoffish, became playful and loose, his verbs took on a fresh and central role in his sentences, the organization of his ideas and scenes became sure and cohesive, and the transitions between all elements—

ideas, sentences, and paragraphs—at first forced or awkward, became unobtrusive and then almost indiscernible as the story flowed on with a momentum of its own.

His vocabulary, too, quickly expanded. The range of words he had been using was now too limited for his purposes, so literally hundreds of new words heard or read started appearing in his stories. His search for substance was joined by a search for the proper words with which to build his scenes, his people, and his ideas. He needed only to hear an unfamiliar term or word before he would weave it into his narrative.

Just as his vocabulary and use of language were being propelled ahead, so did his awareness and skill in the craft of short story writing steadily improve with his skills. Those forbidding terms climax, denouement, suspense—so torturously explained in the classroom—were discovered and applied effortlessly in his stories. In the same way that he had worked by himself at his basketball lay-up or at his tendency at bat to pull too hard on an inside pitch, Adam worked at improving his craft of writing. And it was a craft that he, like most children, was fairly familiar with, having watched TV, and listened to and read hundreds of stories. Only now, in fashioning his own stories, he, unlike other children, was making good use of these experiences.

Some high schools do offer elective courses in creative writing to gifted students and, once in college, a handful of students manage to find time free from obligatory courses to indulge a lingering creative interest. However, even these courses are too often closely supervised exercises where a few labored pieces are produced with much effort and even more discussion and the whole sluggish business usually smothers rather than fans creative fires. Few students can stay long enough with their own ideas or stories to really develop a skill or talent. A spark flies up into the air and then the remaining embers are doused and all is dark again.

But for Adam the experience was different. He not only improved his writing skills and learned to write short stories with unmistakable craftmanship, he also reaped important side benefits. Through his stories, he created a world of his own, a world in which the people and their lives were subject to his will and values. He discovered what it was to be creative, enjoying in the process a marvelous affirmation of his individuality. And as he created his own world, he strongly sensed the blank areas of his life and the need for new knowledge and understanding—a humbling as well as a broadening experience. He also learned something of his own capacity to work independently and enthusiastically for long periods. Finally, the completed manuscript provided Adam with a sense of private rather than prescribed success. He had passed no exams, received no marks, fulfilled no requirements; yet by his own awareness of how much he had learned and grown while scribbling these two hundred pages of adventures, he was satisfied, perhaps even quietly triumphant. Writing had become a fascinating tool that he could use skilfully for fun or purpose.

PHOTOGRAPHY

One of our purposes in taking the children out of school was to expose them to values that had been untouched by classroom education. Among these values was the freedom to follow one's inclination to learn wherever it led.

We had a variety of occasions to test out this view, and one of them resulted from a gift to Adam from Grandma Lillie. It was an expensive Instamatic camera. Adam already had a Brownie camera. I recall using the occasion of the gift to inveigh against people who bought expensive, consumable goods not according to need or utility but according to what they could afford. As far as I could see the camera was an improved Brownie sporting a few automatic gadgets.

Normally, I would have held my peace and tried to share Adam's enthusiasm for the new possession. But the present was given in the last few days before our departure. We were all harried and excitable. Adam, no doubt, sensed some reservation on my part concerning the gift and kept prodding me, "What's wrong with it? Tell me! Don't you think I'm old enough for it? C'mon, daddy! Tell me!"

So I told him. And there were many tears. I tried to explain how the more automatic a camera became, the less control you could exercise over it. I suggested that if his grandmother wanted to give him something better than a Brownie she should have bought a camera that allowed him to manually adjust lens opening, shutter speed, and focal distance. I pointed out how the Instamatic mechanically balanced all these factors and the result was a bland, characterless photography in which the photographer did little more than frame his pictures.

In short, I was cruel. Later, the only way I could think of to assuage his hurt feelings was to suggest exchanging the Instamatic for an inexpensive manually controlled thirty-five-millimeter camera. Though there was little time—we were to leave for Europe in a few days—I decided we could arrive in New York City on the day of departure early enough to return the Instamatic, purchase another camera, and then dash to the air terminal.

So, on the day of our departure, we checked our bags at the terminal, returned the Instamatic, and inquired about other cameras. To my chagrin the store's least expensive manually operated thirty-five-millimeter camera cost sixty dollars—more than double what I had expected. There was no time to comparison shop at other stores. Remembering how I had browbeaten Adam into returning his grandmother's gift, there was nothing to do but swallow hard and say, "We'll take it." And thus Adam acquired a camera more expensive and versatile than my own.

I might also add that before leaving the camera store, I took the precaution of buying Adam twenty rolls of black-and-white film to emphasize that I expected him to make good use of his new possession and to work toward professional standards. With black and white film, I explained, he could later reprint his negatives and blow up and crop his photos. I also had a defensive purpose. I wanted to ensure heavy usage of this investment in equipment and thus psychologically dissociate myself from the addicted consumer syndrome of more and more purchasing and less and less utilization. A sixty-dollar camera for an eleven-year-old smacked of waste and luxury.

I don't think Adam fully appreciated my reservations until weeks later, long after he had learned what all the controls and dials were for, how to load and unload film, how to set shutter speeds and lens openings, and how to focus. He was on his second roll of film as we drove down the coastal road of Spain on a rainy morning.

The rain was thick, thudding against the roof and hood, splattering against the windshield, blinding the car. Though I was at the wheel, there were four other heads straining forward to see the road as it serpentined round the cliffs. There were no shoulders, just a sheer two-hundred-foot drop on our left and a high rock wall on our right. Along the narrow, tortuous course, occasional trucks and cars suddenly emerged careening forward out of the mist and forcing us to the wall. There seemed more ruts and potholes each mile. Before long we were bypassing washed-out sections of the road and trucks pulled over to the side. We wondered why we hadn't turned back long ago. It was now too late because the distance back to Alicante (the last city passed) was twice as far as the distance ahead to Motril. A half hour later, as we entered a small town, the large number of cars and trucks pulled to the side clearly indicated serious trouble.

We moved slowly forward until the problem was visible. A rushing stream of rocks and water was tumbling down the main road of the town and clattering across what had been the highway. The road was brutally hacked through, and water cascaded freely through a gaping ditch. Clustered around the ditch was a good number of local men and children—the women could be seen looking on from their doorways, many with sober eyes and hands raised pensively to mouths. Two members of the *guardia civil* (green-uniformed policemen with comical black plastic Napoleon-style hats) were casually conversing with the townsmen. The road was clearly impassable. I found an alley between two buildings, parked the car, and jumped out to learn what I could about going forward or returning. Adam, I found later, had jumped out behind me.

As I talked with the policemen, I first noticed Adam moving purposefully toward the broken section of the highway. He wasn't doing anything wrong or unexpected. Yet I could see that he was being given extraordinary attention by the local townspeople, particularly the children. He was dressed in a heavy overcoat, new corduroy trousers, high thick-soled buckskin shoes. He looked warm and comfortable in the bare, wind-whipped little village and no doubt a little odd with his Beatle-length hair (in much of Spain, children with long hair are taken by the ear by the local policeman to the barber shop).

Perhaps the most important feature of his appearance was the camera he carried in his hands and the businesslike way he went about planning his photographs. He had taken two shots of the raging water before he noticed the crowd of little boys slowly collecting about him. It wasn't fear or antipathy on their faces—or on those of their fathers, who didn't move forward but just stared. It was awe that a little boy could possess and use so matter-of-factly a valuable piece of equipment.

I observed all this as I spoke to the policeman. A few moments later, clearly frightened and puzzled, Adam hurried to my side. Then as we walked together to the car, Adam, head down and tightly holding my hand, looked as though he were going through the mill—a game in which the person who is "it" must crawl between the legs of a line of punishers thus affording them the best position for whacking him on the behind. I leaned over and drew the camera strap over Adam's head and suspended the camera from my own shoulder. With that simple movement I seemed to have relieved him of some terrible burden. He smiled broadly, released my hand, and with some return of spirit continued walking back toward the car. When we reached the car, Adam was insistent on probing what had happened to him, and it was difficult for me to tell the others what I had learned about the roads.

He said he understood that we would be curiosities in any town—even in the States—as outsiders, perhaps foreigners. But he was unprepared for this open amazement which he quickly recognized was associated with his camera. He had never so vividly seen himself as something other than just a boy. Clearly to these Spaniards he was a little rich boy.

That night we had a lengthy conversation in the small hotel in La Rápita, Adam sitting cross-legged Indian-style on his bed, Seth and Ariel sprawled out beside him, and Bea and me on the other bed in the darkened room. (Because of the washouts the hotel had no running water and no electricity.) We discussed comparative wealth at some length. Although we were traveling abroad, Adam knew that back home we had little real money and that my job, teaching, was known to be a poorly paid profession. He had never felt deprived, yet he thought we were closer to the bottom than the top of the economic scale. It was a good time to point up our comparative affluence even at home. The blacks, the migrant workers, the Puerto Ricans, and the Indians he knew about—we had been diligent in discussing their problems. But it was clear we had not sufficiently emphasized the millions of unskilled workers, the small town and rural families, the sharecroppers, the day laborers and handymen. Too often we had pointed out the extremes of poverty, of hate, of illiteracy, of ignorance and neglected the great middle mass of restricted-income families; neglected the presence of quiet intolerance, of limited education, of misinformation; neglected the great bulk of people who formed nations. We were in fact too close to the metropolitan, professional, and corporate executive milieu to have a clear view of our relative position even in American society. So when we came to Spain—to a small isolated village—it was no wonder that whatever image Adam had of our economic position was shattered. The lesson of comparative wealth was driven home in a manner that would probably never be forgotten.

Adam talked long and well about the limited prospects of these La Rápita children simply because of their place of birth, their undiscovered talents, the terrible waste. As he spoke I had the uncomfortable feeling that he would suddenly burst into Gray's lines:

> *Full many a gem of purest ray serene*
> *The dark unfathomed caves of ocean bear;*
> *Full many a flower. . . .*

But I resisted telling him that he was not alone in having these thoughts.

After this incident many weeks passed before Adam again started working with his camera. His interest was rekindled finally when he saw me setting my own camera for a night shot of the town of La Herradura. I had never tried a long time exposure and ran into many difficulties stabilizing the camera, estimating the time exposure, and holding the shutter open. Adam, watching me, offered a few suggestions but I took only one of them. He asked me if he could use my camera and try shooting himself. Of course, I agreed and with much preparation he took two shots. The next day he took his own camera out and became absorbed in a whole series of trick photos. When our film was developed we found that both our night photographs of La Herradura had worked out well. However, Adam's roll of trick shots—with two exceptions—had turned out uniformly bad: under- or overexposed, out of focus, poorly framed, blurred, or dull subject positions.

Adam asked if we could get a book on photography. I sent for it, but a month and a half passed before the book arrived from the States. Meanwhile, he had continued experimenting with his camera, finding and creating shots, learning to adjust for light conditions, and later for light conditions of his focal point, balancing shutter speed and movement of subject with lens opening, and playing with depth-of-focus problems. When the book finally arrived much of what it offered Adam had already learned. He showed some interest in the technical discussion of lenses and artificial lighting, but his real interest now was in saying something—not just recording, but in making a statement about a person or a locale.

He would take picture after picture of Seth reading, in the bathroom, on the deck chair, on the lawn, on the beach, in bed, at night or early in the morning—trying to find the right one to best express Seth's love affair with the printed word. Or he would quietly study, camera in hand, Ariel and Bea working together on arithmetic, trying to determine the most significant visual interplays between parent and child: mommy—smiling, stern, instructing, listening, pensive, questioning, or bemused; Ariel— happy, tearful, insistent, studious, passive. He had to decide what combinations he was looking for, the correct angle, distance and framing to capture it, the settings for speed, light, and focus. And then he had to exercise patience, to outlast his subjects' consciousness of being photographed, which would pass when they once again became absorbed in what they were doing. And then catch the scene—a moment of reality he had isolated and given meaning to.

His work was not only becoming technically more demanding, it was also searching for more subtle and intellectual approaches to measure up to his own rising expectations from photography. He moved on to portrait photography; close-up work with flowers, insects, and sea life; trick shots using mirrors and time exposure. But his underlying interest remained the ability to make a statement through his photos.

Adam spent considerable time with photography, just as he spent much time designing and drawing up architectural plans for a dream house. But in both cases the rewards went far beyond those of a hobby. For example, the benefits in science and mathematics were immediate. Through his close-up photography, he became involved in biology and botany—not only identifying living species found near the house, but in dissecting many of them, carefully studying their parts so that he could know organs and systems when he took his cross-section shot or highlighted a species habit.

In attempting to capture the sense of height on top of a cliff that dropped precipitously three hundred feet to a stone-strewn, rugged beach below, Adam realized that his camera would record a scene without drama because there was no point of reference to fix size or distance. He needed a person, a goat, a rowboat down below. From this observation stemmed a series of discussions and experiments on relative size and optical illusion, dual vision and depth perception, the anatomy of the eye and mentally reversed and blended images.

The brain's trick of reversing images had intrigued Adam before. He had learned a few weeks earlier—when with the help of Ariel and Seth he had done an experiment suggested in a science book—how the camera lens and the human eye both record an upside-down image. He had placed a lighted candle behind the base of a cardboard box lying on its side with its top open and covered with tissue paper. When a hole was punched through the box base and the room darkened, a reversed image of the candle was thrown on the tissue paper. At that time I had made much of the fact that the brain automatically reverses this upside-down reality. I stressed that it was another example of the magical properties of the brain in bringing order and intelligibility out of a chaos of sensory impressions that constantly bombard it. But it was Adam who saw the corollary danger in the brain's potential for disorder. He clearly perceived how the brain could convincingly distort reality as well.

A similar interplay of book and experience occurred in relation to light reflection, only this time the book experiment simply explained a phenomenon that Adam had already observed and utilized in his photography. In shooting interior photos he had discovered that reflections on our living room's large glass windows provided him with a technique for taking wide-angle shots of the room from within the room itself. He later matched his experiences to the book's explanation of reflection and did two textbook experiments which gave him precise information on angle of reflection and focal distance of reflected object from camera.

Sometimes ideas for photography were stimulated by other activities. The entire family had in a two-week period gone out five or six separate nights—bundled up in blankets and coats against the raw night winds that whip the Costa del Sol—to observe the stars. The chart of the heavens I had secured was small and lacked detail. As a result all the children—but particularly Adam—had trouble matching what was in the chart to the numberless stars visible in the clear Mediterranean night sky. Proud of his own increasing ability in photography, Adam decided to set up his camera and take some time exposures of the stars. I tried to dissuade him by stressing the incredibly exact requirements of astronomical photography. In the process we discussed the relationship of light to size, distance, and time. Adam seemed strangely at home with concepts of relativity. He already knew of the concept of light years and was aware that many stars that can be seen actually burned out millions of years ago. But the science fiction concept of going back into time by jetting out into space faster than the speed of light really won his attention. In any case, all my talk about the difficulty of photographing stars didn't prevent him from setting up his camera and photographing four constellations. The local camera shop in La Herradura chose not to print these shots since the negatives showed no light. When we insisted that the four shots be printed, the proprietor dutifully complied and the next day returned four uniformly black prints with a shrug of his shoulders and raised eyebrows as if to say, "You wanted this?" Adam decided at this point to put off astronomical photography until we reached home.

But this sort of technical application was no more than a by-product of the real benefits that were accruing as Adam worked with his camera. He was moving more and more into areas of logic, of creativity, of complex decision making. He was developing an appreciation of precision and control, sharpening and broadening his powers of observation.

KEENER OBSERVATION. Because a photograph reduces a many-faceted subject to a single image from a fixed perspective, it is as much related to the subject as a phrase ripped out of the context of a paragraph. Of course, if the photographer knows his business, it will not be a random image, but one that catches an essential flavor or aspect or characteristic of the subject. He must be aware of the subject in depth so that as the images of the subject change from moment to moment, he can quickly sort out and weigh a full range of essential subject details before stopping and extracting one image as his—the photographer's—statement on the subject. He must learn to conclude, to bring the random sensory impressions together, and to formulate an opinion or idea that can then be represented by isolated images.

To do this well requires an interest and close attention to

detail in one's subject. Adam was forced to observe each member of his family, people he came in contact with, and his entire environment with an increasingly comprehensive and critical eye. He looked out at the world, even without his camera, with a fresh awareness of the infinite complexity of detail that makes up life and a sense of his own power to select significant features out of these details, to bring order and meaning out of a welter of information. With his camera he could make his individual view of a subject intelligible and memorable. And following quite naturally from this discovery was the fact that his individual view could be made significant. It gave him a feeling both of power and of self-assertion.

COMPLEX DECISION MAKING. As Adam studied his subjects more closely, he became progressively more sophisticated in seeing possibilities for different statements on a single subject. Simultaneously he was becoming technically proficient as well, thus enhancing flexibility. In the few seconds between recognizing a potential shot and taking it, he was concerned with a host of considerations: what he was trying to say; framing the picture; setting the lens opening and shutter speed; checking light and shadow areas, backgrounds, depth of focus; maintaining naturalness in subjects or getting a particular effect. If any one factor was neglected, he knew the entire composition would be marred. And when prints returned from the developer each of these factors was visible in each of the separate areas of decision. For an eleven-year-old—for anyone—this was complex and instantaneous decision making. The number and variety of decisions to be made, often within seconds, offered Adam invaluable training for efficient and decisive action in all areas of life.

BROADENING EXPERIENCES. Thanks to his camera, Adam became an intense, curious, and searching observer. It was he who frequently wanted to inquire further, to climb a Spanish lookout tower, to return to an aboveground graveyard, to speak to construction workers, to stay behind to work with a gardener, to dissect a sea urchin. And much of his interest was either directly connected with taking a picture or triggered by the photographer's general curiosity about things around him from which he could draw later.

He was no more immune than other amateur photographers to the lure of seeking out an unusual or new scene or situation, be it village schoolhouse or peasant's home, in an effort to broaden his subject material. In the process he learned how to gain the cooperation of a variety of new and strange people, he spoke to village teachers in his halting but expanding Spanish, he saw the kitchen utensils and living quarters of a farmer's family, he discovered how much milk a she-goat produced and how many pesetas a goatherd received for a liter of goat's milk, he estimated the goatherd's modest income by counting his goats and relating this to the high cost of milk in the marketplace, he even figured out how much profit the small-town distributors and shopkeepers made on this toiling goatherd's family. From this he concluded that high retail prices for meat, fish, eggs, and vegetables made these foods unavailable to the very people who produced them.

One morning he woke up early and roused Ariel. The two of them slipped out of the house with an empty milk bottle in hand. They were headed for a goatherd's house a mile down the beach. The night before the five of us while walking on the beach had stopped to watch a goatherd and his flock of she-goats returning from pasture. At the herdsman's hut, we saw the goatkins, eager to suckle, jumping and leaping out to meet them. It was dusk and the goatherd, a man about sixty, was clearly fatigued after his long day in the hills. Nevertheless, he enjoyed the romping goatkins and the stir around the hut at his return. I'm sure the presence of five admiring strangers added to his pleasure that night. We fell easily into conversation and before long he had called out his wife and children. It grew darker. We made a tranquil tableau, four adults speaking softly and five children, quietly busy and lost among the sixty or seventy goats and goatkins. The woman at one point disappeared into the hut and returned with a jar and funnel. Then without a word, her husband left us, moved through the herd and returned dragging a she-goat with bulging udder and taut teats. He dropped to one knee, positioned the funnel and jar, then began milking the patient goat. The children were again by our side now. The man offered Seth the first jarful. He tasted it cautiously, then gulped down large draughts so that before long his face was covered with the foam from the body-warm milk. The children disliked the store-bought goat's milk so that disguising the taste or finding milk substitutes had remained a continuing problem for us in Spain. But it was clear that fresh goat's milk tasted similar to cow's milk and all three of our children were embarrassingly eager to take their full share of the proferred jars of warm, fresh milk.

We talked for a while about factory processing and how in America, too, cream was skimmed off before milk was packaged. We learned how different types of feeding grounds produced different quality and flavoring in milk. During our conversation, Adam was quiet but attentive. He asked me to find out if we could purchase some milk. And I did as graciously as I could without offending their hospitality. After some shoulder shrugging the couple agreed between them on a price per liter. Adam eagerly volunteered to pick up the milk each morning and everyone seemed delighted with the arrangement. Then after much hand-shaking and shoulder clapping, we waved goodbye and continued our walk home in total darkness.

So the following morning Adam was up and out of the house, camera on his shoulder. He returned with a bottle of milk and a wealth of information about the goatherd's hut, the neighbors, the village children, the suckling habits of the young goats, why and when the male goatkins were sold for butchering. And for much of what he had observed and reflected on he had taken photos to capture his feelings. When the film was printed one could easily see in household items and village scenes, in the distinctive features of the faces of older men and black-shrouded women, what Adam had been impressed with. He had seen, and with his camera he was trying to make others see as he had.

CREATIVITY. Perhaps the most important aspect of working with a camera—and in learning generally—is to participate and to sense the joy and need of participating creatively. Once the camera gadgets and controls are understood, the cameraman is thrown back on his own imagination, intelligence, and quickness of perception. Photography can be unmistakably creative work, easily distinguished from the smile-and-face-the-camera picture taking of the Sunday amateur. In Adam's case, as the photos in this book suggest, the photographer wanted to say something; he was out to create the setting, lighting, angle, framing, and subject expression that would make a point. He was alert enough to seize upon existing scenes or situations and put his camera to work to make them meaningful or to painstakingly put together point by point the elements for his photograph—a meticulous, carefully articulated piece of craftsmanship. Yet the product must be art rather than artifice, singular reality rather than a platitude.

REFINEMENT AND CONTROL OF ACTIONS. No small benefit in providing a youngster with a delicate and complex piece of equipment is that the need for discipline and control becomes clear. It may be foolhardy to entrust an eleven-year-old with an expensive and fragile instrument, but it can also be viewed as a daringly effective way to dramatize the nature of responsibility. Most children readily accept and follow through on responsibilities for pets or for prized sports equipment. Of course, the proper care and responsibilities for Adam's camera were carefully detailed and the consequences of omissions or negligence made clear. But once this was done, an occasional reminder was all that was needed to keep Adam alert to the continuing need for care with his camera.

Perhaps I should relate an earlier event that helped impress my warnings on Adam. When he was eight I had bought him a sturdy bow-and-arrow set. Before turning it over to him, I had carefully spelled out the correct procedure for safe handling of the equipment and then vividly conjured up the outcome of a careless act. For the first hour or so nothing untoward happened, though I did harshly caution him one time to keep his drawn arrow pointed at the target. Then as his enthusiasm for target practice mounted he became wild and careless, whooping like an Indian and sweeping his drawn arrow around in a semicircle. Then suddenly, the taut string slipped from his fingers and an arrow went streaking by my head, missing my eye by half an inch. I ripped the bow from Adam's hands and snapped it in two on my knee. Then I took the other bow and did the same. Then I broke every single arrow as well. Finally, I told him he would never shoot an arrow in my presence again.

It would be hard for an eight-year-old to forget such a scene. So when I cautioned him about using his camera with care, the lingering dread of irresponsible action played no small part in making Adam appear capable of assuming responsibilities. A capacity for responsible behavior is not the result of any one event. Long after the bow-and-arrow incident, the lesson was still being played back as reinforcement.

Equally important was the opportunity to use a fine and flexible piece of equipment. Children are quick to learn, and learning that requires continued practice and exercise by an adult is often absorbed in a fraction of the time and with far more facility by a child eager to know how. So with brief explanations, Adam became quickly familiar with and fascinated by the variables in taking a photo. It was a new game with an endless number of possible answers. There was a sense of mastery in knowing that by rearranging these elements he could make countless variations on the same subject. Yet for each of these variations not only artistry was involved, but logic and craftsmanship, a sure knowledge of the relationships among all these elements. It became an amusing pastime for Adam to observe people working with cameras and to guess what they were doing right or wrong in taking a shot. He acquired the jealous craftsman's pride in his art and instruments.

ART. Photography is a creative art that uses many of the judgments and senses that identify an artist or one who appreciates art in any form. As Adam continued to work in photography, his appreciation of design, of symmetry and asymmetrical balance, of gradations of gray tone and sharp black-and-white contrast, of the added dimension of color providing new opportunities as well as more complex problems was enriched and refined. He began to use soft focus and silhouette, to establish mood by foreground touches or meaningful backgrounds. In one photo of Bea and the children on the beach, he moved far away and high so that his photo showed the family close and united against a vast, bleak, rock-covered beach. In another photo of the hard-lined face of a Spanish laborer, he waited patiently until the man walked in front of a brilliantly white, sunlit wall of rough-textured stucco to complement the man's clean, coarse, simple character. There was not only meaning in his photography, there was an attempt at poetry. And of course, like any artist proud of his work, Adam came to understand his materials and the possibilities of his craft. He noticed how some prints were streaked and spotted, how the same negative when printed twice produced totally different tones, and he determined to know more about the printing process. One afternoon he asked the photo store owner if he could watch him develop some film, and when we picked him up hours later he was beaming and babbling about what he had learned. He had discovered an additional assortment of techniques and skills available to the photographer who cropped and developed his own photos. He also had an answer to why prints were smudged, spotted, and streaked. From this point on he would be a critical purchaser of photo services.

We had one embarrassing experience as a result of Adam's rapid progress in photography. It resulted from our decision to have a professional photographer take a picture of the entire family so that we could send a photo back to the children's grand-parents. We had shots of three or four of us but had never asked someone to use our camera to shoot the whole family. The idea of snapping a family picture in this way reminded me too much of those family grin-and-bear-it photographs of my youth.

Since the local photographer had some good shots on his studio walls and his rates were one sixth what they were at home, we arranged for him to come out to our home to shoot an infor-mal family scene. He came and took about eight poses. It was the same store where we had a roll of Adam's film being developed, and it happened that when we came to look at the professional proofs Adam's pictures were also ready. The photographer was uneasy because his shots had turned out poorly—too distant to provide sufficient facial detail, badly exposed so that faces were lost in shadow or against a rugged, sunlit coast. Every picture was clearly faulted. And what really humiliated him was that Adam, who was eagerly examining his own photos oblivious of all else, kept rushing over to us with this shot or that—all of them not only better pictures but often evocative, sharply focused little gems of photography. Realizing the awkwardness for the photographer, we shooed Adam away and seriously set about selecting one of these studio shots. Despite our insistence that we wanted to pur-chase one of them, the photographer made it clear that he couldn't allow us to and begged us to arrange for another sitting. We agreed and later that week he took another series of shots in his studio. This time they were fine studio portraits. But they didn't compare with Adam's.

16.

ARIEL—OUR

SPECIAL CHILD

Ariel's education back in the Lakeland schools had been a slow-motion version of the regular academic program, three or four skips behind and moving sluggishly forward. To us, this emphasis on academic work seemed particularly wasteful, since Ariel's needs loomed so large in other areas of ordinary living that the school pretty much ignored. What she urgently required, if she were not to be permanently shunted off into a life separate from the rest of us, was an upgrading of her basic communications skills and of her competence in social and personal behavior. With these shored up, she might be able to slip back into society and remain there happy and unremarked.

Before we took her abroad, Ariel had been categorized by the system as intellectually unfit for a normal school program and had been sent miles away from *her own* school and friends to a strange building to learn with other slow learners. Of course, lack of everyday access to average children widened the gap between Ariel's new world and theirs and made continuing contact with her old friends more difficult. And she was sensitive to what was happening. A few days before we left for Europe, she wrote this little piece on "Who Am I?"

> I am a girl. I lev [live] in Peekskill. I am dift [different] then an bote [anybody]. I sleep in a dift room. I play by my slef [self] on the swing.

Whatever potential she had, which had formerly been pricked and prodded by exposure to a demanding and real world, was now being boxed into an unreal environment of slowed-up, sheltered living.

So when we took Ariel out of school, our job, unlike our approach with the boys, was sharply defined. We had to improvise a curriculum that would equip her with everything she would need to be reintroduced into a workaday society: not the school society of reading, writing, and arithmetic—after all she would be out of that world in seven or eight years—but the neighborhood and community society in which she would be spending her entire life.

Ironically, our plan centered on taking advantage of many of the conventional and personally damaging values of this society that, for the boys' sake, we had come to Spain to escape. We hoped to provide Ariel with a range of skills and behavior patterns that would give her a look-and-act-alike normalcy. It would certainly be an easier life style for her to emulate than the curious and independent lives we wanted for the boys.

SOCIAL BEHAVIOR

Our first concern was her social behavior, her ability to participate in social situations, to control her emotions and fears, and to acquire the niceties, the tastes, the manners with which she could lose herself in the anonymity of "womanliness."

Our family provided a social environment that was not threatening, yet exposed her on a twenty-four-hour basis to verbal, physically active, and alert people. We were a family of five, and *five* had taken on for each of us a mystical wholeness. If one of us was sick or away from home, all family life seemed to grind to a halt until we were whole again. And because she was unquestionably felt as one-fifth of the living tissue of the family, and not an appendage, each of us separately used his energy, his will, and his skill to keep her up with us. We were determined that no part of the family be left behind.

We sought her comments. We insisted on her participation, whether in a discussion on sex, an arduous mountain climb, hauling food from the marketplace, a dissection of a sea urchin, or a night of astronomy under the stars. We wouldn't allow her to fall back into a posture of helplessness or feigned interest.

And it wasn't just doing what others did; we wanted her to feel what others felt. Ariel was already capable of jealousy, resentment, exhilaration, and despair, but there were other emotions, major holes in a normal network, that she had learned to simulate without really experiencing them. She couldn't distinguish between liking and loving, between the affection offered by and to a member of the family and that offered by a stranger. On a few occasions she had seemed perfectly ready to leave her brothers and go off with a strange child or even an adult who seemed to like her.

I remember an afternoon when we had stopped to have a drink at an outdoor café in Almuñécar. Ariel was staring and giggling at a modishly dressed French expatriate couple at the next table. They made some perfunctory comments about how charming Ariel was and then proceeded methodically and superciliously to probe our social credentials. Obviously we didn't measure up, because they soon paid their check and with studied disdain said goodbye. As they were leaving, Ariel ran after them, grabbed the woman's hand, and shouted happily, "I want to go with you. I want to live with you always," and embracing the woman simpered, "I love you." The woman disengaged herself, dropped Ariel's hand like a dirty rag, and simply walked away. Little Ariel, so eager for attention or praise in the outside world, willing to give up parents, brothers, everything and go off with a total stranger, just for the hope of a few more words of praise, stared after them.

How does one teach a child proportion? How does one distinguish between careless words and true feeling, between lasting associations and passing interests, between family and stranger? Scenes like this one in the café were not just causes for wan smiles and momentary discomfort. They were wincing reminders that the edifice of skills, acceptable speech, and physical grace that we were so painstakingly constructing could be toppled instantly if Ariel's weak underpinning of values and feeling was exposed.

She not only returned our concern and affection with indifference or worse, a comic-strip parody of what she thought was expected, she also felt no compassion or gratitude—not because she was cold or self-centered, but simply because she didn't know what exactly she was supposed to feel.

These were serious shortcomings—far more worrisome than an inability to use the nine table in multiplication. And we decided, rather than await the sluggish progress of her normal growth pattern, to expedite the learning process by consciously adopting the very educational techniques we had turned away from with the boys. We would use exercise, imitation, and rote learning—the conventional educational tools—to equip Ariel for a conventional life.

We began identifying, discussing, and using ourselves as models for emotions that Ariel was not experiencing. We would associate an event calling for an emotion with a clear expression of the emotion and point out why and, more important, *how* one followed the other logically and swiftly. Before long Ariel was indeed translating the meaning of an event more and more quickly and accurately into demonstrable feelings. And after a while it was difficult to distinguish between her learned reactions and her spontaneous bursts of emotion. B. F. Skinner would have been delighted.

Here are a few examples.

One afternoon, after she had at first denied and finally admitted sneaking candy from the refrigerator—she was supposed to be dieting—she was chided by Adam who called her a "big, fat liar." Previously, if she felt abused or misjudged, she would invariably burst into tears or retreat with whimpers and a tragically turned-down mouth. But we had been prodding her for some time to meet her problems by expressing her anger rather than translating every difficulty indiscriminately into a crying jag or a sulk.

This time, too, her mouth was turned down, but she managed to say, softly, "I'm a liar, but I'm not so fat." She was tentatively trying out her anger. When she saw that Bea and I, who had overheard the interchange, didn't reprimand her, but smiled and complimented her for fighting back, she shouted her fully verbalized anger, "I'm not so fat!" She even threw a powder-puff punch at Adam, something she had never done before. And at this even Adam smiled. Thereupon Bea opened the refrigerator, handed round a fresh piece of candy to each of us, and we all celebrated Ariel's introduction to anger.

Another time Bea had made identical pantsuits and bikinis for the two of them and then, with Ariel, modeled the outfits in front of a cheering, foot-stomping family. Previously, Bea had made skirts and dresses for Ariel, and the child had taken them without thanks or comment. But this time Ariel, with no hint of playacting but a little embarrassed by her own feelings of gratitude, said quietly, "Thank you for making me [look] like you."

Again, after a dancing lesson in which she went through a whole range of movements gracefully and faultlessly, she was so excited by her feeling of competence that she threw her arms around Bea, her teacher, and gave her a huge hug. Previously she had used the hug primarily as a way of gaining attention or affection from others.

This and the other scenes of emotional awakening were the progress we were looking for. Ariel was starting to react the way little girls reacted.

In some areas, however, we still had a long way to go. We had been able to get Ariel to express some emotions meaningfully, but she still had difficulty using others with discretion. Her feelings of love and pleasure were still only fuzzily attached to people and events—displayed to please others rather than to express something felt. Being open and warm with everyone might well be part of her charm, but we felt she'd need some reservation, even suspicion, if she was to function in a world unprotected by parents and brothers.

FEARS

On the other hand, we hesitated to cultivate any sense of fear in Ariel because once she was visited by fear we had found ourselves almost helpless to allay it. When she was seven years old in Peekskill, Adam had pointed to a daddy longlegs spider that was moving quickly along a ledge next to Ariel's head and frightened her by saying, "Look, your hair is alive." From that moment on not only was she afraid of all spidery bugs, but at the sight of any loose hair in her bed or in the sink, she would run screaming out of the room. To reassure her we tried everything including taking hairs from our own heads and holding them for her to examine. Nothing worked. For Ariel, any loose hair might suddenly quicken into life; the fearful image was indelible.

So too with motorcycles and strange toilets. When she was six, a boy on a roaring minibike had chased her all over a schoolyard, zooming in on her so that in terror she screamed, then blocking her retreat and zooming in on her again until she was driven into shrieking hysteria. The gunning of motors and any loud sound brought back that terror, and she bolted to the nearest wall, wild eyed and ready to run. The phobia of toilets was another example of teasing gone awry. An acquaintance in Spain had said jokingly to her just before she entered an outhouse, "Little girls sometimes fall in and are never found. So be careful." She never forgot and would squat in a field rather than sit on a strange toilet.

These were fears that had to be overcome. Loud noises, hair, and toilets were parts of everyday living. Yet we had little success with explanation, demonstration, or ridicule. Only when we came to accept her fears did Ariel begin to work on them herself. It was as if feeling this emotion and knowing it had nothing to do with reason, she feared being intellectually manipulated out of it. Whereas before she would run from the sight of a bug and beg me to kill it and remove it without her seeing it, even dead, she began watching me; then she took the flyswatter warily and made a few passes at a fly herself; and before long, seeing their vulnerability to her, she was picking up with her fingers insects the rest of us would hesitate to touch. Today the fear is operating almost conventionally. You'll only see her scamper, a little more actively than most youngsters perhaps, from bees, hornets, snakes, and jellyfish.

So, too, with water. She feared nothing more than the possibility that she would be forced to swim. Until we went to Spain she would never enter water higher than midcalf. When we stopped urging her to swim, however, she gradually ventured into deeper water, tried kicking while supporting herself, tried flailing her arms, and eventually learned by herself how to stay afloat. Only then did she accept our help. She had mastered the element and overcome her fear and could now trust intellectual guidance.

As for minibikes and strange toilets, she's still not very secure, though she makes a conscious effort to face up to her fears by standing tautly by my side when a minibike is heard and by bravely entering strange ladies' rooms though she returns often ruefully unsuccessful.

WOMANLINESS

Our friends in the women's lib movement are no doubt already braced for this one, squinty eyed and implacable. And they may be justified. More deliberately than wife beaters, all-male labor unions, university faculties, the AMA, and *Family Circle* we were out to take advantage of womanhood.

We found in womanliness a collection of skills and attributes quite within the reach of a slow child. I don't mean to downgrade either Ariel or womanhood, for most of us no longer hold that housewifery, sexuality, and consumerism are of sufficient importance to occupy a grown woman full time. Any alert vigorous woman who would not balk at such a life is simply ignorant or wretchedly intimidated by a system that hobbles women and prefers men. But we were not at all interested in preparing Ariel for independent actions and bold initiatives, for comprehensive awareness and high opportunity. We wanted simply to ensure that she could get by. And since the great majority of society conveniently holds tight to the idea that women are decorative, unaggressive, and not terribly bright housewifely things, to be petted and caressed and cared for, we had a far easier task than if we had tried making her into a free but far from equal spirit. If we kept our eyes on the conventional world's continuing prejudice toward women, we might be able to use femininity as a shield for Ariel's serious deficiencies.

There was no levity in our intention. Bea and I had agreed that this was a crucial factor in winning Ariel acceptance in the workaday world. And so we set about consciously feminizing her; encouraging her to take an interest in cooking, keeping house, caring for children; teaching her how to shop and count change, how to dress, how to listen, express warmth and friendliness, and be helpful; how to make herself more attractive.

Of course, appearance was a key element. Most contacts in life are brief and superficial—with storekeepers, the postman, fellow workers, neighbors—so that the immediate impression a person makes, based in good part on appearance, is a critical factor in his or her social viability. For most women, their clothes, carriage, poise, grace, and particularly their good looks determine whether their overall impression will be favorable or unfavorable. To call a woman a "dumb blonde" would hardly be a condemnation in most male lexicons. On the contrary, it would suggest womanliness without the handicap of intelligence. Women, too, often judge other women solely on physical assets: dress, grace, youth, figure; later husband, house, car. Our purpose was to use these superficial judgments as a way to protect Ariel from possible abuse from the passing world.

So with calculation, Bea set about improving Ariel's appearance. Bea made her conscious of clothes by making her outfits, by modeling them with her. She had Ariel diet to trim her figure and take full advantage of the fact that she was indeed a pretty little girl. She encouraged the child to improve her carriage by correcting her walk (Ariel walked flat footed as if to secure each step until Bea insisted that she climb along the rocky shores and scale mountains with the boys to make her more nimble; had her walk a straight line with a book on her head, toe extended; and watched her relentlessly for weeks until the heel finally came down first and consistently). Bea taught her to sit with legs closed or crossed, to keep her shoulders straight, her neck extended. She made the child aware of the importance of cleanliness, of combing her hair, of keeping her clothes neat and her shoes shined.

And by insisting on her feminine role Bea also helped to create a separate identity for Ariel, which she desperately needed to distinguish her from her brothers. Ariel learned that her life could be quite manageable. Boys might have their schools, their jobs, their books, but she had only herself, her home chores, and her shopping to worry about. Indicative of the change was the day she voluntarily came to dinner in a dress; before then she had always insisted on wearing long pants or shorts like the boys. She was clearly on her way to womanliness.

EVERYDAY SKILLS

Ariel couldn't button her coat, pour milk, fold a towel, or brush her teeth. Her speech was ungrammatical, her pronunciation haphazard, her ability to order ideas infantile; she made little effort to follow conversations and seemed unable to follow instructions. So even if we were successful in implanting a sense of womanliness in her and creating a viable set of emotions (or if you will, emotional responses), we had also the no less important task of providing her with the everyday skills needed to handle the routine activities of day-to-day living.

PERSONAL HABITS. For example, besides brushing her teeth, Ariel had to learn how to bathe and shower by herself (taking a shower was another of her phobias), how to dress herself (she had trouble with pullover sweaters, with zipping and buttoning), and even how to eat (she chewed food with her mouth wide open, grabbed for what she wanted, used her fingers even in soups and desserts, and stuffed her mouth with large chunks of tougher food because she had trouble using a knife). These had been continuing home problems that we had tried to work out before, with limited success. But they were even more important to us now that we had undertaken her entire education because we realized how crucial personal habits were in making Ariel's differences less conspicuous. A continuing failure to perform routine activities might seriously threaten her chances for an independent life.

At first we treated her acquisition of each of these skills as a major educational undertaking but could see little improvement. Later we took a different approach concerned more with her general manual dexterity than with any one skill (I'll discuss this shortly), and our results were far more encouraging.

On her return to the States she could zip, button, and pull sweaters over her head; had learned to use a knife skillfully and eat decorously in company (alone she still picked up choice morsels with her fingers); she loved taking showers and sang with abandon as she soaped herself; she combed her own hair, tied her own shoelaces, flushed toilets, changed her clothes when they were soiled. To someone looking for giant strides in education, these may seem like memorabilia on baby's first steps. For us they were major advances because each time Ariel acquired a personal skill, it meant that another door would not be shut in her face and we could continue her methodical advance forward.

BASIC MENTAL FUNCTIONS. We were equally concerned with Ariel's basic mental skills: her ability to follow simple instructions, to listen with intention to understand, to observe carefully, to order her impressions. Each was an accomplishment an ordinary child would acquire without help; yet for Ariel all remained unexplored. Neither Bea nor I had a background in child psychology or behavior patterning. All we knew were the day-by-day shortcomings in our child's behavior and our own day-by-day attempts to change or eliminate them. We had no educational jargon, no carefully delineated objectives, though perhaps I may be suggesting the latter here. These notes are set down after the fact, looking back and trying to analyze what happened. At the time, all we knew was that Ariel didn't follow instructions, that she kept interrupting conversations, that she seemed to see nothing unless it was called to her attention. And this situation needed fixing.

I wasn't troubled too much by her inability to follow instructions because I suspected that, like most kids, she had already been trained by the schools to suffer politely through periods of instruction, offering as little resistance as possible until they passed. It is a rare schoolroom in which a child feels comfortable enough to say, "I don't understand," to a teacher who is trying to get on with the work and who seems to have won the understanding of twenty-nine other youngsters. Better to remain silent and try somehow to work around the murky instructions when you have to. And sure enough, when we repeatedly went over instructions with Ariel to be certain she understood before starting any task, she came to understand that we would not make demands that were beyond her capacity and would not let her wander off alone without fully knowing what was expected of her. Under these consistent conditions, she began to listen.

An example of this is a long entry in her notebook in which Ariel describes how "To Make a Omlet [Omelette]. First you crak a egg. Den . . ." Bea had spent an entire morning with her showing her, coaching her, and reviewing each of the steps. The result was that Ariel could prepare eggs, she could tell you how to prepare eggs, and she was more likely to listen to further instructions.

Of course, with any change there are problems of balance. And we soon discovered that Ariel began to welcome total instruction because it often eliminated her need to think for herself. But we were taking one step at a time, and she had learned to follow simple instructions.

Another area in which Ariel was weak was ordinary conversation. Granted, she often had trouble following discussions. But she frequently betrayed her disinterest or incomprehension—to the annoyance of those participating in the discussion—by suddenly interjecting a completely unrelated comment or asking a question out of context. It was her way of maintaining her one-fifth right of participation. We usually tried to keep her in the conversation, so it was even more irksome to have her suddenly blurt out an unassociated remark revealing we had obviously failed.

Her inability to concentrate was compounded by the fact that she had only a small fund of her own experiences to draw upon. She observed and thought little unless sights or impressions were brought to her attention.* So with our family activities increasing and becoming more important in our discussions, we found her able to play an increasingly active part in our conversations. As time went on her tendency to interrupt with nonsequiturs—which quickly gave away her difference even to casual acquaintances—lessened. However, it remains a problem and I suspect the only workable answer is her silence—which Ariel, with reason, is resisting.

Bea had far more success dealing with defined areas of knowledge that Ariel would need in everyday living. She worked with the child on practical terminology: months, seasons, measures, money, time—creating ingenious clocks for learning, devising shopping games, designing new calendars. She worked on the concepts of opposite and similar, emphasizing sensory terms that Ariel could immediately understand (hard–soft, loud–noisy, bitter–sweet). It was not unusual to find the two of them in the kitchen sampling sugar, salt, oregano, ground coffee, and deciding on the texture and taste of each. Bea worked on identification of materials: wood, straw, metal, paper, fabric, pottery. Ariel once spent an afternoon listing every item in the living room under each category of material. Later Bea had Ariel look at a wide range of objects and describe them in terms of shape, size, texture, taste, and function.

Interestingly, as Ariel became better able to name objects in her environment and articulate their qualities and functions, she seemed to have more new impressions of them and be able to recall a larger number of these impressions.

SPEECH. Still another skill by which Ariel could be judged as

---

*Nevertheless, in certain areas such as family and social activities her memory was oddly sharp and even today startles us with its unerring accuracy.

different was her speech. I say *skill* intentionally because I still remember the Briarcliff Manor high school kids who scored well on vocabulary tests thanks to their materially and educationally rich home environments, and thus despite weak comprehension scores placed in the highest aptitude percentiles. If Ariel's useful vocabulary could be enlarged and her pronunciation and usage made standard, she too could enjoy the quick approval of a society concerned more with style than substance. She had a large number of usage peculiarities ("What happen if the store is closed," "I want go too") and a number of pronunciation oddities (*th* pronounced as *d* or *f*, consonant inversions). Our tack with each was to stop her while she was talking—trying not to disrupt her flow of thought—and to have her either rephrase or repronounce the problem word correctly and then repeat it before she could go on. All four of us were doing this in all our conversations with her, and after a while some of the mistakes started disappearing. The more persistent problems recurred so frequently that it became unnecessary for us to correct Ariel with the right pronunciation or phrasing—we needed only to interrupt her and she would backtrack and correct herself so as not to waste time and to be able to continue with what she was saying. She didn't seem annoyed with the process because we all subjected her to it, and I guess, poor thing, she had no escape from monitoring. In any case, more and more of the speech problems began to disappear and today she is well on her way toward standard usage and pronunciation.

Ariel's limited vocabulary was another problem. Before we took her abroad her exposure to words had been restricted to the conversation of slow children at school, simple reading material, slight contact with her brothers (who were busy with school and friends), and brief dinnertime conversations during which she was often too intent on eating to listen or participate. But once abroad, she was constantly drawn into conversation, made the object of innumerable parental explanations, and inducted into the boys' circle as a regular playmate. So it was no surprise to find her usable vocabulary expanding. There also seemed to be a correlation between her new awareness of words and her increasing ability to listen. I recall, when Adam was reading his adventure stories to the two children, hearing Ariel twice stop him as he was describing the antics of a little monkey he had named Cautious to ask first what *cautious* meant and then what *pouch* meant. The questions were not meant to interrupt; far from it. She was listening, trying to understand.

You could sense the cracks and squeaks of expansion in her vocabulary each day. She pointed to the horizon and exclaimed, "Look at the mist over the ocean." Or later, "The sky is all hazy." Or when I was describing what it was like to be blind, she said, "If I walked with my eyes closed, I would tumble down the stairs." *Mist, tumble, hazy*—such words would have been unbelievable just a few months before.

PHYSICAL DEXTERITY. Still another set of skills in which Ariel was noticeably deficient centered around physical dexterity. It wasn't that she was born with some irreparable failing in coordination, but rather that the process by which she gained mastery over each separate physical activity seemed to be inordinately protracted.

We had been working on some problems involving manual dexterity, such as tying shoelaces, writing, buttoning, and zipping, long before we left the States and in Spain, where we had more time for Ariel, we simply concentrated more attention on them. But to watch as taskmasters as Ariel attempted to force her unresponsive fingers to do what we willed ("cross the left lace over and under the other, then pull it up") and what she, with her complete and painful concentration, could not manage, time after time after time, brutalized Bea and me and made us realize that even if we succeeded, too much else would have been lost.

We decided that another approach had to be found. Rather than concentrating on separate activities, perhaps we would do better to engage Ariel in a whole new range of manually demanding functions, to loosen up her fingers and build up their separate muscular responses, to give her a sense of general control rather than the all-or-nothing skill we had insisted on her mastering in a single activity.

So Bea began involving her in kitchen and other household tasks: pouring milk, opening packages, beating eggs, stacking dishes, unscrewing caps; she had her fold towels, arrange her bureau drawers, make her bed, and every once in a while without fuss, try buttoning, zipping, or tying her own shoelaces again. The more Ariel did, the more she seemed able to do. Today, she still can't handle a manual can opener or beat the white of an egg until it's stiff, but most other kitchen chores she can handle without help.

We were also concerned with Ariel's general physical dexterity. I've already mentioned how Bea worked to improve her walk and used dance as a vehicle for instilling grace in her movements. Before long Ariel had developed strong extensions, was doing leaps and triplets and could point her toe and balance in an arabesque. She was not only becoming more lithe in movement, she was also building up needed muscles and improving her coordination. Even more important, in promoting her physical competence, she was a participant in countless physical activities undertaken by our family. Ariel wanted neither to be left behind nor, because of her own timidity or ineptness, to be a drag on an active family. So she tried gallantly to keep up with the boys and with us. As a result during the course of the trip she was scaling mountains (on her hands and knees for some time, though later upright, careful, and proud); leaping from rock to rock across running streams; regularly climbing up and down a precipitous drop of two hundred and thirteen treacherous steps to an isolated beach; swimming; fishing; playing soccer, volleyball, baseball.

What we had feared would be a major obstacle to a normal life—her poor physical coordination—we began to see as possibly turning into one of her major strengths. These were nonintellectual activities that Ariel could readily enjoy and, with concentration, perhaps actually excel in—a possibility that has since become reality. Ariel has learned to bicycle, shown continuing growth and ability in dance, readily picked up most of the conventional sports, and become an outstanding swimmer, exhibiting not only speed and endurance but astonishing grace.

HOUSEKEEPING. Finally let me say a few words about housekeeping, since it has played such a significant part in our discussion of Ariel's needs thus far.

I've already indicated how Bea and I saw the conventional woman's life—in its most limited sense—as an attainable and manageable goal for Ariel to work toward, and how we planned to use housekeeping as a central activity through which to improve her manual skills, her basic mental functions, and her sense of identity. To these ends I should like to add one more—the ability to function as a consumer.

Consumerism has assumed an awesome importance in the average woman's life, and it would be essential for Ariel to be at least competent in this area. That's why, when Bea was teaching

Ariel arithmetic and spelling, she created a variety of shopping and housekeeping games as major teaching aids. The emphasis quickly shifted from proficiency in the disciplines of arithmetic and spelling to the everyday usage of household skills. Bea involved Ariel in estimating costs, counting and changing money, anticipating home needs, judging weights and measures, sampling foods. By the end of our stay in La Herradura we were still unable to send Ariel shopping without items listed and prices indicated, but she had started making independent shopping trips for three and four household items, felt increasingly competent in womanly activities, and enjoyed a new sense of responsibility in family activities. And that was all we wanted for her—simply to become confident and competent as a housekeeper-consumer. To reach this end there were no insurmountable obstacles ahead—we'd worry about job training and husband at some future time—and there was real promise of success. Ariel would be well on her way to a life no different from that of millions of other housewives all over the world.

CHARACTER UNDERPINNING

There was still something more we wanted to do for Ariel in this year abroad. When we returned to the States, the type of hothouse learning environment we had provided in La Herradura would no longer be available to her. The boys would again be going to a different school and resuming their old friendships, I'd be back at work, and Bea would be caught up in her own interests. We would, of course, have our family life—hopefully, richer than before—but each of us would again be leading a separate life. Our full attention and the entire atmosphere of intense learning would no longer be available to Ariel.

If her progress was to continue, if everything she would be able to accomplish was not to become simply the curious results of a year's experiment in an otherwise uneventful life, we would have to carefully provide her with the motivation and the character underpinning that would permit her to grow with far less help from us. We would be there to encourage and assist, but she would have to take on responsibility for much of her own progress.

The immediate problem was that she was so poorly motivated. When we first took her abroad, she had literally no interests of her own—not in dolls, playing house, jumping rope. Her pleasures were sleeping, eating, and sitting on the toilet. The one thing that enlivened her some was being with people—particularly strangers who hadn't yet realized her slowness and were initially charmed by her broad smiles and exuberant warmth. And this eagerness to socialize, without the ability to hold her own, made her the ever-present spectator of other people's lives. She was an untiring, usually unwelcome, follower. And apart from this unsatisfied social appetite she showed scant interest in anything. I remember Bea in her frustration with Ariel making a list of all the things she could do with her spare time—make lemonade, practice ballet, write letters, pick flowers—and then trying to get Ariel to follow through on them. As long as Bea was present Ariel would persevere with the activity. But as soon as Bea left, the child would lose interest and stare vacantly ahead waiting for dinner, for the boys to interrupt her, or for drowsiness to overcome the waiting.

Later we looked back at our initial efforts with Ariel and realized that we were attempting to get from her something she had never experienced—a sense of private purpose. We had failed to see that the tasks we suggested were often beyond her own sense of what was possible and that because of past experiences the expectation of failure was so strong that it was discouraging for her to even consider undertaking new tasks.*

We decided that the problem was ours first before it could become Ariel's. We had to provide her with a range of comprehensible activities and establish a sense of pride in her accomplishments before we could look to her for self-motivation. Then perhaps she could start developing interests and a sense of purpose and be willing to accept criticism, to exercise self-discipline, and take on personal responsibility for her continuing education.

So our first job became to shore up her self-esteem. And she did have some delightful qualities. For one, she had a marvelous

---

*This same sense of self-protection may account for much of the poor motivation we hear about in our schools. Many of the youngsters who are so poorly motivated in school show keen interest and persistence in less demanding activities, like hairdressing or home auto repair work, where there are no comparative grades to humiliate them and where they feel they can gain the competence to handle the work. Perhaps if we gave these students a surer sense of success in all areas of the school curriculum—regardless of their comparative standing—much of this fiction about unmotivated children would disappear.

sense of humor. If something funny was suddenly said or remembered, her mouth would turn down, barely containing her hilarity, her eyes would widen with delight, and at the slightest response from anyone she would bubble over with giggling and carry her audience along with her. Bea recalls one time when she and Ariel, sitting side by side at the kitchen table, were going over some spelling words. Bea would say a word and Ariel would write it in a sentence:

> As I came to the word _farmer_ Ariel said aloud as she wrote, "If I know how to spell _farm_ then I know how to spell _farmer_."
> Then I gave the word, _meaner_.
> Next I gave the word _made_.
> Ariel started saying, "If I know how to spell _made_ then I know how to, . . ." and she looked up at me and giggled a little, ". . . how to spell _made_."
> And both she and I burst into a giggling jag.

Another strength was Ariel's memory, which, as I've indicated, on social and family matters was more dependable than any of ours. And we made much of each of these qualities.

We also made much of her smallest achievement (unlocking a bathroom door, cracking open an egg), no matter how insignificant it might seem on someone else's scale, and this added to her continuing sense of progress. Even on some of the larger scales we could see signs of an expanding capability. Imagine her enthusiasm as she identified more constellations than Adam and Seth or her pride when as we all searched the sea she was the first to spot and shout out, "A dolphin, a dolphin!"

But perhaps most important in giving Ariel a clear sense of pride and achievement was her concentrated effort, with Bea's help, in a few specific fields: dancing, buying, matching and modeling clothing, and housekeeping. These were areas in which the boys would offer no competition and areas through which Ariel could become conscious of separate interests and a separate identity.

One day while Ariel was helping Bea make lemonade she said; "When the children go to school does the mother have to do work—like arithmetic?"

"No!" Bea responded, "She doesn't do schoolwork but she does do housework like cleaning and cooking."

"Oh, good," chortled Ariel, "then I can be in the house."

Later that afternoon Ariel used her new information with me: "When you're a mother you don't have to work, you don't have to do arithmetic," she declared.

"Oh! There's some use of arithmetic, when you're a housewife," I warned.

"Only for shopping," she promptly answered, "to buy and get change. But there's no studying."

Ariel obviously was already distinguishing her role from her brothers'. They didn't stay home, but had to go to school, to work and to handle lots of arithmetic. But she was now seeing her role as separate—she no longer had to compete with them.

She began showing a dogged perseverance in the tasks and assignments associated with these separate interests, as if she knew she now had a beachhead and was out to protect it. She hovered around Bea in the kitchen, eager to be used. She asked Bea to write out and go over with her a list of fattening foods and from that time on, ducking her head or blushing with embarrassment, she refused to touch "fatty" or "starchy" dishes, foods she had previously eaten with greedy concentration. She was the first to make her bed and straighten up her room and often volunteered to make all our beds as well. If there was an errand to be run, she would jump at the opportunity and insist that it was part of her job as "mommy's helper."

The same self-discipline was carried over into some of her academic work, particularly as Bea spent long periods of time with her going over assignments to be absolutely sure she understood and could handle the work before turning her loose. Ariel enjoyed these assignments because they were so thoroughly structured that she had only to stay with the task to achieve success. Under these conditions she proved herself responsible and conscientious. She would work for one- and two-hour stretches, tirelessly plodding through addition and subtraction problems.

Bea began having Ariel help in making up these assignments, and before long Ariel was suggesting things she wanted to do or reminding Bea if anything was omitted from a day's work. For a typical day the list of activities might include:

Dance
Shopping game

Letter to Grandma
Read to Mommy.

After three months of working with her in this way, Bea found that Ariel was able to make up her own assignments sometimes for two- and three-day periods. Of course, Bea continued to review what Ariel wanted to do. But Ariel was often pretty much independent in completing her self-assigned schedules. It was startling for us to compare this Ariel, concentrating for long hours on "her" work, with the quiet, unresponsive girl who had started out on this trip.

No doubt the example of a busy father and mother and her industrious brothers, working without supervision on their own tasks, helped show her how and motivated her to work independently—quite different from the situation back in the States in which teachers prodded, threatened, and pushed and the peer group imposed its sense of dislike or disinterest on learning.

But it wasn't all roses. The days were not all carefully planned assignments and assured successes. Even in our idyllic retreat Ariel ran into countless problems and remained the target of a never-ending barrage of correction from the family. She had so many weak areas and we were so eager to continue her progress in each of them that we seemed to be perpetually correcting, reminding, and chiding her. Her speech, her walk, her mannerisms, her work habits—every move she made or thought she expressed—might well become the target of more criticism. It was heartbreaking to hear her say, "I can't do anything right," because we knew if she came to believe this we would be back where we had started with a defeated, apathetic little girl. However, she usually said it with a little pout to indicate things weren't all that bad. She knew she needed criticism if she was to continue her rapid progress, just as we knew she needed her own sense of worth confirmed day by day in order to accept the criticism.

When we corrected Ariel, it was always on the basis of our expectations of her and her special capacity and never on the basis of any norm. The norm was certainly our goal, but our eyes were always on the next step in her progress rather than on an end. And the next step was what was realistic and possible. We were determined to consistently stretch her capacity by setting higher and higher incremental goals, but never goals beyond her reach.

In this way we managed to make considerable progress with her in speech and other personal and social areas where she accepted correction quickly and without resentment. But when it came to school-associated work, her progress was slower. Bea's approach at first had been a methodical step-by-step, drum-it-into-her-head curriculum. But as the emphasis shifted away from academic work to Ariel's special woman's curriculum, the general approach to learning softened, and Bea purposely avoided any critical remark or sign that might suggest to Ariel that she wasn't succeeding in her schoolwork. Her academic work was treated in the same manner as dancing and housekeeping, an ongoing process in which she was experimenting and expanding her abilities, with Bea there to help her steer around problems that cropped up. Bea frequently went over Ariel's work, but when she circled any mistake she did so lightly in pencil so that Ariel could find the error, erase Bea's mark, and correct the mistake herself.

When Ariel misspelled a word, Bea never marked it wrong or corrected the mistake. She simply helped Ariel find and correct her own error. Sounding out the syllables, using similar-sounding words, Bea would work with Ariel to discover the correct spelling. She avoided an either-right-or-wrong attitude, but tried rather to make learning an ongoing process in which more and more things were slowly grasped, understood, and made reusable.

17

SETH—THE

OMNIVOROUS LEARNER

Seth was a child whose appetite for reading matter had turned voracious; whose joy in mathematics had carried him swiftly through multiplication, division, and fractions and into algebraic equations, where he had to be halted for fear of what would happen when he returned to the classroom; whose letters back home ran on for three or more pages crowded with details, complex thoughts and sentence structures, crossouts and bad spelling; whose taste for whimsy and introspection found full expression in a string of original short stories; whose studies of flowers, animals, and insects showed the budding of an exact and inquiring mind; whose chief problem seemed to be in having someone always by his side who could and would answer an endless succession of questions and listen to an interminable stream of comments on everything that Seth felt, saw, heard, thought, or read.

When you have a boy like Seth you always imagine there is more you should be providing—more love, more experiences, more excitement, more involvement, more time. Like a mysterious seedling with a frail little leaf revealed and a fine network of roots spreading underground, you only guess at what it really is and what it can become. Only in this case the seedling happened to be our son, and there was no accidental fall to earth in shade or sunlight, in rich or poor soil. Our little patch of ground was his unalterable lot, our will and means now surrounded and limited him.

No doubt these early years of questioning, of indiscrimate interests and momentary involvements are a child's way of reaching out and positioning himself before sinking roots deep and reaching up, sometimes far beyond the limits of what his parents or his hometown can offer. But it is this period of positioning, of getting ready for a burst of independent life that will thrust branches high in the sky and finally produce a fruit, that makes some parents wince at their neglect and the opportunities lost.

Seth's interests were indiscriminate. Anything new was exciting and would be pursued with fervor. Like most children, he was predisposed to learn. But unlike most, he was self-propelled. He needed little stimulation or prodding. He was the sort of boy the schools say they want; but when they get such a child they inevitably cow him into dull submission or turn him toward sullen defiance. At the age of seven and after only one year of formal classroom work, Seth was already finding the routine and regimentation of the classroom less than exciting. Before he was completely soured on education, something had to be done.

He was in a fill-up stage. Unlike Adam, who welcomed the discovery of strong personal interests and wanted to plunge into a few fields and acquire a sense of competence, perhaps even mastery, and unlike Ariel, who had problems in self-esteem and basic learning habits, Seth was not ready for deep involvement. There was too much to do and see and experience. He was interested in painting, sketching, and handicrafts; he was fascinated by nature as well as textbook science; he would read anything, from the *Herald Tribune* news columns and biographies of Columbus to fairy tales and comic strips; he worked with Adam on his city planning models, with Ariel on her arithmetic assignments, with Bea preparing a table centerpiece; he liked contact sports like soccer, football, hockey, and enjoyed no less activities that were contemplative and more solitary like fishing or hiking. So it is hard to indicate just what Seth's improvised curriculum really was. Perhaps it might best be described as an almost total freedom to pursue his interest or fancy at an age when everything is yet to be discovered.

Seth enthusiastically engaged in a wide variety of activities, each of which could be interrupted, temporarily displaced, or crowded out by new activities but rarely was abandoned. All his interests seemed to remain very much alive ready to catch fire and totally involve him again.

To illustrate the way Seth's interest could flare up and stay brilliant for long periods or be banked and ready to rekindle at any moment, I'll deal in this chapter with only one of his interests —keeping a diary.

SETH'S DIARY

Each morning for an hour or two Seth was nowhere to be seen. Occasionally he was discovered by Adam or Ariel, and there would be a howl of protest and we would all know that Seth had been interrupted again. It was his allotted time for writing up the previous day's experiences in his diary and he hated being distracted from his work. And for him it was work. Not onerous or school-type work, but good, important work. Keeping a record of the family adventures abroad was a major responsibility.

He first started working on this diary in mid-May and continued making daily entries on page after page of looseleaf notebook paper through July. In that short period he wrote more than thirty-six thousand words, cramming about two hundred laboriously hand-printed words on each page. Anyone glancing through these pages could see the way his spelling, vocabulary, punctuation, and grammar skills seemed to lurch and leap ahead. But more tidy and far more significant was the evidence of a growing comfortable relationship with writing as a medium. The entire process of learning to write could be seen telescoped in these pages from the first halting, fragmented, and bare facts of his first entries to the lucid, thoughtful, and keenly observant entries toward the end when we left Spain and before returning to the States spent a few weeks in Russia.

The idea of keeping a diary had started inauspiciously when Bea, seeing that Seth was losing interest in his magazine-picture stories, suggested that he try writing up what was happening to him each day. Adam had tried keeping a diary after our visit to the Anne Frank house, but the further we got from Amsterdam the more burdensome the daily chore became and within a few days he had given it up. Seth, who took on most assignments with alacrity and only after some exposure showed his interest or disinterest, was understandably reluctant to start the diary because he knew of Adam's failure. But, agreeable child that he was, he went ahead anyhow. His first entry was enthusiastically received by Bea, and of course he was pleased. But after reading his second entry, the following day, Bea was so impressed, she said she wanted him to read it aloud that evening to the entire family, and he was goggle eyed. He reported, unabashedly, in his diary:

> While we were eating, I read. It was a very long one. It took me like an hour to read. [More like twenty minutes but that's still a long time for a seven-year-old to hold the attention of four older people without interruption.] They all loved it. It was like Adam reading his adventure to us.

That night Seth came into our bedroom and we talked.

SETH: [Referring to his initial disinclination to keep a diary] Do some people have to be forced and then as soon as they start doing it they like it?
DADDY: Did that happen with you?
SETH: No, but I didn't know what to write. But when I got into it there was so much to write. (Pause) It did happen with me today. I didn't want to do it because of the trouble I had with arithmetic. But as soon as I started I forgot all about arithmetic.
DADDY: Yes, I know.
SETH: (Decisively) I should have started that diary earlier.
DADDY: It would have been nice if we had it earlier. Then we could have had a record of our travels, a family record.
SETH: But I wrote letters and they told all about the things we did. (Considers a second) I could combine the letters and diary all in order.
DADDY: Yes! Having a record of what you see is a good idea. Mommy and I have traveled a lot and we've forgotten so many good things that we saw and did.
SETH: Now when we travel I can keep a diary. Then you'll remember what we saw.

That's how casually the idea of keeping the official record of the Rowland family adventure started. But it was no small matter to Seth from there on in. He now had a serious job. It was not to be busywork or a school-type assignment, he would be fulfilling an important family function.

Often at dinnertime we would have him read his latest entry on what had happened the previous day, and by that time it was far enough away so that his retelling of the images and happenings seemed to take on a story-telling quality, as if he were recounting the lives of a legendary family. We all shared in this sense of witnessing our own lives mythically through Seth's chronicle and he loved his dual role of historian and narrator.

Of course, he had to put up with some critical comments: "Why didn't you tell about? . . ." "You go on and on about one little thing. . . ." "That's not the way it happened. . . ." But Seth wouldn't budge. It was his version of what had happened and that was that.

Food and bedtimes were always prominent features of this private view. If he had eaten "three juicy oranges before lunch" it was a memorable part of his day. In one of his diary entries Seth discussed our hunt for a suitable restaurant and showed his amusement with the antics of adults. He quoted Bea or me three times saying, "No, not here, let's try another one," and you could sense his mounting hunger. When we finally entered a restaurant, the writing almost burst with excitement.

> *I ordered a tunafish sanwich. It was really good. Not too sweet. Not too strong. But just about right. It had a tamatoe on it. It all so had an egg. I tried saving the egg and tamato for last but after the first peice I was temted to take the tamato. I took another bite and ate it and then the egg. It was delisious. When we finished we left for the cafe with the display of cakes.*

And he then detailed the next food adventure. Like all active and growing seven-year-olds he was always a little hungry.

So too with his standardized ending: "Then I soon fell fast asleep"—which for a seven-year-old captured storybook-fashion how each night, after the ritual of bedtime kisses and hugs, of remonstrances to "shush and stop talking and go to bed," of last giggles and promises to be quiet, after finding a cool spot on his pillow, he indeed fell fast and happily asleep.

I once suggested that he drop the ending and I mentioned a number of happenings from the previous day that he might have included in his diary entry. Seth listened with interest and in his next diary entry faithfully recorded the scene:

> *At breakfast I read it out loud. It was very short. Daddy gave me a whole list of things. Then I started re[me]mbering things. But I said to Daddy. You know. Once I finish a diary and read it, I can't add things in the middle of it. Only when I'm writing my diary and remember it.*

Seth was proud of his diary and determined to keep it his version. He once said that when I drove the car or Bea cooked a meal, we didn't like "butinskis." Clearly, now that he had his own family responsibility he wanted the same freedom from being prompted or corrected.

Of course, we had been moving him in this direction for a while. When he had started writing his magazine-picture-based stories, we stopped correcting his mechanical writing errors— spelling, vocabulary, punctuation, and grammar—feeling that exercise in writing would take care of these problems automatically. And all along we had encouraged each of the children to find his own interests and go after them without supervision or daily coaching. So this sudden flare of independence was not really unexpected—perhaps it was overdue. Now that he had found an activity that was distinctly his alone, that was removed from schoolwork and therefore not just practice or make-believe and that actually served a meaningful function for the family, he didn't want anyone tampering with it. Perhaps that's why he guarded his privacy so jealously when writing down his entries.

Each day he would seek out a quiet place: curling up alone on a beach chair in a hidden corner of the deck, sitting hunched over and tense on a rock by the shore, or on a rainy day locking himself in a room determined to get it all down without distraction. Because I too complained unless the house was quiet while I was reading or writing, the children had jokingly printed a sign for my working room that read, "Silence! Master at Work." On one of those rainy days when Seth emerged from his room with the latest entry in his diary complete, he found taped to his door a page from a notebook with Adam's scrawled words, "Little

Master at Work." Seth feigned anger, but obviously was delighted and the paper stayed up for weeks.

There were a good number of peculiarities in his writing that made us want to offer a little coaching: his need to fill up every line and even scrawl in the margins, his factual reportage of events rarely centering on his own feelings or thoughts, and perhaps most annoying his inability to discriminate between routine happenings and uncommon events. He was so intent on making his diary complete that he would report anything he might recall, even his bowel movements:

> *In the middle of lunch I made a B.M. [our family euphemism].*
> *While I made I listened to what mommy was saying to Adam and*
> *Ariel in the otherroom."*

One time he was unable to make his diary entries because we had been traveling for two days. He was so concerned about forgetting a single detail that he broke his own rule and asked me to remind him of what had happened. When I made light of it by saying, "Nothing can be too important if it's forgotten so soon," he started to cry. He didn't want to forget anything. Each day had to be complete otherwise the continuity would be broken, the importance of his special interest diminished. It was as if he feared that the family history, which he had been entrusted with and which he had until now so methodically woven together, would start to unravel.

Typical of this mania for detail was a June 6 diary entry that ran on for more than a thousand words. He described a before-breakfast pajama adventure (they tracked down the home of our stray cat Cautious, hidden on the underside of a cliff and discovered her two kittens, and Seth noted, "We didn't quite get a look at his [the black kitten's] eyes. He was very shy"); their efforts to construct a man-sized tunnel to get to an otherwise inaccessible stretch of coastline; a family incident in which Ariel was discovered lying; an experiment with Adam on light refraction; beginning a new book while Bea and I were in town; a dusk walk with Bea into the hills to visit a cemetery. It was the sort of day "I want never to forget," he wrote.

But even the dull days received his sharp and critical attention:

The day was very boring till lunch. All we did was shop and wait. Stand still and die of thirst in the sun.

He was obviously impressed by his power to arrest time, to catch what had happened and set it down in his book. But he was also delighted that he had so much to say, that he could sustain a writing effort for hours. He had always been fascinated by quantity, and keeping a diary provided all kinds of quantitative achievements: the number of consecutive days he had made entries, the number of details he had been able to include each day, the total number of words he had written thus far. When Bea said he had enough pages written to make a book, he was thrilled.

But the diary had become more than a cumulative total of words and impressions, it was also an instrument Seth could use to bring together the pieces of each day and to make a final statement on each before it slipped irrecoverably away. It was his way of holding on to the separate moments passing so quickly in La Herradura.

He began jotting down little notes to remind himself of what he wanted to write each night. You could see at the top of many diary entries six or seven words such as these recorded after a day's visit to Málaga: "museum, walk, eat restaurant, sugar cane, runes [ruins], winding road."

At one point Bea tried to get him to give up recording every detail of each day. She suggested the idea playfully: "Why don't you pick out the most important things that happen in the day, not every part of the day? Otherwise it will take you all of Tuesday to write about what happened Monday and you'll have nothing to write about on Wednesday except writing about Monday." And Seth did laugh. But then he turned serious: "But I want to tell everything that happened." Meeting resistance Bea quickly backed off: "All right. I was just telling you about another way a diary could be written. This is *your* diary and you should keep it the way you want to."

However, treading gingerly and not overstepping that fine line between counseling and telling, we continued suggesting ideas to him such as making more use of description, writing about books he had read, including more about what he thought and felt. Some of these comments were never picked up. Others gradually found their way into his writings. None were immediately incorporated. He was very conscious of his prerogatives as an independent writer. However, since we never insisted, he was willing to listen and in his own good time use what he thought worthwhile.

For example, Bea's point about eliminating the petty details, though dismissed out of hand by Seth, could be seen gradually taking effect in his writing. Whether it was because Bea had said it or because, like so many of his other writing problems, this one too corrected itself with exercise, Seth stopped piling up random details and began concentrating his attention on just a few prominent happenings each day.

In a long July entry he introduced just three items: floating on a rubber raft, reading a book, and building a sand castle, and each was discussed at length:

> Once in a while a big wave would come over my head and all I would do is flap my hands softly and I would rise like a feather above the water. . . . Then I started reading. I was very excited by the book . . . [four paragraphs of description follow]. We tried building the biggest castle yet.

But there was more involved in his progress than picking up ideas from us. We could hear with each reading an emerging freedom and joy with language and a progressively surer control of what he wanted to say. His sentences were no longer terse, disconnected factual statements. They varied in length and complexity, flowed more logically one into another, seemed richer with reaction, observation, and detail:

> The hot chocolate was hot. I loved to watch the steam curling up into the air.

> On our way back from getting real goats milk straight from the goat we walked home by the dimlight of the moon. Cautious [our pet kitten] was like a little white mouse crawling on the snow in winter. I could hardly see her. All I saw was a moving object moving on the ground slowly but slowly. I drank the milk straight from the goat. Slowly but slowly I got tired. The bottle seemed to waigh 3 times what it should. I slowly got drowsy. I was happy when we got home. I soon fell fast asleep.

He reported in detail of his fear when, riding his float, he was suddenly swept out a little way from shore:

It was very rough. The little drop that used to be there [the shallow beach suddenly deepened] seemed gigantic. When I went on the float and tried to get back it seemed all most inpossible. It was like being stuck on an island or being marooned on an island, not able to get back. I tried jumping over the waves. When I was trieing to get back I felt like I was drowning.

He was also discovering a bit more of himself. I imagine most children his age have no inclination for self-evaluation or introspection. There's simply too much outside to experience and digest first. The facts, the outer life seen and heard, are the memorable things. Of course, eating, sleeping, and the simple daily pleasures are also part of the important happenings. But there's little need for the critical subjective understanding that adults make so much of. It may well be their inability to judge themselves personally that lends to children the ingenuousness we admire so much.

Seth reported on what he and we did as an observer, rarely as an interpreter, of events. Nevertheless, even within these limits it was curious the way the process of writing and expressing himself seemed to accelerate his maturation. One could feel his senses awakening as he reported in greater and greater detail on how things smelled, tasted, looked, felt.

I sat at a chair in mommy's room while the rain sang.

We found a path going to the see of ice [a glacier] and took it. It was gigantic. A man looked like an ant in the tall grass. A boulder bigger than a man looked like a pebble squashed together. We saw rushing streams with snow water.

One could also detect a balanced self-awareness developing as Seth looked openly at his weaknesses and tried to deal with them.

I was very bad at swimming but floating, I could float fine. I tried diving and opening my eyes under water. It was no use. I couldn't do it. So most of the time I was busy floating around. Sometimes I would bump my head but I hardly felt it.

And a persistence:

When daddy saw me swim he thought I realy inproved. I would say to my self "I can do it. I don't want to drown." Tired or not I swam. I stil swam till I reach[ed] the pole.

*How much I love ducking under waves. I used to hate doing that.
I feel like a fish in a pool. I can touch the bottom.*

He could discuss endlessly things he *liked:* not just food,
swimming, and bedtime, but pillow fights, experiments, soccer,
"disgushens," Bible reading, rolling down hills, "snuglin in bed
with daddy and mommy." But little attention was given to complaints. He may have felt there was something mean and unpleasant about such thoughts that would have clashed with his diary's
storybook quality of "everybody lived happily ever after." Or,
being a happy child, he may have simply found it more agreeable
to concentrate on the good things in life rather than whine about
its injustices. There would be time to change the world. For now,
he was thrilled to discover it.

We tried not to interfere with his sense of discovery and
success. We dwelled almost entirely on the good things in his
writing so that keeping a diary remained a consistently enjoyable
experience. For example, rather than chide him for misspelling
big new words in his diary, like *under toe* (undertow), *graduwal*
(gradual), *asoomed* (assumed) *recanized* (recognized), *manyouscrip*
(manuscript), *inclewding* (including), we complimented him on his
burgeoning vocabulary. Later, we found, his misspellings seemed
to clear themselves up as he continued to see these words in his
reading, to listen to them more carefully in our speech, and to
use them again and again in his writing.*

As for his usable written vocabulary, we found it virtually
exploding. What words he heard and understood, and many of
those he read, began to appear in his pages. Of course, a certain
amount of cryptographic skill was required to decipher his spelling licenses, but his work was a far cry from the vapid writing
exercises that resulted from prescribed second-grade vocabulary
lists and simplistic classroom assignments.

There were other benefits, too. The more words Seth used,
the more ready he was to read difficult books, since the unfamiliar
words no longer made the reading unmanageable, yet exposed
him to ever more words in meaningful contexts. Thus the range
of understandable reading matter in a variety of subject areas

---

*After Bea had mentioned that he was accumulating enough pages to make a
book, he began coming to Adam, Bea, and me with words he knew might be
misspelled because, he said, "I don't want to be embarrassed if somebody reads
it."

constantly expanded. History, science, biography, and other subjects were opening up for him.

As in our discussions, we were finding that the block in his understanding was often caused not by subject matter as much as by the big words used by adults, words denoting no more than the complex jargon, rather than the complex thought, of contemporary living. As children become familiar with the full range of words used by adults around them, we've found there are few discussions that are in fact above their understanding—though they may remain outside their areas of interest. The progressive recognition of more and more new words offered our children the means to expand their interests and knowledge of the world. That was why we let Seth spell his newly acquired words any way he wanted to. Our object was to have him see words as building blocks and not obstacles in expressing his thoughts.

We acted similarly with his handwriting. If I had it my way every child would have his first writing experiences with a mechanical gadget like a typewriter, requiring no more effort on his part than identifying and touching a letter on a keyboard to begin the writing process. But as we are presently set up, children have to go through years of calligraphic apprenticeship learning to manually form fifty-two complex individual symbols, then learning to reshape and join the letters, to rapidly increase the pace of writing while preserving legibility. After all this, it's no wonder that most children find it difficult and unpleasant to use such a complex skill for something as simple as expressing oneself.*

So we let Seth print in his clumsy writing style, cross out, erase, do whatever he liked as long as we could still read the words. And again the process proved self-correcting. Over a period of time, his writing speed rapidly increased as, through so much exercise, he gained better control of his pencil. And with speed providing a closer approximation to the rapidly churning thoughts in his mind, there were fewer erasures and changes and more evidence of coherence and purpose.

It had been painful to watch this quick and alert child laboriously form each letter of each word. The whole process was so protracted that he frequently forgot what he wanted next to say. But with the spelling and penmanship roadblocks eliminated, he was able to put his thoughts on paper rapidly and gain a sense of continuity in the writing process. Unlike most children who

*Since our return Seth has been learning to touch type.

learned the mechanics of writing, Seth learned to write what he wanted to say.

His diary not only served to improve his writing skills and order his experiences, but also to reinforce other areas of learning. He recorded with the precision of a scientist the steps he took in dissecting a flower; he told of his impressions visiting a museum and being excited by pop art; he outlined—while describing a sand castle he built—his ideas on planning a sea house; he retold the Bible stories he loved to hear at night:

> *There was a man called Samuewole [Samuel]. He was a young man and he had a sun. The sun soon grew up. The gews [Jews] were now begging the lord to give them a king and the lord was trieing to stop them. He said it was going to be a terrible king that would take away all your servents for his servents, all your land for his land and make you his servents. This did not convince them.*

Even the tales of the family in the days before he was born were resavored as Seth reported them. I remember Bea reminiscing with the children one afternoon about our courtship, how we met, dated, broke off for a while, introduced our parents, planned for our marriage. Seth reported it all, magically distilled through his child's eyes, remembering clearly that, "their parents were sad when they heard that they were not going to have a fancy wetting."

Nevertheless, time moved on. And with it our obligations to finally move on ourselves. On our cross-Europe trip toward Russia Seth often had no opportunity to make entries in his diary. He took notes each day hoping to catch up and managed at first to keep the continuity going by holing up in a hotel room while the rest of us were eating breakfast or staying up a little later at night.

Bea noted:

> *He clutched that book everywhere with him but he was either too excited by what we were seeing or too tired to write.*

Seth's apologies for keeping an erratic diary were charming:

> *I'm sorry but we were to busy running around for our Veasas [visas] and I want to look around. So I fell 4 days behind. So when I couldn't do it I skipped it.*

I'm sorry but I fell for day behind and are skipping three.

I'm sorry. But I fell seven days behind and are skipping 5 days.

And finally he gave up, before the integrity of what he had done unraveled any further.

One evening just before we were due to board our plane back to the United States, Seth was rereading some of his diary entries and magazine-based writings. He suddenly looked up, stared at us, and said reflectively, "Do you know, in a diary all you need is memory. In a book you have to think; it's a challenge. You have an idea, you combine two ideas—it's not only what happens. I haven't put my ideas in my diary."

Bea and I looked at each other and laughed. Seth wanted to know why. But it was one of the few times we held back. It was the one area of his writing that we had had reservations about, the fact that he hadn't used the diary as a sounding board for more of his feelings and ideas. And here was Seth looking critically at his own work and coming to that very conclusion himself.

V.

REBUILDING FAMILY AND

INDIVIDUAL HABITS

Some years ago I spent a few hours with a tenth-grade English class discussing values. The discussion had been triggered by a rash of thefts in the school, but we were shortly engaged in a noisy argument about where each of us picked up his working set of values.

We had the catechism students write the Ten Commandments on the blackboard, and we examined those tenets one by one, first against contemporary adult practices and then against each student's individual beliefs. There was hardly a commandment that didn't sound anachronistic, sentimental, or unsophisticated to most of the students. And even the Sunday churchgoers, after a brief analysis of current mores in business, education, the home, and the media, grew flustered and then silent.

We discussed other sources of values: the church, the community, the nation, the school. The students quickly, almost categorically, dismissed each as equally ineffectual, even laughable. What was left? What were the contemporary determiners of right and wrong? The consensus was that TV and the kids around them kept young people's values up to date.

And the family?

The students' attitude was ambivalent. The family was a museum of outdated customs and beliefs, yet still a place where one might discover some true values. What these values were no one seemed able to define adequately, though most youngsters agreed that they would emphasize the family in bringing up their own children.

They all seemed troubled and embarrassed, once it was brought out, that TV and the peer group were so prominent in their scheme of things. They admitted mocking nationalism, religion, and community responsibility and recognized that many of their classmates were far more influenced by the values of a peer-group leader such as John O'Hagen, the football player, or Jan Hurder, the class swinger. Yet they thought it unfair when I juxtaposed the values of John and Jan against those of Patrick Henry, Jesus Christ, or Martin Luther King.

What struck me most in our discussion was not so much the shoddy base on which many of these teenagers stood but the wistful quality with which they looked to the family—often not their own families, which they dismissed out-of-hand, but some idealized family unit, perhaps the one they would head, where a sense of order with well-defined values would be at work. They might openly scoff at all the old codes, from the Boy Scout oath to the ritual of baptism, but they were still looking for order, something to believe in and trust, something to belong to.

Their developing fascination with communal living or the back-to-Jesus movements was not surprising. These were fashionably radical groups, and joining one fell within the bounds of "in" things being done by peer trend-setters. What was not said was that these groups were among the most austere societies imaginable—stripping participants of personal possessions, limiting their contact with other people, confining their movements, and forcing uniform behavior, code, and ritual on all. Anyone entering such a society would not be looking for individual fulfillment or private values, but for an escape from the moment-to-moment demands of living without values. These young people clearly wanted to lose themselves in an organization in which what was right and what was wrong would be rigidly defined for them.

No less frightening was that other group of young people who confidently believed in nothing and operated from moment to moment, designating certain attitudes or beliefs as "operative" or "inoperative" according to whim or immediate need. This was the Watergate mentality that judged every action simply on the basis of whether it would work, without thought of whether it was right.

FAMILY VALUES

Earlier in this book, I discussed my misgivings about the values of both these groups as well as those of TV and the schools. Although we too believed the family offered the best hope for establishing a value system, we differed in defining what these values should be. And values were at the center of our concept of a total education. We wanted our children to be neither thoughtless joiners nor pleasure-seeking pragmatists. We hoped our family could provide a loose moral structure in which they could feel comfortable making their own decisions without feeling muddled or ill equipped for the responsibility. We wanted them to vigorously maintain their freedom, to decide and act according to the needs of the moment and their own perceptions. But we felt that to exercise this freedom confidently they needed a framework of values that they had lived with, helped affect, and could use as a firm base of reference.

Here are some family values that developed in La Herradura.

LOVE. Our experiment abroad was in part a reaction to the uncertainty and loneliness that characterized so many youngsters back home. We wanted to reshelter our children, to build a world of love and consideration where each could be taken in completely, as he was, without ratings or qualifications—a society where there was no question about being accepted. In La Herradura warmth and tenderness were encouraged, not suppressed, the children were free to express the full range of their emotions without embarrassment or fear of exposure; they could touch and kiss and fight and shout and be completely free with us and each other. In La Herradura there was no need to win love. It was enjoyed as an unquestioned right.

BELONGING. Another unquestioned right was that of belonging. Many confuse this right with a narrower concept, *deserving—*

as a member of the family *deserving* food, shelter, clothing, and a share of the consumable goods.

We had seen too many families where children had little expectation of receiving more than tangible goods from their parents and where parents had no idea what more could be offered. But there was a larger sense of family and what it was to belong to a family, and it was this sense that we set out to establish. We wanted to make the family again a center of love and ritual, of festivities, joint activities, and adventures; a miniature society with a clear, workable code of values that prized each member as an individual and encouraged each in pursuing his own interests. It was in part our antidote to the lonely, self-serving, cynical crowd we had left behind.

LOYALTY. We hoped that each child would assume a protective and loyal attitude toward the other members of the family. One of the curious failures of young people, I believe, is that they feel no obligation to defend their country, community, school, neighbors, even members of their own family, and yet can involve themselves passionately in the causes of South Africans, Vietnamese, Israelis, and the Bangladesh. They are engaged by dream visions of remote causes rather than the grubby work at hand. Bea and I wanted no child radicals marching on distant roads to right remote injustices. There were local injustices enough in their own schools and hometown that first needed righting. We wanted to dramatize their obligation to defend and protect what was their immediate concern, to build loyalties from the ground up before stretching them across oceans. Let the children be true to themselves. Then let them extend this loyalty to the other members of their family. Once this little ship of society was afloat and well, we might hope for some meaningful loyalties and true commitments on a larger scale.

REINFORCEMENT AND ENCOURAGEMENT. Even beyond a sense of loyalty to one another, we hoped they would experience a joy in each other's success, a concern at each other's shortcomings. Whatever happened to one of us affected all of us. Ariel's triumph in learning to swim underwater was a family triumph. Seth's asthmatic attacks and his inability to overexert himself in damp weather was our weakness, and our misty-day activities had to be arranged accordingly. I still remember a family celebration after I had returned the galleys for a book I had written, when Adam proposed a toast for "our new book." It was this identification of the family as an extension of the individual that prodded Seth to help Ariel with her letter writing, that made Adam want to teach Seth advanced math, that made Ariel beam when a professional photographer complimented Adam on some photos he had taken. The family acted as coach, teammates, and cheer-leaders for each member—the family was always on your side.

ESPRIT DE CORPS. We saw our family as a distinct little island with its own rules, its own procedures, its own perspective on the world—and we were proud of it. Some may call this elitism, and well it may be. But Bea and I were not out to stress the common-ality or futility of life. We were out to establish an emotional climate in which children could feel secure and free and happy. If being part of a family that all five of us were proud of, were loyal to, would fight to protect was elitist, so be it. I would cer-tainly expect any good family to take real pride in the successes, large and small, of any member of the family without measuring them against what the neighbors had accomplished. I didn't want an objective view of my family. There was only one Howard-Bea-Adam-Ariel-Seth Rowland family, and there was no other family like it.

We relished our differences with the world and enjoyed our shared songs and dances, our family jokes, our special celebra-tions, the whole range of activities and attitudes that were dis-tinctly Rowland-family ways of thinking and doing things. We were a family apart and each of us was proud to be a member of it.

MUTUAL ENDS. Tying all our family values together was the knowledge that we had stolen ten months from our lives in order to share them fully with one another. I had left my job, Bea had dropped her writing, the children had been wrenched from school. Though five separate individuals, we were moving as a tight little group toward some new life that we would have to construct together. It was clear from the start that such a journey demanded that each of us subordinate some of his private inclina-tions to the general interests of the family. But for the children, the fascinating development of the trip was that though they were intimately involved with a larger order—one that made demands on their time, energy, and loyalties—they found themselves free as never before to learn and discover themselves. The family had its own full life of play and work and adventure that propelled all of us forward. But simultaneously and as a result of the momentum of the family ship, each child's range of inquiry expanded, his private interests deepened, and a set of individual values started building.

INDIVIDUAL VALUES

In Chapter 2 I listed the sorts of values Bea and I intended to bring alive in our trip abroad. What I'd like to do here is provide a little more detail on a few that assumed more importance during our stay in Spain.

A FULLY INTEGRATED LIFE. Psychologists and sociologists have warned us of the personality fragmentation that attends a contemporary life in which husbands and wives play a multiplicity of roles, each separate and distinct in locale, associates, intellectual and emotional climate, dress, cuisine, and code of behavior. The frenzied housewife who acts as mother, lover, chauffeur, hostess, social worker, maid, and office manager is a cliché of commercial TV. And the husband who shifts from businessman to lover, to fraternal club man, to family man, to church deacon is no less stereotyped. What has been given little attention, however, is the effect these familiar adult types have on the children.

My aim is not to condemn adults for performing a variety of functions well or to deny that variety is indeed the spice of life. As a matter of fact, most of us take particular delight in changing costume, visiting a strange town where we are unknown, assuming a new role. It is often not a matter of losing oneself as much as a hope of discovering a new part of oneself. But ultimately what we all want is not a parade of images that we flash to a changing public but an integrated, honest self—perhaps with many facets but with a solid and unified core. Complex, yes! Multicolored, yes! Woven from a variety of yarns, yes! But of one fabric.

In our stay abroad the children saw Bea and me with each other, alone, in a crowd, with friends, arising from bed, eating, sleeping. They saw us housecleaning, playing, writing, teaching, bargaining, adventuring, learning; they saw us arguing, exulting, embracing, teasing, joking, concentrating. We weren't monolithic types with a single overriding function. They saw us whole.

They saw us functioning in a multiplicity of ways that provided no single image but a kaleidoscope of impressions. We were complete, no part of us hidden from view. It was no classroom teacher presenting a classroom teacher's image ("I wonder what she looks like kissing her husband?"); no cop on the corner with only a scowling face and a uniform to identify him ("Does he yell at his own kids too?"); or the minister talking down his nose at you ("Would he use a public bathroom if he had to?").

We wanted the children to see us whole and we wanted them in turn to be able to present their own total, honest, many-faceted, disagreeable-agreeable-sided selves. We wanted them to feel complete and intact with us, with all their beauty and ugliness exposed. So that in all the years to come they would know what it was to be whole and known and accepted. Perhaps then there would be less shame in their lives, less need for pretense and compartmentalized living.

A NEED FOR PRIVACY. It is not just the young, but grown-ups too, who dread being alone. The concern used to be with not having a date, a friend to visit, or a place to go where you were welcome. It wasn't so much that you were alone, but that your aloneness was evidence of social failure. But today the antipathy to being alone has a far more disturbing quality. What is feared is the boredom and implicit waste of being with oneself. All that is important, enriching, and stimulating is out there someplace —at a bowling alley, on TV, downtown, at a hangout, with the crowd. It is as if each of us denies any type of worthy private life. We live outside ourselves. The desperate attempts to reach some kind of shock identity through sex, drugs, or reckless driving are much more in evidence than the quiet reflective attempts to come to terms with our workaday selves.

What has happened to those old images of people content and reflective walking alone in the woods, fishing, enjoying a hobby, reading? Some speak of young people again finding themselves in music or guitar playing. But few youngsters in fact use music as a reflective or private experience. Their music is more like a tribal ritual, so loud and piercing as to blast out any private thoughts, or so soothingly familiar as to make more onerous activities such as reading tolerable. For the young as well as the old, the case for privacy is bleak. We look askance at anyone we see alone, as if we could imagine no reason for finding moments with oneself useful or refreshing.

The fault is not just in attitudes. It is in our fading ability to act alone as individuals. We've all seen the way committees function, how the majority of the members contribute nothing but body heat to the proceedings. Committees seem to have won their popularity by offering large numbers of people benefit from the work of a few. The group is fully credited with the excitement, the ideas, even the hard work of these few, so that the credit can be evenly redistributed to all members who by definition are participants in a group effort. It is a neat system for providing dull, inactive people with a sense of accomplishment.

Perhaps in an adult society we need masses of hangers-on and followers to keep our political parties, our factories, our women's clubs and fraternal organizations going. But we certainly shouldn't encourage that sort of follower's instinct in the education of our children.

Bea and I both felt that the overemphasis in our schools on committee projects and group efforts—which may indeed have useful social ends—had to be counterbalanced by an emphasis on individual contributions and separate efforts. We wanted our children to be given the opportunity to discover their own interests and the limits of their own understanding and talent before being shoved into a group where for any number of reasons they might not react well and thus end up following someone else's lead or turning passive. We wanted to extract from our three children all they were capable of.

That's what we were about in La Herradura, and that's why we saw such great importance in developing a need for privacy in each child. We had done much to strengthen our family life. But we were keenly aware that each of our children must also develop an equally strong and vital private life. If they spent time alone and used this time enthusiastically for their own purposes, it would be our surest indication of their health and stability. And even if they were troubled, there would still be some merit in being alone and being able to puzzle through their own problems. They needed this privacy to build up their own checks and balances, to reflect and make decisions, and to arrive at an appreciation of what they were capable of managing alone and where they needed help. We couldn't do this for them. Growing up required being alone.

It's curious that schools find this need so threatening. Many of them actually have bathroom toilet cubicles installed without locks—even without doors—to deny students even this privacy. Implicit is the question, What might the child do alone with himself? We too asked that question, but with expectation rather than fear. Our children were not only trusted, they were surrounded with opportunities and large chunks of time that were unaccounted for or abandoned to their private interests. They saw us jealously insisting on our own times for privacy and often returning from these solitary periods with something done. And before long they too were welcoming long periods of privacy and emerging from them refreshed and ready to rejoin the family.

CREATIVITY. Most people have special fields in mind when they think of ideas or actions that can be called creative. My use of the word is much looser. I see creative people as those who have a sense of discovery in things they do, people who are curious, probing, and fresh in their approach to life. Creativity was high on our list of values during the family's stay abroad. But it was encouraged in the most humdrum things, not just in poetry, music, and painting. The conventional creative arts were encouraged, of course, but as specialized efforts different from the generally creative approach to life we wanted to foster. We were just as excited when the children produced a distinctive work or a new idea in home decoration (an artful table setting), science (the dissection of a flower), sports (the creation of a water soccer game), or cooking (a new spaghetti sauce) as when they wrote short stories, choreographed, or designed birthday cards.

For us creativity was synonymous with having a will and perception of one's own, a confidence in one's own insights and inspirations. The creative person says, "This is what I see, this is what I can do, this is my own." Everything else is imitation or picking up usable skills, a denial of individuality, a harnessing in. But those sudden moments of personal illumination, of insight, of private vision—these were the affirmations of life we were looking for, the moments when the children might feel uniquely separate and alive.* For despite Robert Frost's injunctions about taking the less-traveled road, it's not always so rough or lonely. There are lots of followers and often they welcome someone up front to brighten their lives a little, to reach out beyond where they are and find out what's there. And even if Frost were right,

---

*Such moments belie the behaviorists' view of man as a complex toy that only needs proper winding to perform as predicted. The creative person is the one who has not been conditioned to view and respond to life predictably. He is the person with the capacity for surprise, for inventiveness, for change because he views life proudly from a vantage point uniquely his own.

at least our children would be alone and rejected because of what they were and not because of what they couldn't become.

A SENSE OF TRADITION. When we left the States, determined to establish a new set of values for the children, we had given no thought to that thing called tradition. In the 1970s the very word smacked of the shtetl mentality of *Fiddler on the Roof* or the exhortations of the DAR to return to founders' principles. Who would have thought that our little renegade group would find tradition creeping into our lives in a Spanish fishing village?

It started inconspicuously. The children, tired of our make-do family odyssey and relieved to settle in La Herradura, obviously welcomed a little more order and continuity in our lives. They would sometimes ask us to repeat an outing or continue an activity that we had all found pleasant—as if they didn't want these rich moments to slip away into the past. Some activities became favorites and were incorporated as periodic features of our life abroad: family walks along the seashore at dusk, climbs to high points in the surrounding mountains, the lighting of candles at dinnertime, the building of fires around which we lazed or told stories at night. Each seemed to add to a sense of stability and continuity in the children's new life so far from home. Once Seth, who had been reading a good number of new books, picked up *Black Beauty,* a story he had read early in our trip; after half an hour of reliving his first moments with the book, he came to Bea, book in hand, bursting with excitement: "I could read this again and again. It's so good. And I love everything that's going to happen."

At the time it struck me as odd that I and many people I respected were spread out so thin trying to read and do and experience as much as possible, and often as a result experiencing so much superficially. And here was Seth, reliving an experience and fully savoring it again, even more intensely because it was now familiar. I wondered whether we might not be wrong to move him on so quickly in pursuit of knowledge and expanding interests, whether there wasn't much to be said for quiet moments with familiar thoughts and objects, when he could enjoy and seek renewed pleasure from what he had or already knew without forever looking toward the horizon. Shouldn't there be room for both? I wondered how we might reinforce such an attitude so that in years to come Seth would not, like his peers, measure everything by its novelty, but find time to reread other

books or return to a favorite hill or community or group of
people and find not just old memories but a familiar excitement
in each return.

Of course, there was more than this one incident with *Black
Beauty* to account for the increasing respect we began paying to
tradition. We were, after all, cut off from our home, friends and
relatives, country, and familiar customs. So whatever we could
hold on to, whatever we could recreate from our pasts, became
favored moments: celebrating national holidays, preparing traditional dishes, retelling old stories.

Perhaps this desire to hold on to the past is best illustrated
by the children's increasingly sentimental attachment to our
home back in Peekskill. It wasn't just the pond, the barn, and the
forest. It was where the family had left "our" books, "our" collections of rocks, "our" handiwork; where rooms and objects silently guarded their memories; where trees they had hung from,
bushes they had planted, birds and squirrels they had fed were
nowhere else to be found. Unlike most American families, we had
lived in one house for much of the children's lives, and they could
conceive of no other house as home. They knew that if we moved,
of all their roots sunk deep in Peekskill, few could be taken with
them. So when we talked while abroad of perhaps selling the
Peekskill house and moving further into the country, the children
were appalled. From three thousand miles away, with all ties
severed except for an occasional copy of *Time* magazine and the
few letters we received from friends and relatives, that house was
their lone anchor, their most solid connection with their past. It
could never leave the family. It was only a question of who would
live in it when they all grew up.*

The same sentimentalization took place in regard to their
national attachments. Like all travelers, we often found ourselves
acting as unwilling representatives of our country rather than just
as people. And without a right wing or moderate group to strike
some balance in the scene, it was often necessary for us—despite
our free-wheeling convictions—to supply a more tempered view
of what was happening in the United States than would have been
the case back home. The harsh stereotypes of America and the

---

*Curiously, when we returned to the States and talked again of selling the Peek-
skill house, it was no longer so disturbing. Returning to their own country, to a
larger circle of family, to familiar foods and customs and language made the
prospect of changing homes far less uprooting.

facile simplifications of what was wrong with America forced us, as simply a matter of fair play, to spend considerable time explaining what was generally known and accepted back home but which, over a distance of thousands of miles, had been reduced to blacks and whites. Being intellectually honest forced us in short to explain, and when our explanations were dismissed, to defend our country. I've seen many young Americans embarrassed by their own discovery that there was so much right, after all, with America. I remember my own surprise when, after being subjected to a long diatribe by a close Swiss friend on the violence, racism, and materialism of the United States, I attacked his Switzerland as a smug little country free of conflict because it had sedulously avoided commitment; as a country that cleverly remained aloof from serious problems in the world and stayed quietly at home exploiting Turks, Greeks, and Italians as cheap labor while righteously denying them any possibility of citizenship.

As never before we felt American. Looking around at the mirthless efficiency of Switzerland, the quiet order of Spain, the dreary tempo of provincial France, we discovered there were many things that were right with America besides our plumbing and our packaged foods. And if America had problems, they were never buried, they were splashed across our front pages and agonized over for the whole world to see.

It was this sudden access of patriotism that most surprised us in our rediscovery of roots and tradition. From our perch in Spain we could still feel the pull of that vast nation and its two hundred million people we had left behind. And its two-hundred-year schism from Europe was our schism as well. Our roots were back there. They were not only back in America, but they went back through America to an even more distant past. As we probed America's past and our own we found a parallel history of Jews. The children found their Jewishness fascinating. They weren't at all interested in dogma or religiosity. But they were proud of their identity with Rabi and Einstein and Oppenheimer, with Schopenhauer and Buber and Marx, with Miller and Ginsberg and Mailer, with Heifetz and Bernstein and Horowitz, with Freud and Dayan—with the bright galaxy of famous Jews. And the idea that they could trace their lineage and the lineage of all these other Jews back through thousands of years, through a common history was the stuff that dreams are made of.

However, in La Herradura the children were immersed in an alien religion, and it was a religion of fun and color, pageantry and ritual. The small village seemed to have an endless succession of religious festivals, patron saint holidays, church services, stately processions, choir practices, weddings, baptisms, and funerals—all with a deeply religious character and rich with ceremony. And the omnipresence and importance of religion contrasted sharply with the neglect of religion in the children's own background.

That was in part why we decided to hold a Passover service. And since we had no priest or rabbi, no church, no proper guidelines (a King James Bible was our only tangible resource) we had to make do, to remember, to recreate. The reading of Exodus (the flight from Egypt) and the lively family discussion that accompanied it initiated one of the favorite family activities in our stay abroad, Bible reading.

These readings usually took place after dinner at the cleared dining room table, two candles used for illumination and the children bunched around Bea. She would read a few lines at a time, explaining what was happening, answering questions, and move along at a quiet, unhurried pace. Frequently issues of ethics or morality were introduced. Was it right for the sons of Jacob to trick the Canaanites into circumcising themselves and then to attack them in their weakened condition? Was it sufficient reason to claim that God promised the land to the Jews when they took other people's land by force? Later Bea sent away for Thomas Mann's trilogy *Joseph and His Brothers,* and as she read it she reported to the children on the events and implications of the lives of Jacob and his sons as Mann saw them. Seth's curiosity was so aroused that he read on his own a text on ancient history—though he complained that the book's treatment of the Middle East was too skimpy to be really enjoyable.

And so traditions closed in on all sides of us: personal memories, family rituals, home ties, national loyalties, religious history. The past with its cycles and traditions was demanding recognition and a prominent place in our new lives. We offered little resistance. We found that these forces of tradition provided the children with a sense of belonging and a surer foundation from which they could extend their interests and test their own values.

RELIABILITY. Reliability, a venerable virtue, is still approved of today, though its primary function seems to be in routine or ceremonial matters. The people we call reliable are those who send birthday cards, pay their bills, and get to work each day on time. The meaning generally goes no deeper. However, the reliability Bea and I had in mind was quite different. It was concerned with the whole range of commitments and small details that make up daily living. It was an attitude we wanted the children to have about giving their word or expressing an intent so that anyone hearing them would have reason and precedent for expecting them to follow through. With it, they would enjoy not just the reputation for keeping their word but more important, a concept of themselves as being fully responsible for their own actions.

Too many people have lost this sense of responsibility. They fall back comfortably on a feeling of helplessness in a complex and unmanageable world and use it as a justification for sloppy planning, half-finished projects, and unkept promises. They talk of interest, involvement, conviction—but when finally it comes to commission they are not to be relied upon.

I'm not suggesting that we hoped our children would keep their word at all costs. We simply wanted them to be intelligent enough about their time and powers and confident enough about their control over the future so that they could make statements about what they believed and what they were going to do, and fully expect to follow through. Certainly, if war or natural disaster or some kind of totally unpredictable event prevented them from fulfilling a commitment, their reliability would not be questioned. But the broken promises and shabby assurances of many people are rarely the result of grand, unforeseen circumstances. More often they result from a change in mood, a waning of interest, or a feeling of boredom with matters that may have warranted a firm pledge only hours before.*

We believed that this erosion of will had to be stopped. Not only did it deenergize people and make their efforts contemptible in their own eyes, but it also accelerated the process of losing control to outside agencies.

*This attitude well may be the outcropping of a deep vein of helplessness felt by many people in the seventies. With so much of our lives controlled by remote and virtually unapproachable forces such as government, big business, and a runaway economy, it would seem naïve to regard consistency or kept promises as significant virtues. Rather the man who accepts change and unpredictability and his own insignificance would appear more in tune with these times. And thus many indeed end up with flaccid wills, chancy commitments, a sometimes yes.

We wanted to restore the children's confidence in the individual's ability to contend with and maneuver against those outside forces, whether the force was a dull school system or a TV-foisted fad, and to see their way clear to their own goals. We wanted them to be able to express an interest and hold to it, to take on a task and complete it, to assume responsibility and fulfill it—and always to do what they could, regardless of unforeseen circumstances or grand forces. These were the sorts of commitments they would be making hourly in countless small matters, and how they followed through on them would determine whether their words or intents could be valued not only by others but by themselves.

To add a little balance to these lofty objectives, let me append another example of how our practices sometimes went askew. Our children had come to know that when they were asked to clean up the grounds or their room, we expected them to be thorough. The message had been driven home a number of times when we actually threw in the trash can one of their favorite belongings left out of its proper place and then made sure it was picked up by the garbage truck. After losing a toy tractor, two balls, and a favorite game to the garbage men, the children came to understand that when we said, "Clean up everything!" we weren't kidding.

However, such stern measures sometimes breed overreactions. Adam once left his flippers overnight on the beach and when he looked for them in the morning they were gone. He came home not just in tears but ashamed and bitter with himself. I assured him that each of us sometimes lost things and that we would simply buy him another pair if the flippers didn't turn up. He was inconsolable. They were prized possessions and he felt he had been unforgivably careless with them. I would have liked nothing more at that time than to buy him a new pair just to make the point that we all err and that mistakes are understandable. However, that same day a village boy came by to say he had found and been using the flippers before learning whose they were. The opportunity to restore some balance to the business of reasonable responsibility passed. A lesson can be driven home too well. Finding a middle ground that encompasses high values and human weakness is no easy matter for a parent or a child.

INDIVIDUALITY. We wanted each child not just to hold but to act upon the conviction that he was unique and had something precious to offer the world. There was no substitute for Adam

Bruce Rowland, for Ariel Robin Rowland, or for Seth Gabriel Rowland. Each brought something special into the world that had to be discovered, developed, and worked with—that could become a personal stronghold of individuality. From this true center could come not just creative sparks but a general confidence in the child's own reasoning and a freedom to express honest emotions. It would prod him to follow his own path whether that meant marching alone or with others who had found the same path.

We didn't want the children to automatically shun groups. However, at the same time, we believed that they had to guard against being absorbed, becoming too much a part of any group by which their private view of the world would be colored, perhaps turned upside down simply because they were eager to belong. We wanted the children's minds to be always open and receptive, and so we mistrusted most groups simply because by their nature most had an interest in continuity and conformity rather than change. With the membership committed to a modus operandi, any major change in a group's ideas or practices could threaten that unity. So if an individual, initially pledged to a group because of a general concurrence of views, later had some new perceptions at variance with the group's, he might easily find himself rebuffed not because he was wrong but because his deviation threatened a precarious juncture of all members around a few common beliefs and interests. The more perceptive and personal his views the more separate he would grow from the group. On the other hand, in a group where the leadership was dynamic and rife with change, the individual would be treated with no less hostility. When the leader proclaimed changes, regardless of the members' continuing convictions, each member would be expected to close ranks behind the new ethic or practice or else have his loyalty questioned—on important issues most groups would make no allowance for individual positions.

The alternative, of course, was to accept the fact that we were essentially alone in this world, to choose our groups according to a temporary concurrence of views or attitudes, and to extend our loyalties and energies only in areas of clear agreement. And where commitments must be more permanent, to be far more rigorous in our selections.

Does this stress on individuality contradict my earlier stress on family and belonging? Values often collide. They are not truths but guidelines. We felt that the family was a safe ground on which to practice belonging. It was a group that could make demands on the individual in specific areas of mutual concern—sometimes even counter to his own immediate interests—and yet warrant his loyalty by continuing to prize his separate opinion, his unique interests. But we also believed it essential that each child should feel strong enough to stand alone, to be able to hold his position in the face of family or group pressure unless he were fairly reasoned out of it. There was no shame in that. If you were wrong, part of being an individual was to recognize it, to feel free to make mistakes and correct them—to accept oneself. We wanted the children to know that each of us was a good and bad mixture. An inseparable amalgam of elements—not a few distinguishing good or bad qualities—made up an individual. We wanted them to know unmistakeably that we accepted them whole, and that that meant accepting every element intact as an integral part of their individuality. We wanted them to accept themselves whole, to understand (and where possible to correct) their weaknesses and to explore their strengths, but to deny nothing.

UNDERSTANDING. Our children, like most, were naturally curious—they wanted to know about most things around them. And since they felt confident in our interest and judgment, they asked questions easily: "How does a refrigerator create cold air?" "When does a farmer use contour plowing?" "Why is there so little crime in rural Spain?"

You could see the fascination in their eyes when a question was satisfactorily answered or when they had a new insight or a sudden sense of comprehension. It was as if a piece of knowledge had leaped out of the darkness, crossed the threshold of their understanding, and suddenly become a usable part of them. They were growing.

Children aren't to be measured once a year in the school nurse's office for accrued pounds and inches. They are creatures of logic, of association, of creative insights. They are not meant to be trained as beasts or insects or efficient machines, performing well at fixed tasks. That's why if people prized man's unique capacity to grow intellectually and emotionally, his capacity to probe and inquire and change—they would insist that each of us earn his humanity.

Bea and I thought it wrong to expect our children to complete a task or take on a responsibility without fully understanding what they were being asked to participate in and why. We didn't want obedient children who responded well to orders. We were planning no armies, no suicide squads, no mass movements. We hoped that a sense of control over their lives would result in an appetite—perhaps even a need—for understanding everything that might affect them.

Of course, there are always contradictions in high-sounding principles. Other values occasionally conflict.

I remember a bitter argument with Adam that resulted from his having disregarded Bea's sudden command to jump into a doorway on a narrow street in Amsterdam when a runaway car careened toward us and nearly ran him down. He insisted that he hadn't heard the car, that Bea hadn't explained, that the driver was at fault—in other words that *his* understanding was properly acted upon. My argument—difficult for Adam to accept because of our indoctrination on his duty to understand—was that there are times when, for people we trust and respect, we do jump, and on command.

The general rule, however, still held. And Adam understood this: *usually* you shouldn't perform as commanded. You owed understanding not only to yourself but to those around you. It was a civic as well as a personal responsibility. The less each of us delegated or assumed that things would be properly worked out, the more we could maintain personal control of our lives and collective control of our institutions. The Ehrlichmans and Haldemans who were supposed to be coping with this complex world for us turned out to need careful watching.

This heavy emphasis on understanding and being responsible for what is happening around you does not mean, of course, that we thought reason and logic should be the driving forces of our children's lives. We were just as intent that they become sensitive to the world of emotion, that they be fully capable of expressing fear and outrage, hurt and exhilaration, peace and wild abandon. Whether it was an emotion expressed or an understanding acted upon, we wanted their responses to be as true to themselves as possible.

HONESTY. One of our chief complaints with Ariel when we first went abroad was her habit of making believe she understood. She would follow what you said with wide-open eyes, smile, and then turn to other business. Unless you had reason to check her understanding, you might never know that she either hadn't been listening or simply couldn't follow what you were saying. The fact that she was a slow child was not the problem. Early in school she had been conditioned to put on an understanding face and had thus been able somehow to blunder through. Many fast adults use the same technique. However, in the adult world the pretense is not simply the result of incomprehension; much of business, friendship, and even family life is based upon false relationships. The winner is not the honest lover, but the successful lovemaker; not the honest merchant, the more convincing one; not the honest parent, the controlled father or the psychologically attuned mother. Honesty has little significance anymore. It's a word used by rural preachers, cutrate stores, and used-car agencies.

But we had nothing to sell the children; we just wanted them to laugh freely when they were pleased, to complain when they were offended or misused, to be themselves. We didn't want them to establish slithery relations with each other or with us. There were far too many men and women already leading gray lives of accommodation or resignation. If my feet stank or my advice was unwanted, I wanted to be told good and loud. Then there would be a chance to change my ways or argue about them. I was not proposing to tell all always. Each of us was obligated to be sensitive to the needs of each situation. And if indeed the conditions called for it—in case of rape, humiliation, physical danger—of course, we had to be ready to lie, cheat, do what was necessary. But I didn't want civility or little niceties to slowly choke all expression of honest feeling among us.

Covering up or prettifying is always harmful to one party and sometimes to both. The dishonest person often resents the need to lie, and some of the resentment may well be directed at the very person he is trying to please or protect by lying. It is far easier to extend our love to those we needn't deceive. And it is this trust that results in fewer excuses, scenes of embarrassment, and disappointments, and that makes a child and a parent comfortable with one another.

It also enables parents to deal effectively with opportunities and problems that are no longer hidden. Bea and I wanted the children to feel free to initiate a discussion or inquire about anything at all and hope to get an open response. It was the way we approached sex, religion, death, bodily functions. We wanted no hidden subject areas, no parts of their lives that they felt shame in exposing. We would not expect them to confess crimes of thought or temptation, but we did expect them to feel they could talk easily about most things they thought or worried about without feeling we would misuse or abuse their confidence. We didn't want the taboo or embarrassing areas of life to pile up unspoken in their minds until like their peers, they were dumb with unarticulated thoughts. If as youngsters they could express their concerns, we felt that later in their lives we might hope they would be able to articulate and cope with the more complex concerns they would be dealing with.

OPENNESS. We wanted the children to be open to not only our knowledge and influence but to what others offered as well. That didn't mean turning them into gullible foils, easy prey in an impersonal world. On the contrary, we felt that by observing and listening to all kinds of people and being exposed to a wide range of thoughts and appetites, the children would be better equipped to deal with the real world. It wasn't innocence to be open to new ideas or willing to accept the other fellow's point of view. It seemed a likely approach to wisdom. There was excitement in moving beyond the chemistry of your own brain, with its eyeball and fingertip witnesses, to this larger arena of alien ideas and unfamiliar impressions. It was an excitement rarely experienced by the single-track people for whom things are either familiar or forbidden; who know what they believe, what they like, and where they're going; and who remain cold or hostile to any new influence. Too many of our young people view all of life through critics' eyes. They look on, cynically detached, picking apart people and ideas and institutions as if there were nothing but sham and deceit and weakness around them and they will not be taken in.

It is an ugly stance, one that puts the entire world in the position of first proving its innocence. We wanted the children rather to see a complete spectrum of good and evil in life and then by choice, simply because it made living more pleasant, to concentrate on the brighter parts of the spectrum. Certainly they would still see ugliness, sloth, and stupidity. But they wouldn't dwell upon these aspects, and their focus would readily shift back to the happier colors in the scheme of things.

I have a sister, Alayne Badian, who has the remarkable gift of bringing out good traits in the most unlikely people. Her approach is simply to expect nothing but the best from each of her many friends. And almost invariably they measure up to her good opinion. It is as if her strong belief evokes, from the infinite possibilities for noble and ignoble acts within each of us, only noble responses. Some of the most despicable people I know have eagerly sought her friendship and tried gallantly to reflect her wholesome image of them in their relations with her—yet to the rest of the world they continue to offer only their usual snarling responses.

Her secret should be shared. It would certainly be more pleasant to think well of people—and perhaps bring out some of their good inclinations—than to walk around in a state of siege for the rest of our lives.

These are a few of the values that the Rowland family emphasized in an effort to counteract what Bea and I believed was wrong with our schools, our families, and our life styles. However, the day-by-day implementation of high-sounding ideas is always the true test of their value. I present more tangible evidence in the next two chapters, where I show how two major themes, sex and death, around which many others have built value systems, played a part in our stay in La Herradura.

18.

SEX

Sex begins the life of each of us and seems to provide much of the momentum that carries us through. To deny sex is not only to deny love and lust, but to delimit living itself. Even the schools have belatedly recognized the need for sex education. But it has taken the pill, drugs, and the youngsters' abandonment of all restraints and taboos to force the schools into some response.

Unfortunately, the response has been token and, as usual, mechanical. It is still the biology teacher's approach to animal reproduction—and a little bit more—translated step by step into *Homo sapiens* reproduction. And since familial, marital, and moral problems, the nature of love, and the interplay of passion and reason have little part in animal reproduction, our current spate of sex-education courses has little reason to move beyond the mechanics of human reproduction.

Perhaps if the course were titled, "The Nature and Responsibilities of Screwing," the teachers would be jolted into understanding what is really wanted. Parents who insist that schools offer sex education are concerned not that their children know that the sperm ascends the uterus to fertilize the human egg, but that they know that when both the boy and the girl neglect to use contraceptives properly abortion or an unwanted baby may result; not that there is a nine-month cycle between conception and birth, but that pregnancy involves discomfort, pain, a narrowing of life's options. What these parents are asking the schools to do —though many of these very people would declare it far beyond their intention—is to rationalize sex and enunciate standards about what is desirable and what is not desirable (rather than the old-fashioned what is permissible and what is not permissible).

An occasional teacher may temper the personal hygiene and biology approach with some discussion of values in relation to sex. But too often, even here, the emphasis is on prevention or containment rather than on a total view, which would include the excitement, the wonder, the beauty of sex—the very things the kids are looking for. When the positive features of sex are denied, a teacher's timid forays into sexual attitudes become boring or quaintly amusing to students. The youngsters are told what not to do and the consequences of disobedience. They hear only a harsh moral or practical tone; the pleasure of sex is dismissed with such homilies as, "Yes, you can enjoy yourself quickly and suffer at leisure."

At La Herradura there was no calculated attempt to inject sex education into our discussions. Sex was all around us, and wherever it was met we tried to deal with it openly. We were available to the children for questions, and our comments never skirted ticklish or taboo areas. If the children were ready to ask questions, we were ready to supply answers.

This didn't mean that when the subject of whorehouses was broached—which it was—we would respond with gratuitous descriptions of fifty positions for copulation and graphic explanations of deviant practices. But it did mean we would try to be honest in dealing with the children's immediate concerns.

The subject of whorehouses did come up in our second evening in Europe as we walked unwittingly through Amsterdam's red-light district on our way to an Indochinese restaurant. Adam and I strolled in front; Bea and the two other children walked behind us. We passed a number of large picture windows that opened not on a room, but on a shallow stage—much like a display window of a store, only furnished to look like a miniature room. Seated in the middle of the window frequently when the curtains were not drawn was a woman reading or musing or crocheting and occasionally staring boldly out at the passersby. The ages of these women, their attire, even their races varied, but it was clear even to Adam that their exposed positions in these windows signified something. He asked me directly whether they were prostitutes, and I said they were. The transformation was instantaneous. His movements quickened; his eyes sparkled. At one point Adam heard Seth, who was obviously delighted with the ladies in the little windows, ask Bea, "Why are the curtains drawn?" Over his shoulder Adam intervened, "Because the ladies are busy."

Adam told me how on a few occasions at summer camp the kids had heard the counselors talking about a whorehouse in town as if it were a place for real adventures. The campers, too, had snickered and joked about whorehouses, but Adam said he doubted whether any of them had actually ever seen one. He stopped at one window, which seemed empty, to look around and was startled—I should say frightened—by the sudden appearance of a middle-aged woman's garishly madeup face whose leer turned to puzzlement at the sight of Adam. After this we moved more rapidly through the area, but Adam's curiosity was now fully roused so that by the time we reached the restaurant he had questioned me thoroughly enough to elicit how some women sold their bodies for money, reasons why women become prostitutes, why men seek out whores, why it is frequently unsatisfying, problems of disease and crime, and social attitudes toward prostitution.

Now this is not the sort of sex education I would recommend to other parents eager to do what the schools are not doing. In any case the locale and the characters might not fall into line so conveniently in each hometown. But I do suggest that when situations dealing with sex arise parents meet their children's questions then and there rather than rely on some formal presentation later on divorced from the immediate event that produced the question.

For example, Mr. and Mrs. W, an American expatriate couple we knew living not far from La Herradura, had taken the initiative of buying a book called *Human Reproduction* for use in educating their eleven- and thirteen-year-old children. We had then given no thought to incorporating sex as a significant part of our own children's education while abroad, though as I've indicated, as sex-related situations arose we were quite willing to discuss them with the children. When Bea saw this book with its handsome illustrations and big readable print, she saw an opportunity to bring together what until then had been random discussion and to stimulate further questions. It would be better, she thought, than the street-corner education she and I had had or the two or three solemn lectures on the facts of sex that progressive parents treat their children to. Bea asked Mrs. W if we could borrow the book. Mrs. W, who was also educating her children herself but with lesson plans and textbooks, said, "I made it one of their reading assignments. But typical of my kids, they read the chapters but then said nothing about it." No doubt she had waited—braced herself—for their questions, but they hadn't come. Not a question, not a comment. She wasn't really surprised. As a matter of fact, she was probably relieved at how painlessly she had been able to do something progressive in educating her children.

Many weeks after this family had left our area, I learned from some of Adam's remarks that Mrs. W's eleven-year-old boy had a strong and healthy interest in anything dealing with sex. It was enlightening for Adam because he and his friends back home were totally wrapped up in football, baseball, and basketball. It seems that while Adam and the boy were swimming, exploring, or talking in their room at night when one slept over at the other's house, they frequently discussed girls and breasts and making love. Adam was puzzled that the boy should show such a keen interest in sex yet be so ignorant of elementary facts. He told me the boy had laughed at the idea of talking to his parents about sex. As for the book his mother had assigned, he had only glanced at the pictures.

We were using the same book. Only in our case we had some discussions on sex already and this text became simply a convenient summary of some of the factual information. Both Adam and Seth, who have an aptitude for science, read through the book—and thoroughly. Seth, throughout his reading, would shout out new discoveries from the patio where he was cuddled up in a deck chair, the book opened wide on his lap. Occasionally, he came running into the kitchen or my room to make a comment such as: "Daddy! Daddy! Did you know that women have two breasts in case they have twins? They can feed two at a time." Big smile. Then suddenly serious again, "If they have three babies they have to use a bottle."

Adam was far more reserved. Bea and I were quick to see that the book might be giving him much information but it was leaving him dissatisfied. The treatment was heat tempered and antiseptic. It was as if his interest had been caught up and then shunted into some long detour, informative yet somehow separate from his original purpose. I felt responsible for having given him the book and thus tacitly having endorsed a dry and almost irrelevant—for his immediate interests—treatment of sex. Adam probably felt that the book—and we, in turn—were trying to cover up the excitement of sex with a thick overlay of facts. Manipulation of this sort we had always shunned, so I felt called upon finally to talk up and explain my own attitude toward sex.

I tried to indicate how right he was in feeling cheated by a biological account, how not just children but adults were forever learning and being stimulated by sex in what they read, in the movies they saw, in songs, painting, fashion, in almost every sphere of life. No, it wasn't to be relegated to a hard-nosed discussion of human reproduction. It was an exciting range of experience to look forward to with all kinds of sensual delights of taste, of touch, of smell, of warmth, of intimacy, of affection. It was a mystery and private discovery for each of us.

Adam listened intently and then almost challenged me: "Then why is everybody so hush-hush about it? Why are teachers and everybody so afraid to talk about it?"

So without looking for an opportunity to spell out all the dos and don'ts society worries about inculcating in the young, there I was with a son demanding fair treatment for the conventional point of view. We talked for a little while more and touched on premarital sex, fears of pregnancy, Victorian morality, and the new attitudes toward sex. But more important, the conversation opened these subjects to many other unguarded questions and discussions throughout our stay in La Herradura.

Ariel too followed these conversations and was quick to pick up terms and meanings. Her real interest in the subject was evidenced by her many questions, often pertinent and surprisingly thoughtful. Once Bea was trying several dresses on Ariel for alteration. They were in the living room, Ariel just clad in underpants as she changed from dress to dress. As Bea was adjusting a skirt on her, she looked up and saw Ariel moving her hands back and forth over her bare chest. Ariel noticed her glance, and when Bea smiled up at her, smiled back broadly. Ariel asked, "What are these things for?" and pointed at her nipples.

"Those are called nipples," Bea said. "When you get older, you form breasts and when you have a baby they hold milk. Then the baby can get milk from the nipples."

"Oh, like Missy," Ariel exclaimed, her eyes shifting to the cat curled up on a chair. (The children liked nothing more than sneaking up to observe Missy nursing her kittens.) Then after a moment, "Then, why do men have nipples? They don't need them for anything?"

Bea faltered. She started to mention vestigial remains but then admitted she really didn't know. Ariel looked very pleased with herself.

We were delighted with this interest because we realized we faced a serious problem in preparing Ariel for puberty. We had observed that because she couldn't win attention like the boys by being quick and verbally alert, she had tended increasingly to establish new relationships by excessive warmth and friendliness. This often took the form of holding hands, touching, and smiling —open signs of affection through which she could quickly win interest. I imagine that, like any handicapped person, Ariel experienced a faster and richer development in functions that were perfectly sound. Her hearing, her visual memory, her taste, all her senses were almost preternaturally acute. Part of this compensating process was also a precocious curiosity about lovemaking and boy-girl relationships.

Typical of Ariel's eagerness to please was an incident in which she had been asked to serve as the patient in a game of doctor. Adam was not present when a friend and his sister—both older than Ariel—suggested the game to her and she eagerly complied. When Bea and I learned later of what had happened, we reacted sharply, not because there was anything wrong with children exploring and playing games of sex but because it suggested the possibility of a pattern developing in which Ariel would become increasingly compliant as she strove to make and hold friends.

Of course, we lectured Ariel about how a little girl should behave when asked to expose herself or play touching games. But it was Adam who received the brunt of my words because he tried to defend his friends. I made it clear that sex play was expected and perfectly wholesome in young boys and girls. However, there was a distinction between playing with children your own age, where you take the normal risks and opportunities that come with your age level, and playing with someone far younger than yourself, someone who is trusting and unwary and of whom you can take advantage with your more mature knowledge of sexual proprieties. In such a case, I pointed out, it wasn't sex play. It was calculated, malicious abuse.

My language was harsh. It was another case in which I was not acting the part of a textbook father but venting my own frustrations and fears in regard to Ariel. Adam simply happened to get in the way. He walked off in silence—no doubt feeling the injustice of guilt by association. Nevertheless, something must have passed between him and his friends because in a few weeks we noticed a distinct change in the boy's and girl's attitude toward Ariel. Their mocking, impatient tone with her was gone, yet they were not overly considerate and polite as if she were a maiden aunt. She was simply included in play as Adam's sister who, if she were a little slow, was otherwise okay and besides, you had to put up with her.

We may have gotten her safely through this situation, but we knew there would be others. The problem was how to break the link between Ariel's desire to win attention and her precocious use of her body.

At the same time we saw the rich opportunities offered by these tendencies. It was right for a person to be hot and alive. D. H. Lawrence had made much of the other, nonrational side of our lives that is given such limited play and yet is often more central to our well-being than all the intellectual and logical processes. And here was Ariel, not rebelling or seeking thrills, but naturally inclined toward this other side. All she needed was a personal code, a set of values that could provide her with the protection necessary to ward off those who wanted to abuse these healthy inclinations. She could turn her heightened sensuousness into a marvelous personal asset. It could lead to immense physical gratification, the true affection she sought, to marriage and a fulfilled life. For many men it is no small matter to find a capable homemaker who is also devoted, warm, and richly sensual. And just as I would want Adam and Seth to find pleasure in their intellectual tendencies without ever diminishing their emotional and sensual lives, so too with Ariel. I hoped she would derive a full measure of satisfaction in sensual matters while still functioning at her maximum in intellectual matters.

And so we were happy when Ariel showed such interest in our discussions of sex. Much of what was said we hoped would give her a sense of well-being and wholesomeness in regard to sex that otherwise could be too easily distorted into forbidden fruit. Simultaneously, we hoped to build the foundation for a system of safeguards that would prevent her from being hurt too easily. We realized that we were only at the beginning in this part of her education and the result could be harmful to her. But it seemed no more harmful at its worst than trying to frighten and humiliate her into shunning sex and denying her the benefits of a natural warmth and sensuousness.

By being open about sex we found that the tendency to giggle and make jokes about organs or screwing practically disappeared—but not completely, thanks to our book, *Human Reproduction.* One morning we heard Seth, running around nude in the house, taunting Ariel with, "I'm going to put my penis in your vagina." We bided our time until evening when a related subject allowed me to easily broaden the discussion to include taboos on sex between parent and child—a subject we had touched on before—and brother and sister and the genetic basis for the taboos. I made no reference to the morning's scene, but the scene and its general overtones were never repeated.

Often the children watched birds and frogs copulate back home so it was no sudden revelation when they observed goats and sheep up close in La Herradura. The difference was in their increasing awareness of sex and in their acceptance of it as part of the natural order of things. One of the distinct advantages of living in the country—and in Spain you are almost always within walking distance of the country—was the ability to live intimately with plant and animal life. The business of obtaining food, providing shelter from the elements, living, and dying are all more visible and present in the countryside. And so too with sex. It was all around the children. Like the seasons, like the day's cycle, like the chatter of birds, copulation was part of the rhythm and order of the earth. I believe the children sensed this more strongly in Spain, and it helped develop in them a quiet acceptance of their bodies and an anticipation of their own natural role in the cycle of birth, copulation, and death.

It wasn't titillation—their curiosity was aroused by the open, beckoning flowers with their gorgeous coloring and intricate structures, the bursting fruits, the scattered and windblown seed; by the swarming insects and the darting, infinitely numbered schools of newly hatched fish that covered vast areas of the shallow waters like thick webs of seaweed. Sex and fertility were everywhere—not smutty or clandestine, but essential and fascinating.

Once Seth, after reading a passage on puberty in *Human Reproduction,* remarked, "Girls can have babies when they're fourteen. Why do they wait?" It was a natural extension of his observations of lovemaking and life generation all around him. It was one of the many questions children must ask stemming from their confusion at trying to reconcile what is good and natural with what is social, legal, and wise. It's a lesson that is never learned, forever confronting adult as well as child, and each time it must be freshly answered. This time it was Seth's father's turn to try to explain the dichotomy in life—the need for balancing passion and reason. Soon Seth would be alone with this problem.

I remember speaking of the drawbacks of having children at an early age, premature marriage, the differences between copulation and love. Throughout my discussion, Seth continued stabbing with questions. Both Adam and Ariel were soon part of the interrogation. A question of Ariel's turned out to be the hardest to answer. She inquired, after I had mentioned birth-control pills, "Does Mommy use them?"

"Yes," I replied.

"Why don't you want to have babies with Mommy?"

I paused—more accurately, I slowly winced—and then paraded a number of conventional arguments against having more children. Bea, fortunately, joined in, too. However, the more thorough and self-justifying our explanations became, the more our children—all three of them—poked and probed at our reasons. Population explosion, family economics, added responsibilities and chores, future limitations and inconvenience, adults' increasing impatience and lack of flexibility were all somehow beside the point. The children were clearly entranced by the idea of touching, fondling, having as their own a baby, and despite all my strong beliefs in planning and reason regarding conception, I couldn't help feeling drawn to their view of the magic and mystery of bringing new life into the world. Curiously, Bea said later she felt the same way. And we all knew there was more, much more to be said on the subject.

19.

DEATH

"Poor Daddy!" Ariel said, with exaggerated feeling. "You're going to die soon."

After a momentary plunge into the dark abyss opening beneath me, I realized Ariel was simply trying out a new emotional pattern, just as another child might try out an impressive four-syllable word in conversation. I was balding and over forty, but I was still healthy. However, in her eagerness to win some praise for a show of feeling, the kind she had seen others express, Ariel had manufactured my imminent death and was now simply aping the words and tone of consolation. She had essayed false sentiments like this before—concerning fatigue, sickness, hunger —unknowingly comic as she imitated the mannerisms used by others. It was nothing more than a developing awareness of how others reacted to situations and her own attempt to match the correct emotional tone to each situation. She was practicing on me.

Of course, I insisted on my health and my expectations of living long enough to give her "at least a hundred more spankings." Then to probe her real feelings I said, "You know someday you'll die too."

But Ariel didn't react to the remark as one might expect. The finality of death was clearly beyond her comprehension. All she could visualize was a ceremony and some temporary inconvenience. "Do they put you under the ground?" she inquired, squinting her eyes and wrinkling her forehead.

"Yes!"

"They cover your face with dirt?"

"All of you."

"Then how do you breathe? Do you hold your breath?"

I imagine most children today are no better equipped than Ariel to deal with death. American parents anxiously guard their children from the subject as well as the presence of death. They view anything related to death, whether it be humans dying, or animals being slaughtered as morbid and thus by inference unwholesome for children. Our view was different. We didn't want death to become an important concern in their lives, but at the same time we knew it shouldn't be ignored or pushed to the side as some remote, incomprehensible, and thus meaningless event.

In La Herradura we found ourselves in the presence of death frequently and without any of the intermediaries that back home were placed between the dead or dying and the living: a fisherman's body washed up on shore, a matador playing with death in the bull ring, animals living and feeding on one another, goatherds slaughtering and skinning goats.

In the States, we buy our meat neatly packaged like cereal or soap, we turn fishing and hunting into play and relegate survival to an abstract concept. But in less developed parts of the world, death is unaffectedly present as part of the everyday business of life. Many families in La Herradura had their own pigs—often housed in a small cubicle in the central room—a few chickens and occasionally some rabbits. These were raised and then slaughtered for food by one of the family.

A shopper entering the marketplace early in the morning would see a few lambs or goats herded along through the narrow stalls; a few minutes later he would see their bloody bodies dragged from behind a stall and hung on a hook to be sold.

Or take a more particular sight, a cat bolting forward, crashing her paw to the ground on a lizard, and then gracefully arching her neck to study the wriggling creature before, with calculation, snipping off half its body. Or the twice daily passage of a large black crow, flying from the forbidding mountains in the east, over our house, to the fertile delta surrounding La Herradura. He would pass, beak open as if parched or insanely hungry, and return a few minutes later with a limp mouse or other small animal held tightly in that once empty beak. Fulfilled, purposeful, black wings flapping loudly above us, he held his dying prey.

The children not only saw death in the natural world, they were able to observe it closely in a human setting as well. On the very day of our arrival as we stood with a real estate agent on a mountain high above and overlooking the town of La Herradura, Ariel pointed out to us a line of men—neatly dressed, some even wearing suits—walking single file and silently up a hill into a mountain dip and out of our sight. From our vantage point we had a panoramic view of sea, mountains, and the little fishing town, and in the vast still spaces open to our view, all specific movement was muted, barely discernible: a few ships ten or twenty miles away inching imperceptibly across the horizon; tiny dots of life barely noted and then lost to sight—dogs, children, perhaps adults—in the white sun-drenched town rising up the hill from the beach; high up in the surrounding mountains flocks of goats made visible only by squinting to bring them into focus; and this line of men—closest to us yet more than a third of a mile away—slowly winding into a sheltering dip in the hills.

The last of the men disappeared over the knoll. Then after a few minutes we noticed them coming out still soundless because of the great distance from us but this time moving irregularly alone or in twos or threes and more rapidly. Before long they had all scattered and disappeared, most heading down toward town, some over the adjoining hills; there was no further movement in the area immediately below us. None of us had seen a casket but, as I told the children, it was probably a burial procession—someone had died in town and the men had taken off from work in the late afternoon to bury him.

A few days later after we had settled in the town, we climbed a neighboring mountain and walked deliberately to its inland side to confirm what I had assumed when we had lost the procession of men walking silently into the hills. Indeed, it was a small graveyard, and the children were fascinated. They peered down noting the raised beehive structures in which the dead were entombed and the more elegant chapels that housed the bodies of wealthier townspeople, and they insisted that we walk through the cemetery itself. The economical beehive arrangement had produced whole walls of dead people and the children closely examined some of the shallow, square glass cases at the exposed ends of most of the entombments. Some contained silver vases, religious articles, photographs of the deceased, personal mementos, and even whiskey, wine, and beer bottles intended, we assumed, either to make the journey more enjoyable or to good naturedly suggest the deceased's earthly tastes. The children were surprised that people were buried aboveground, but more curious to them was the idea of capturing the essence of a man's life in a few mementos. We moved from one glass case to another examining the items displayed and trying to translate the words that were sometimes visible on yellowed photographs or other items within. We all tried to puzzle out the character and life of the dead person from the articles we could see on exhibit. It was pleasant in the graveyard and none of us felt morbid or squeamish during this or subsequent visits to the Almuñécar cemetery and other graveyards.

Bea and I accepted the need for death and wanted the children to find it necessary and proper that everything should die. We wanted our children to become familiar with death rather than have it hidden or hushed up as if it were an embarrassing or perverse happening. Besides, one of our children was already somewhat morbidly concerned about dying.

Ariel's fake emotions about my coming death were little more than echoes of Seth's continuing preoccupation with death. Seth had three uncles and each of them had children with whom he played. When Seth was two years old two of these uncles— both in their early thirties—had died of cancer leaving his cousins fatherless. The previous summer while attending a seminar in California, I was suddenly called back to New York and had to leave my family behind. A few days later I returned with the news that Grandpa Martin, my father, had died. Seth hadn't spent much time with grandpa but enough so that the thought of his being no more made him occasionally speak of missing grandpa and later, more frequently, make references to my dying soon. In Seth's case it wasn't playful or forced. He was really fearful, to the point of tears on a few occasions, that his daddy might also disappear and never come back. He had preconceived my death and its effects on him and was morbidly fixed on the eventuality.

Adam's attitude was far more wholesome. He noted my changed manner after my return from New York, digested some of my acerbic comments about the commercialization of death and the carefully planned elimination of feeling from the ceremony of burial, and was sensitive enough not to intrude his own misgivings about death on top of my raw feelings.

As a result I'm still unsure of his feelings. However, both boys had expressed regret at not being at the funeral and I had to assure them I would have had them there if it hadn't been three thousand miles away. Clearly they felt deprived of some final ritual, to mark the end of their relationship with grandpa. It was as if he had been stolen away behind their backs, a victim of some mysterious adult game where people suddenly disappeared and were never seen again. They had been "spared," but in a more important sense they had been cheated. A body had been shoved underground and the less said the better.

For a number of years I had been assuring Seth of my health while at the same time saying that of course some day I would die, as he would, and his children, and his children's children. But however matter-of-fact or philosophical I was about death, now that my father had died Seth became somehow fixed on the idea of death, mine in particular.

Bea had previously discussed with Seth how long life really was—in an attempt to break into this block Seth had formed on death's imminence. She had spoken of the many years that he would live and how each year was divided into whole seasons: cold snowy winters, hot summers of swimming and playing, the springtimes of lilacs and rabbits and forsythia, and the school days of autumn with new friends and teachers. Each was a new, exciting big block of time and each was made up of a full month of beginning and two long months more before the next season rolled around. And each day contained twenty-four separate hours, each hour sixty minutes. "Look at my watch," Bea said, "and see how long a minute is." And if you thought in terms of seconds, the possibilities for life could not be comprehended, the numbers were so vast. And that was but one year. It was this numerical view of life that Seth finally grasped. Bea had luckily hit on just the right imagery to turn his fear of the future into a wide-open view of life.

The change became evident to me in a conversation Seth and I had on the beach soon after this. From our house we had noticed vast schools of foot-long fish cavorting near the surface of the water not far from the shore. When we climbed down to the beach, we were astonished to see even more numerous schools of sardine-size fish close to the shore; and knee high in the water swimming all around us were millions upon millions of baby sardines, moving rhythmically together in thick, deep, green waves of life. It was a nightmare of fertility. There was almost no water to be seen, just a writhing sea of fish bodies head to tail, one on top of another endlessly. As we moved, the brilliantly green translucent water opened momentarily around our legs only to be engulfed again by a returning deluge of fish. Many had been flung up on the shore during high tide and had died and Seth marveled at both the numbers alive in the water and the numbers dead on the shore.

"Death is very important," I said, as I watched him examining the dead fish. I had wanted to say something clear and intelligible to him, I recall, but somehow it had come out in this awkward generalization. In any case, either my puzzling words or what followed had some effect, because the occasion marked a turning point in Seth's attitude. I spoke of plant seeds, of fish and frogs' eggs, of nature's way of ensuring continuity through vast numbers; I spoke of climate, tides, predator fish, birds, and men; of hunger, disease, and chance as agents of death without which the world would be quickly overwhelmed by one species or another; of how one form of life could not live without destroying other forms of life; how the old grew weak, unable to reproduce, more subject to pain and difficulty; how death was central to the cycles of life and so necessary to relieving the accumulating hardships of age.

During my long soliloquy, Seth said nothing, just stared into space, mouth and eyes wide open, occasionally picking at his nose. And when I paused too long and he realized I had stopped, he simply looked up at me and with eyebrows raised murmured, "Yes, daddy," as if emerging from a dream.

Not long after this conversation by the shore, Seth again spoke of my father, as he was wont to do. There were tears in his eyes. But without any consoling remark or attempt to redirect his thinking on my part, I noticed that this time he seemed to check himself. Then he said reflectively, "But death is very important." I asked why, too much like the rote schoolteacher. And Seth replied, "Because you said so."

"But don't you think it's important?"

"Yes." Long pause. "I suppose when you have to use a cane like grandpa you get tired like a plant that gets old and wrinkled and then freezes in the winter. But then in the springtime other plants all young and green spring up and they have a whole summer to grow. And for a plant a whole summer is a lifetime. It's a long, long time before they die."

20

FATHER AND SON

We followed the path that dropped rapidly to the rocky shoreline below and then stepping and occasionally leaping from boulder to boulder at the water's edge the two of us separately worked our way toward the near end of the mile and a half long beach of La Herradura. The small whitewashed town—building exteriors, rooftops and interiors were spotlessly white—nestled in a mountain crease at the far end of the beach was our destination.

Anyone seeing the tall man casually strolling along the pebbled beach accompanied by the eleven-year-old boy might easily have mistaken the scene for an idyllic vignette of father and son. But for the two of us it was a protracted period of silence, of taking stock, of trying to reforge links.

There had been a series of incidents involving the two of us in the last few days that had brought tears to Adam's eyes. One evening the entire family was star gazing and with the help of a seasonal star chart I was pointing out some of the lesser-known constellations and taking particular care that Ariel and Seth could identify each of them. Adam was both impatient with them and jealous of them and showed it by rudely humming a tune loud enough to make it difficult for the children to hear. I curtly told him to stop, whereupon he decided he wasn't interested in constellations and walked back into the house.

The following day Bea happened to run across an algebraic problem. Knowing that Adam and I had worked together in algebra and flaunting her own privileged feminine ignorance of mathematics, she asked—really challenged—us to come up with the answer. We hadn't talked about algebra in two months but I was confident Adam could quickly solve the problem. We were having dinner, so taking a napkin I wrote down the essential information and then in a manner which I now see was a little too cocky turned to Adam and said, "Here you are. Show 'em how it's done." He must have been shocked by the abruptness of this test of ability. All four of us were looking at him, waiting. Either he froze mentally or he really had not had enough exercise in algebraic problem solving. Whatever the reason, he could not do the problem at the table. He retired to his room and ten minutes later he had still not returned. When I went in to call him back to the table, he burst into tears, and admonished me for not giving him more exercises, for expecting him to learn too fast, for not doing things methodically.

Needless to say there was considerable truth to his accusations and whether I treated the incident intelligently could be disputed. Again, however, let me insist that I have no illusions about handling children properly. I try not to handle them at all. I try to act naturally with all my weaknesses and strengths freely at play and hope to remain a person rather than an idea to my children. So if I had turned toward Adam with pride and confidence, those were my feelings at the moment. I would never have wanted to coddle or brace the boy for some controlled event. For those who have a carefully planned relationship with their children this attitude may seem wrong. But I knew it was right for me because I enjoyed my son and I felt good about him. I looked for no lurking problems before saying what I felt like saying to him. The fact that I could also feel disappointment in him, or anger, or impatience, or any other unfatherly emotion and show it—rather than play the part of some benign, de-emotionalized sage—was part of the pain he suffered in having a flesh and blood father. The tears and their cause helped bring out the rough and dirty spots neither I nor Adam probably really knew of before. At least now we would be better able to balance out our picture of each other and adjust our difficulties.

The last incident before the quiet walk on the beach took place outside the house where Adam was trying to wheedle Seth and Ariel into acting naturally while he adjusted his lens opening and focused-in within three feet of them. There was so much movement and giggling that he was unable to frame and focus fast enough without jiggling the camera. I suggested that he use my tripod and remote plunger so that he could pivot the camera more easily and release the shutter without too much camera jitter.

He set the camera on the tripod, screwed in the cord release and returned to instructing Seth and Ariel, laughing himself at the professional look of all this gadgetry and obviously delighted by the fact that I was witnessing the shooting. He started clowning like a director, making broad movements with his hands, jumping from behind the camera to arrange Seth's position or to push Ariel back. But in one of those quick movements forward he brushed against the camera so that its loosely locked clamp gave and the camera pivoted sharply forward and cracked against the base of the tripod.

I let out a loud "Shit," which because I use it so rarely the children recognized as pure outrage, and quickly stooped to examine the camera and lens. Adam glowered in the background.

"Damn it, you have to be careful. You're lucky it didn't break. You can't clown with a camera." Then noticing how he continued to brood, his head bent down, I added tersely, "It's okay." The other children stared from one of us to the other. I stepped back as if to indicate he was free to continue shooting. But I knew it was unlikely anything more would come from the afternoon. He rose and said huskily, "I don't want to shoot anymore." Then as he started folding up and unscrewing the gear, I walked away.

An hour later I found him in his room. The door was shut, the window shutters closed and he was sprawled out on his bed reading a book. I asked him if he wanted to take a walk. He refused. I suggested more specifically walking all the way to town to get the mail. He still feigned indifference. But I could see that he sensed I was not trying to coddle him—I remember as a boy resenting worse than anything else the sympathy of mother or

brother when I was emotionally hurt, because it invariably resulted in a sudden welling up of self-pity and then an outpouring of
sobs and cries. He saw I was hurt and puzzled by the incident and
so grudgingly he agreed to accompany me.

And so there we were, side by side, exchanging perfunctory
comments on the tide, the condition of the beach, the rich green
in the hills, but mostly just trudging ahead without any words.
Occasionally Adam fell behind to pick up a shell and examine it
or a stone to fling and skim along the water. And he would stay
there, behind, for twenty or thirty yards, then move a little faster,
come abreast of me, and the two of us would continue in silence.

By the time we reached town we were no longer uncomfortable with each other. The presence of other people, of staring
storekeepers and strange children playing on the beach pulled us
ever closer together. And as new common experiences called
forth questions and comments we found ourselves re-establish-
ing a running colloquy of thought and impression. When we
roused up the mailman's wife and she sorted through the mail in
the pantry of her kitchen, we both shared the knowledge that she
didn't know how to spell our "Yankee" name and was only pretending to look through the mail. Adam offered to help her and
she beamed with relief as she handed him the stack of letters.
Outside the two of us laughed—at the woman and all of us—for
our inability to simply say, "I don't know," or, "Could you repeat
that . . .? Spell it . . . help me."

We climbed to the top of the village and then into the fields
above, at each level examining the houses, the gardens, the crops
and the successively broader vistas. From the highest point we
could see a higher border of mountains behind us, and behind
that a still higher and more craggy range and finally surmounting
even this and rising up into the sky like some massively concentrated, white conical cloud, incongruous in this hot orange and
lemon tree climate, a snow-covered peak of the Sierra Nevada.

Our little journey from the house, across the beach and up
the village hill took no more than two hours but within that time
we had shared so much just walking side by side unspeaking, felt
so similarly being American, being New Yorkers and being father
and son, viewed identical scenes and people at the same place
and time, that we could no longer maintain a false separateness.
On the way home there was much talk about city planning, about
burial practices (we had seen another aboveground Spanish

cemetery), about preservation of beaches (a truck and bulldozer had been busily pillaging sand from the beach for a building project). . . . When we returned we found that we had neglected to tell the others where we had gone and they were angry with us. We exchanged glances that were both guilty and playfully conspiratorial. Two days later Adam had the camera out again and he was photographing the children. He had decided to hand-hold the camera . . . at least for then.

VI.

KNOWING THE

WORLD OUTSIDE

21.

A TRIP TO

MANUELO'S HOUSE

One morning we climbed the mountain to the house of Manuelo, a man who did gardening for the large summer villa of a Spanish colonel, and in fascination watched Bacca, his wife, as she made bread: kneading dough; adding the starter saved from the bread making the Sunday before; slapping and patting the dough into loaves; covering the loaves with layer upon layer of blankets, cloths, and more blankets; then peeking under occasionally to watch them rise; and at the right moment shoveling under them one at a time the long wooden board and inserting each loaf into the outdoor stone-stuccoed oven—all while crowing roosters, a beaming, bereted and tattered husband, a donkey, and incongruously, a family of neatly dressed Americans looked on, studied in turn by Manuelo's two young boys, barefoot and in patched, ill-fitting trousers. But a few minutes later the tableau broke up, and Manuelo's boys were back about their chores gathering scraps of wood for the cooking fire that night, loading up the donkey with four basketed urns and walking a good mile to a stream for a day's supply of cooking and drinking water.

In their three-room cottage Manuelo's family had a large, handsome battery-operated Panasonic radio, some upholstered furniture, a king-size matrimonial bed and three cots for the children, a small butane-gas portable heater that threw some warmth on objects within four feet of it, no books or magazines, no decoration except a framed rotogravure portrait of Christ. Their kitchen contained no sink or refrigerator, only a flat two-burner butane-fed stove, open shelves housing a few bowls, pots and pans, some cracked and chipped dishes, and three drinking glasses.

As we walked home Adam tallied the problems: no electricity, no water, no bathroom, no heat. He had, of course, been aware of such living from a distance and from television and reading. But being there in such a house and knowing the people was another matter. He was clearly shocked. The others, still bemused by the bread making and the farm animals, slowly perceived this new and comparative view that Adam was expressing, and before long each was contributing to a catalogue of differences. And behind all these mounting differences was the central question, Why? Why was Manuelo's family so backward? The discussion started that afternoon as we climbed down the mountainside from Manuelo's house and continued off and on all through our stay in La Herradura. It included the cost of bringing electricity to isolated dwellings or communities, the problems of producing electricity, the need for accessible coal or large dams for power, the slow and painful migration of rural populations to cities and industrial centers, the concentration of resources in metropolitan areas, the difficult transition from an agrarian to an industrial economy, the interdependence of one community on another, one area on another, and one nation on other nations. We considered the complex business of changeover that involved raising the level of education; developing a broad base of skilled industrial workers, technicians, executive and management personnel, and professionals; finding massive new capital; building mammoth power facilities; finding new sources of water; breaking up living patterns and values long established; and somehow orchestrating all these activities so they moved ahead together.

Manuelo could not read or write, had no skills other than gardening, no machines or unique tools, no capital or any way of acquiring it, and because of his primitive form of living, no time to learn or try new things. He could barely grow food enough on his poor land for his donkey, his family, and his livestock and made only a few thousand pesetas (a peseta is about one and a half cents) from his sparse olive, almond, and fig trees. And at his farm and household chores and odd jobs and gardening, the man worked seven twelve-hour days each week—without time, even if he were so inclined, to go to church—and had no energy or appetite for new ventures. He was literally trying to live. If there was to be any change in his life or the lives of the millions of other small farmers of Spain or in countless other backward areas of the world, it would have to be introduced from the outside—by government, new industry, or revitalized schools. Even so it was probably too late for Manuelo. His hopes, his ability to adjust and change, his life patterns had tempered and hardened. Only his children could escape and, as Adam noted, after seven or eight years in one of these local villages, it would be hard for a child to ever catch up.

The more we discussed Manuelo's children and their prospects—how long they would go to school, what they were learning, how they spent their spare time, what hopes they nursed for their futures, what experiences they would have as they grew up, who and why they might marry, where they would live—the more we made up stories and surmised about their future, the more impressed we all were with the idea of propinquity, with the accident of birth, and selfishly and somewhat guiltily with our own incredible good fortune.

The visit to Manuelo's house had broadned out to an awareness of the multilayered differences in life patterns, differences over which each man had little control. It was a theme that recurred constantly not only during our long stay at La Herradura as the children probed the limits of their independence and individuality, but also in our later travels through Austria, Hungary, Russia, Finland, and Norway. They learned how man's character and potential were inextricably tied to the character and culture of his immediate environment.

22

THE WORKING

WORLD

Ideas, like the vocabulary children are exposed to, should be a little beyond their grasp, perhaps even far beyond their grasp to hurry them along. A baby learning to speak acquires a massive number of new words in a short time and obviously encounters and assimilates new concepts and ideas at an equally impressive rate. Yet a few years later the same child is immured in a classroom where for ten months he is allotted fifty or one hundred new words and made to worry over a few new concepts or skills —and we say he is being educated. It may well be that something is learned, but a good deal is also lost by keeping a child in a schoolhouse for twelve or more years and cutting him off from his parents, the adult world, and its institutions. The real world of grown-ups working, talking, planning; of local politics, business, professional life; of hospitals and road repair; of trades and crafts and employment conditions; of motherhood, fraternal clubs, and divorce courts is a world untouched in most curricula.

Our idea was to open this outer world to the children, to

expose them to as many people and ways of life as possible so that
when it came time to think about what to do with their lives they
would have more than TV images to base their judgments on.
Despite brave talk of new values and life in a leisure society,
most people today find that the bulk of their time, energy, and
hopes for the future are still involved with their occupations. Yet
the typical young person emerging from school has barely heard
of, much less explored, the many skills and fields open to him
before he falls into this or that trade or profession, often irreversibly, for the rest of his life. A random comment by a teacher, a
job opening in the neighborhood, or a friend's remarks about a
college is enough to launch a career. But with such a large chunk
of contemporary living still centered around work, it seems irresponsible to ignore its importance, to fail to ensure that each
youngster is given a chance to find a thoroughly absorbing occu-
pation rather than drifting into a job that is something to be
suffered through while fighting for more profit or reduced working hours. There should be more to a man's lifework than a
vacation allotment, a pension plan, and provision for coffee
breaks. If youngsters were familiar with a wide range of careers,
they could discover their own interests and talents and have a
more logical basis for deciding how to spend their forty-seven
working years.

Implementing such an idea would be most feasible in our
large cities, where the whole gamut of adult occupations—factory, office, service, paraprofessional, and professional—is present. It might even be worthwhile expanding the apprenticeship
concept so that elementary level children could be around all
kinds of working adults, who are performing tasks that are palpa-
bly real and meaningful in the community. That would certainly
be a healthy change from schoolrooms and schoolteachers, with
their graded and methodically ordered academic exercises. It was
in part this sort of change we were looking for in taking the
children out of school and placing them in an environment where
they would have frequent contact with the wide range of adults
found outside of school buildings.

Since we were in Europe and in a remote coastal town, the
range of pertinent jobs—pertinent, that is, to children who would
be returning to a highly industrialized and sophisticated society
—was not the same as it would have been had we spent a year
exploring the business, craft, technical, and professional occupa-

tions of New York City. However, if we had tried that the children would have been picked up for truancy. Besides, the benefits of being in an alien land were no less exciting. The children not only saw a variety of people at work, they saw them approaching their work with values and attitudes often quite different from those held by Americans back home. It's true Adam actually spent time with a professional photographer developing film, with a draftsman in an architect's office discussing techniques and renderings, and with a German expatriate TV writer listening to his script ideas and tales of Nazi Germany. And these meetings tied in with Adam's newly discovered interests. But more significant than knowledge in specific fields or subjects, the children's easy contacts with people afforded them fresh insights into the way adults —Spanish, foreign, American—lived and thought.

Among the people who wove in and out of their days were a fisherman, deaf and mute, but nonetheless exuberant, who yowled and bellowed his triumphant return each night from a day at sea and then over an open beach fire steamed a pot of mussels and shared them with passersby; laborers and stonemasons and carpenters and plumbers, people with specific skills and trades whom the children often watched and talked to, who sang, laughed, shouted and argued on the job, then sat silently eating lunches brought hot at noon by their black-garbed wives or mothers who sat by wordlessly watching them eat; a real estate developer who took us on a picnic to the top of a rugged, unspoiled coastal mountain with a commanding view of the Mediterranean and proudly explained, to Adam's barely concealed disgust, how he was going to cover the entire mountain with concentric lines of houses starting from the top where we sat and working down to the very shoreline; a church restoration specialist who stopped work for a good part of an afternoon to talk to the children and answer questions about his work, his training, his use of materials, his need for research; the shoemaker, the butcher, the fishmonger—skilled, knowledgeable tradesmen with a sense of importance in their work, with wives and families whom we often knew—not the faceless interchangeable supermarket and department store clerks of America; the local priest, the mayor, the bureaucratic government officials, the carabinero who patrolled our area each night, the postman's wife, the gardener who had volunteered to fight with Hitler's armies in Russia. These were but a few of the local people—in addition to a whole galaxy of other Europeans—that the children came to know. But it was more than a mix of occupations, people, and values that the children experienced. They had a rare insight— not a tour bus view—into a totally different way of life.

EXPOSURE TO

LIFE STYLES

I mentioned earlier that shortly after we first entered Spain on our way south to La Herradura, a torrential rain had washed out sections of the cliffside road and we were forced to spend two nights at a small family-run hotel in the fishing village of La Rápita. The children were entranced by the strange people and surroundings: men working together down at their boats mending their nets, joking and laughing, surrounded by teasing, shouting, playful children in ragged clothes; hunched-over old women in black, resting in doorways; wives briskly sweeping the narrow cobblestone streets that wound sinuously up the hill between whitewashed walls. As they walked through the streets the children were surprised at one doorway by a pungent animal odor and then the presence of an immense pig, grunting and snuffling about in a dank area littered with straw in the middle of the large family room. At another they discovered a burst of sunlight and air flooding a little room from a bright and spacious inner courtyard where hens and a donkey, sun and clothes and sharp shadows, the sound of running water together quickly jumbled their senses and made them want to stop and order the scene. But they passed on anxious not to cross that delicate boundary between strolling down a street and eavesdropping. No matter how inconspicuous their dress, manner, behavior, they were acutely aware they were strangers. They even lacked the language facility to start the long process of winning some identity as individuals. They remained what they after all were—faceless American children passing through.

Even the hotel seemed mysterious and exciting to them. Except for such a calamity it would hardly have had more than one or two overnight guests at this time of year. But here were the Rowlands and at least twelve other carloads of foreigners wanting coffee, mixed drinks, soft drinks, meals, rooms, phone services. It was more crowded than at peak season, yet there was only one waiter and a cook instead of the normal staff of eight. The young owner of the hotel was so distressed at his inability to supply his usual services that he seemed embarrassed at the windfall in money he was enjoying as a result of the washout. But it was the intense and beautiful woman in black, always on her hands and knees scrubbing and washing the immaculate lobby and dining room floors, who intrigued Bea and me—and as a result the children too—particularly after we learned that she was the hotel keeper's wife. A slim, black-haired peasant girl with remarkable natural dignity, she had obviously been overwhelmed by the sudden influx of people and could think of nothing better to do than put on an old dress, get a pail with water and a rag, and barefoot, drop to her hands and knees—much like Fellini's dream wish in the film *8½* where he visualizes his wife on hands and knees washing the floors amid all his guests. Early in the morning, late at night, and during meal times, for the two days we were there, we saw her washing the lobby or the dining room floor.

Later as we continued our journey south we talked about this brief glimpse into village life, the incredible poverty, the dirt and squalor, the lack of opportunity for children. But we also talked about some of the subtler benefits: the intense private lives of even the simplest people, the four-generation family, the rich and personal sense of belonging in such a community, the natural warmth and playfulness of adults and children. And we contrasted this with our own society back in America, where the massive outpouring of facts, the tremendous speed that attended all activities had produced a nation of people who lacked depth and continuity, who were impatient with detail, who dutifully rather than naturally involved themselves in community life.

It was all very romantic at the time for people passing through. But when we settled in La Herradura and the children were able to observe at length what it was like to be isolated in a remote community, the attraction of simple living faded rapidly. They were clearly unprepared for the full impact of village life: the sewage running down the gutters of the street, the four generations of family housed in a single room along with hens and pig; the tiny schoolroom without desks or even books; the children over twelve, little grown-ups working long hours, haggard, weary, and worldly-wise before they were fifteen; and the universal fear of the carabinero—the one man who was never mocked in La Herradura, who was always treated with deference.

Ten minutes into Spain we had been stopped by motorcycled carabineros in white helmets and black leather jackets. While one waited fifty feet behind, the other politely saluted and handed me a paper printed in three languages stating that I was speeding and that I could immediately pay the arresting officer a fine at a discount if it were cash. When I asked what was the alternative, he replied matter-of-factly that I could go with him to the nearest town and spend the night in jail until the town clerk was available. I laughed and paid the fine, but later in La Herradura we learned that that was indeed the custom, that he didn't pocket the money, and that it was no laughing matter.

We heard only rumors of the punishment the carabineros meted out, but one could feel their presence everywhere. People would talk loudly about girls, church, food, death, marriage, but when it came to politics voices dropped to whispers. If a stranger was present even the whispers stopped. We were told by a proud visiting official from Madrid that unlike the situation in our American towns and cities we would find no crime in La Herradura. But even the children realized that the price that had been paid for safe streets was high.

We would see the carabineros in the most unexpected places —walking through vast stretches of barren countryside, sitting quietly in a cove down by the sea, late at night on a deserted mountain road quietly smoking and talking and staring carefully at each passing car. Once, with the courage of strangers, we walked to the carabinero headquarters located at the end of a cattle path in the battered ruins of a Moorish tower. Inside we were startled to find the offices brilliantly lit, spic and span, and superbly fitted out with the most modern equipment; the captain and his men handsomely groomed and immaculate in resplendent uniforms. They remained courteous and proper during our stay, but we all suddenly knew that no one voluntarily visited carabinero headquarters.

These new impressions at first overwhelmed the romantic picture we had created back in La Rápita. What the children saw clearly was a dirty, impoverished, fearful community. The other picture might be true too, and perhaps television would eventually alert the townspeople to what was happening on the other side of the mountain, but at this moment Adam, Seth, and Ariel Rowland were having none of the romance.

But time passed by and as our daily needs had to be met by trips to town—as the streets so strange and fetid became the streets we walked each day to check our mail, to buy some rope, to pick up a loaf of bread, and see the fish catch; as the little boys so haggard and grown up at work ate, showered, and played soccer with the children on the beach; as the carabineros waved to us each night when taking up positions near our house—some of the stranger's detachment wore off and the life of the village became more and more our life. When we returned from a four-day trip to Málaga, we were greeted by children, storekeepers, and even the dour postmaster's wife with inquiries about where we had been and what we had done, as if we had disturbed the normal rhythms of the community by our absence.

And we ourselves felt the subtle pull of these rhythms, the relentless slow beat of the town contending with our own family rhythm. We had plans and ideas and old habits about eating, working, playing, but all the while there was the cycle of town life and activity pulling at us: the fishermen silently putting out to sea before dawn; the church bells and the marketplace coming to life; the baker's wife selling loaves of fresh morning bread to a steady stream of babbling children and women; the workmen, the farmers, the storekeepers busy at their day's work; the fishermen returning, pulling up their boats, sorting their fish, spreading their nets; the long noonday lull; the hot tedious afternoons; and then at quitting time the slow convergence of men walking toward town, a few dallying behind to pick up a pole and bait, slip down to a special rock at the sea's edge and let the line drop; then the calls to supper, the same call heard all over the bay as men and children were summoned from the streets, the beach, the fields to sit down as a family to supper.

But more than anything, it was the peasant family primitively housed in a windowless one-room cottage on the mountainside across the valley from us that came to represent the mysterious other life—so totally foreign to our own—that we had sensed back in La Rápita. Though we lived for many months as closest neighbors sharing a valley, a stream, and a shore area, we never really talked.

They were a family of four. Occasionally, we met the mother, shrouded in black, bent and steel-faced, filling her large earthen jugs with water from the stream, but as we passed she would only nod her head and return to her work. The daughter, barefoot and thirteen years old, seemed constantly in motion, running, picking herbs, playing with the animals; yet if she chanced to pass one of us on a path or down at the shore her eyes sank to the ground and she hurried by without a glance or word. Even the teenage brother, who sometimes used our fields and hills to graze his goats, was unapproachable. Our children watched with delight as his billy goats bucked and reared and the kids leaped gracefully from ledge to ledge, as he effortlessly herded his flock from place to place, but they avoided coming too near. Once earlier when Seth and Ariel gingerly approached one of the boy's more docile goats to pet it and Adam tried to address the boy directly, the young Spaniard had quickly gathered his flock and left the area. Another time, when I saw the boy seated on a hillside above our house surrounded by his flock, I approached him myself. Though at first he was pleasant and responsive, when I asked if I might buy one of his little goats for the children, his manner changed. I said we would treat the goat kindly and perhaps even return it to him before we left. He shook his head and said it would be lonely and die without its mother, and besides once a kid had left the herd the other goats would never accept him back. He stood up, whistled shrilly to force the herd's attention, deftly threw some pebbles at a few strays that quickly scampered back toward him, and then started walking away. I walked by his side a few steps, the children following behind, and asked if he would ask his father if he were willing to sell a goat. He matter-of-factly informed me it was his herd. When I asked about a price anyhow, he said firmly eight hundred pesetas, a price he knew I knew was five times the price of a kid skinned and butchered in the market-place. After that he didn't come near our house for months though we could see him each day diligently herding his goats on the surrounding mountainsides.

No doubt it was the physical proximity combined with their clear unwillingness to let us share in their lives that made this family all the more fascinating to us. The townspeople were slowly becoming used to strangers, making adjustments to our special needs, but these people were still cut off, still very sepa-rate in the pattern of their lives. We would hear them singing, the daughter's voice bright and bell-like as she moved along a hillside picking herbs, the mother's doleful and Moorish as she hung the family's clothes after pounding them clean on the rocks by the stream. We could hear the laughing banter of brother and sister, their shouts of delight playing with the animals or teasing their mother, who was busy building the outdoor fire, then the muted conversation that always followed the return home of the father plodding along beside his donkey, and when it was dark the quiet voices of the family barely seen, gathered around the fire, eating their supper and finally the unbroken stillness as the fire slowly burned out. But before dawn the hillside was alive again, the goats let out, the chickens scurrying about, the family moving in and out of the windowless house. We could see the boy heading out with his flock, the daughter skipping along a path on some errand, the father with his donkey carefully plowing another ter-raced sliver on the vertical, rock-strewn mountainside running down from the house. And as each season came along, we could watch father and son together building up retaining walls, plant-ing and harvesting, picking the sparse olives or figs or almonds in their meager groves.

We came to know them from afar, not consciously, not as distant eavesdroppers, but simply because like the hills, the stream, the crow that each day flew past our house in search of food, they were there. Adam, summing up his impressions in a letter to his aunt, spoke of "the beauty, happiness and simplicity of family life on a small Spanish farm."

Nevertheless, there were still the old arguments against sim-ple living, which were reinforced each day as we saw more of the townspeople's lives. There was no denying that they led lives of ignorance and prejudice, that their children were cut off from opportunity, that there was little hope for change or novelty or personal growth in their isolated society. I recall one discussion in which Adam spoke of how some of the positive features of our society could be introduced here. All of us were soon speculating on the momentum of change that probably would occur once it was started, of how hotels would be built, roads widened, and eventually values, tastes, customs, everything, homogenized into a dull sameness.

We could already see the homogenization process at work. A new hotel was being built on the beach, developers were buying up mountainsides and planning modern housing developments, and foreigners were now arriving not just for a fleeting glimpse of a distant fishing village as they passed on the high mountain road heading for Granada or Torremolinos but to speculate in real estate, to buy a summer villa, to frolic for a few days in this sun-drenched backward setting.

Jetted from their familiar environments, the newcomers were visible in sharp focus against the hot, dry, unchanging landscape: a young Belgian airline pilot grown flabby, alcoholic, and slack, who had given up his career for an easy life on the Costa del Sol with a wealthy French woman rumored to have been a Nazi collaborator; an American college student and his girl turned hippie for a minimum-cost tour of Europe, scrounging food and a few pesetas indiscriminately from passing tourists and even the wretchedly poor townspeople; two thick-set, prosperous Germans spending an entire day at Almuñécar's Hotel Portamar polishing their Mercedes-Benz until every other car in town was put to shame. There was an American bank clerk who after five years of saving had quit his job, announced his intention of writing a novel, and flown off to Spain with a friend. But after nine months of sunning and getting his thoughts together, he found he still hadn't quite outlined what he wanted to write, and the friend, sleeping a good part of each day, would emerge at dusk to sit on the patio and stare out at sea, would open American cans for meals and if a guest stayed for dinner, invariably produced coq au vin as the main dish. Other visitors included Monsieur X, the French-Canadian builder who had his children each day play in front of the chief hotel in town in order to strike up friendships with touring families and then himself followed up these contacts with a hard sell for one of his apartments; the Belgian TV repairman who with his wife had come to Spain to start a new life, had invested almost all his savings in one of these apartments, and now wandered through town each day wondering why he had chosen Almuñécar to settle down in; Herr Kombosch, a handsome young German who had left his homeland to discover a better life, who methodically bought up all the land along a stretch of mountain highway, and who was—by denying the peasant farmers water and electricity, and if they were too recalcitrant even access to the highway—forcing them to sell to him at hard-driven prices their spectacular sea-front farms.

One day we hiked to the top of the coastal mountain range in order to catch a glimpse of the back country. We worked our way up past farms and grazing goats. The terrain became more barren and rugged as we ascended higher and higher. Looking back occasionally, we each had a feeling of exhilaration and escape as the ships, the houses, and farmed land below grew smaller and smaller. The last of the olive trees were left far behind, and before us lay only rock and little dry patches of sand, inhospitable to any form of life. We passed gorges and sheer drops but kept ascending until we reached the very top. Then we took our first look at the other side, the back country. Below us, set in a sheltered mountain valley, was a massive, thriving, modern development of look-alike summer villas for foreigners, one on top of the other, no different from a suburb of Los Angeles. It was not hard to understand why the peasant family across the valley from us remained wary of strangers.

Time and again we could see instances of cultural clash, and with each collision we could sense a further breaking down of normal village patterns, a wearing away of conventional values, a teasing of appetites, a rising discontent.

I recall one week in May when a jet-set French group suddenly burst on the scene and rented a villa within sight of our house. There were two men in their late twenties, six young women, and a vigorous, fun-loving middle-aged man who seemed to be the focal point of the group. From the moment of their arrival, their existence was all noise and drinking, bikinis, bare breasts, wild antics, and laughter. Some local laborers building a villa nearby stared at first, then tentatively shouted friendly remarks to the visitors. The workers seemed surprised at first to be answered in kind. Emboldened, they moved a little closer to view the strangers' antics, and over the next few days attempted to engage them in conversations and then began making suggestive remarks. When finally they were pointedly ignored, the laborers turned derisive and taunting. During this period the French group became more and more restrained, then gave up their outdoor fun making altogether, and finally, quietly packed up and left.

With children it was no different. When two visiting American children clambering along the rocks by the shore saw a group of barefoot Spanish children in tattered clothes approaching, they veered off to avoid them. The Spanish children followed them and tried to engage them in conversation. But the American boy, who knew no Spanish, tried to push by without even a smile or a sign of recognition. The local children turned surly immediately and blocked his passage. Fortunately, our children were not far away. Adam came up, spoke a few friendly words in Spanish and, seeing that the young Spaniards were carrying a basket of mussels, asked if they knew of a special bed he had discovered in a sheltered cove. Before long the whole pack of children, Spanish and American, were working together at the cove searching out new mussel beds. The afternoon turned into an exciting one for all. An ugly scene was avoided not just because Adam knew both languages, but because he was at home and familiar in the local environment and shared the local children's interests. He was no stranger.

Later that evening, alone with the same American children Adam talked easily about school, baseball, and pizzas with a similar sense of familiarity and enthusiasm.

Adam, and to some extent Seth and Ariel as well, was becoming free of a single value system or life style. Of course, he had a long way to go. But he now clearly had a taste of alternatives. He could start enjoying some of the independence and sense of personal judgment that comes from knowing there are many ways to approach life.

VII.

LESSONS TO

BE LEARNED

John Dewey—who maintained that the role of education was constantly to provide situations that intersect a student's needs and thus assist and to an extent direct the growth of the child— placed major emphasis on discovering the interests of individual students. He indicated that a teacher should strive to understand a child as a parent might. His assumption was that only professionals were equipped to teach, even though they lacked that essential knowledge of each child needed to truly individualize the learning process.

The idea that most parents were capable of educating their children would have been romantic nonsense in the 1920s, but today the idea is not at all farfetched. Millions of parents who are college graduates often have more education and richer experience in the world than does the standard teachers' college product. Even more important, these parents are by Dewey's standards incomparably better equipped to know the needs and interests of their children. Dewey wrote:

[The teacher] must have that sympathetic understanding of individuals as individuals which gives him an idea of what is actually going on in the minds of those who are learning. . . . *[It]* makes a system of education based upon living experience a more difficult affair to conduct successfully. *

Then what would be more natural than having educated parents take on more responsibility for the education of their children? We know that those first few years in a child's development are critical to his entire life, and who's in charge then? The parents and perhaps an older brother or sister. Many of our middle-class youngsters enter school already well educated, able to talk syntactically, aware of a wealth of information, capable of manipulating all kinds of complex equipment from color television sets to electric stoves. If everything has moved along so well up until kindergarten, the obvious question is, Why stop? Why turn children over to a routinized and professional institution where their capacity to continue learning is so thoroughly boxed in? Even in conventional educational terms the family's advantages are unmistakable. We all know that the more provident and educated the parents, the more of a head start their youngsters have in school. Even more significant is the fact that almost all families routinely provide:

. A one-to-one relationship
. An honest and uncommercialized interest
. A twenty-four-hour association
. An awareness and sensitivity to the real needs and tastes of a son or daughter
. An unconditional love
. An integration of everyday living and learning

That's why Bea and I believed that many parents—and not just college graduates—instead of watching TV, gardening, consuming, or sleeping might better use their time to make the education of their children a major feature of family life. Our purpose in removing the children from school was not to take on unnecessary responsibilities or to keep ourselves busy while

* *Experience and Education,* New York: Macmillan, p. 39.

idling abroad, but to assume a neglected responsibility and to discover more satisfying uses for our time. Bea had no thought of turning herself, or more generally the free-spirited American mother, back into a house drudge. On the contrary, rather than trying to emulate the American father—sweating at something he hates, selling public relations ideas, writing up annual reports, or running a drygoods store—Bea saw herself as actually living the noncommercial, leisurely, self-fulfilling life of the counterculturist. Of course, if a woman wants recognition, power, remuneration, she too can find a forty-hour-a-week job and turn her children over to the paid professionals to be educated, or she can even become a teacher herself and try to do for thirty children what she found unrewarding doing for one or two of her own. But obviously, Bea for one found educating her children rewarding. And clearly my purpose was not to reinforce a male chauvinist position, since in our arrangement bringing up the children was to become my central activity too. We did our thing just as we thought millions of other parents could do theirs.

Although I've reported our activities here in a, hopefully, organized fashion, our day-to-day living and the results of our family expedition were far from controlled. The countereducation of our children was as unstructured and messy as kids playing with Hershey chocolate syrup, and any educator looking at the five of us enjoying ourselves in our remote little village would have written the trip off as a long wild recess. But Bea and I didn't care. We were having our fun and the kids were certainly having theirs, and along with the good times, we are now convinced, good things were happening.

The lack of form, the totally unforced and almost random nature of our mode of education uncovered needs and encouraged fresh approaches to learning that weren't resisted by the children—that were in fact welcomed. Originally we had wanted the experience to be loose and free. Then hopefully when the adventure was over we would be able to look back and see within the jumble of experiences and discussions, the happenings and developments, some plausible pattern that could make our experiment significant to others. We hadn't wanted to test a theory, but to discover one. We wanted to see the learning process at work with as little academic or formal tinkering as possible. And if we found something unique, something positive in our family junket, perhaps then we could translate it into approaches and tools and ends that could suggest ways to remake, perhaps even replace, formal education.

APPLICATION TO SCHOOLS

I'm sorry to report that we have come back from La Herradura with no all-embracing theory, no profound insights, no replicable methods for the educational establishment to adopt. However, if there are any general lessons to be learned by school administrators from our experiences—since these persons are usually so keen on planning and methodology—some of the following observations might be considered.

TOTAL EDUCATION. The school's unchallenged monopoly on education doesn't seem to have worked to the children's or society's advantage. Perhaps it is time that the family, the church, the community, the media, and the peer group were recognized as significant educational forces and their influence integrated in a total approach to a child's education. We might first freshly determine what we believe to be a child's total needs—without detouring into a discussion of the realities of public education which thus far have resulted in the exclusion of morality, paid work, love, and religion from school curricula. Then we could study the potential for educational influence of each of these forces so we would be in a position to start pointedly assigning new responsibilities to each and to decide just what the school's special responsibilities in the total educational process should be.

PREEMINENCE OF STUDENT INTEREST. Once a child's interest has been aroused and he knows what he wants to accomplish, he can be encouraged to set about gaining skills and availing himself of useful resources, including books and teachers. However, the order should never be reversed, as it is in the schools, where we insist on the development of teacher-prescribed skills and subject disciplines and hope that interests will evolve from them.

KNOWLEDGE AND CURIOSITY WITHOUT BOUNDARIES. We should unpackage the disciplines and allow the student to pursue his interests wherever they take him. This means breaking down the barriers between subject areas and allowing the student's needs and interests to become the focal point of education.

LEARNING WITHOUT TIME LIMITS. Children should not be made to adjust themselves and their individual inclinations to preset time periods for preset activities in preset situations unless we are conditioning them for machine responses in an automated environment. Their interests cannot be expected to turn on and off in synchronization with school day, course, specified hour, and time period. Nor is modular scheduling the answer since it simply camouflages the school's rigidity by segmenting blocks of time more finely. Interest and learning cannot be confined to blocks of time; they must be allowed to flow freely in time and space.

INDIVIDUAL PACING. A child should always move at his own pace. Waiting for others to catch up and therefore losing interest, or not understanding himself yet being forced to move ahead blindly, is punishment not education. Under this mindless educational system of group progression, each child must moment to moment adjust himself to the system; otherwise he is moment after moment too slow or too fast. We are training him to move docilely with the herd. The damage must be enormous.

A NEW EDUCATOR. The most effective teacher is not the trained pedagogue but the practitioner, the friend, the parent. The teacher is often an authority in a single field—and the field is the teaching of a subject, not the subject itself. He is not a practitioner free to bring his whole experience, skill, and interest to bear on his teaching; he is not a friend or a parent whose keen involvement on a continuing one-to-one basis can awaken and maintain a child's interest. He is an adult who for much of his day is isolated from the adult community and thus tends to make his subject seem even more removed from life in the real community.

THE SUBSTANCE OF EDUCATION. Educational development stems not just from schooling but from playing and working as well. Just as there should be no time limits and no place limits on how or where education should take place, there should be no designation of activities as educational or not. Everything done has the potential for educational dividends whether it is household chores, earning money at a job, playing, fooling, pursuing a hobby, or consciously improving an academic skill or discipline.

LAST THOUGHTS

For us the experiment has worked out well—even the formal academic measuring sticks now glowingly confirm this. On our return to the United States, Adam and Seth were at least two or three grades ahead of their former classmates in all subject areas, and Ariel had been brought to a level where she could hold her own in a regular class. More important each had acquired a strong sense of family values, developed a deep appetite for learning, and discovered an exciting set of individual interests.

Of course, I realize that these results were dependent on our sheltered life, a controlled environment in which personal and family values could take root without the grubby business of blocking and fighting off competing value systems. We were able to place the children out of reach of commercial TV, of their thrill-jaded peer group, of a confused and unprincipled society. And this separation alone may have accounted for the most significant benefits of our ten months abroad.

I also realize that few families can take a full year—and many would not want to—and spend it together as we did. Thus, I am open to the obvious criticism: So what? What has this to do with the rest of us? I can only suggest that some of the things that happened and worked well for our family could become part of the life style of any family and without packing up for Greece or Spain.

Even if most of our experiences are not duplicable, they may prod some parents into rethinking their own responsibilities and opportunities in educating their children. All parents would do well to take a hard look at what the schools are doing with their children and to start at least filling in in those areas that are unattended. There are still chunks of time available to every family—evenings, weekends, vacations—and if enough of us start assuming primary responsibility for the total education of our children, we may lend a fresh personal perspective to what have been until now educational goals set by paid professionals.

Maybe it's time each of us started thinking through exactly what we would like our children to learn as they grow up. For if the school, the church, the media, and the community are failing to provide what is needed, the fault may not be entirely theirs. Perhaps the major responsibility for the education of children is still ours, the parents, and we haven't been doing our job.